The How-To Book

for

SAS/GRAPH® Software

Thomas Miron

§.sas. | SAS Press

The correct bibliographic citation for this manual is as follows: Miron, Thomas. 1995. *The How-To Book for SAS/GRAPH® Software*. Cary, NC: SAS Institute Inc.

The How-To Book for SAS/GRAPH® Software

Copyright © 2003, SAS Institute Inc., Cary, NC, USA

ISBN 1-55544-233-1

SAS Institute Inc., SAS Campus Drive, Cary, North Carolina 27513.

1st printing, June 1995
2nd printing, April 2003
3rd printing, September 2005

SAS Publishing provides a complete selection of books and electronic products to help customers use SAS software to its fullest potential. For more information about our e-books, e-learning products, CDs, and hard-copy books, visit the SAS Publishing Web site at **support.sas.com/pubs** or call 1-800-727-3228.

Acknowledgments

Thanks to the many people at SAS Institute who worked to turn this idea into a book. Special thanks to Caroline Brickley for keeping things on track, Josephine Pope for mastering the details, and David Baggett for his faith in all the Books by Users authors.

Table of Contents

About This Book 1
This book is for you 1
What's covered in this book? 1
In each chapter 2
What you should know before using this book 2
About the author 2

Part 1 - Up and Running

Chapter 1 - Overview of SAS/GRAPH® Software 5
How SAS/GRAPH software relates to the SAS System 5
Components of SAS/GRAPH software 6
What you need to run SAS/GRAPH software 6
SAS/GRAPH checklist 7
More Information 7

Chapter 2 - Using Graphics Displays 9
What is a graphics display? 9
Can I use my display with SAS/GRAPH software? 9
Checking the display device driver 10
Using GRAPH windows and the GWINDOW option 11
More Information 12

Chapter 3 - Using Graphics Hardcopy Devices 13
What is a hardcopy device? 13
What do graphics device drivers do? 13
Testing your hardcopy device 14
Hardcopy device checklist 15
More Information 15

Chapter 4 - Previewing Hardcopy 17
Why preview? 17
How to preview 17
When ready for final output 18
What if you don't know which display device driver to use? ... 18
More Information 19

Chapter 5 - Choosing an Output Device Driver 21
What is a device driver? 21
What device drivers are available? 22
Getting more information on device drivers 22
Naming a device driver in your SAS program 23
Overriding driver settings 24
More Information 26

Chapter 6 - How to Structure Data for Graphs 27

What is data structure? 27
Data for bar and pie charts 28
Data for maps 31
Data for plots 33
Restructuring data for graphs 35
More Information 37

Chapter 7 - Using Graphics Options 39

What are graphics options? 39
Using graphics options 40
When to use global versus statement options 40
What can graphics options do? 41
More Information 43

Part 2 - Working with Bar Charts

Chapter 8 - Charting Counts 47

Bar charts show counts by default 47
Charting counts with numeric variables 48
Making each observation count more than once 49
Showing subgroup contributions to the total count 50
Comparing data groups side-by-side 51
More Information 52

Chapter 9 - Charting Sums 53

Using the TYPE=SUM and SUMVAR= options to chart sums 53
Showing subgroup bar segments 54
Showing bar groups 55
More Information 56

Chapter 10 - Charting Averages 57

Use TYPE=MEAN with the SUMVAR= option to chart averages 57
Showing means within groups 58
More Information 59

Chapter 11 - Charting Percentages 61

Showing the percentage of a count 61
Showing the percentage of a sum 62
Showing percentages with grouped bars 63
Showing percentage within a data group 64
Subgroup percentages with segmented bars 65
More Information 66

Chapter 12 - Displaying Statistics 67

Horizontal bar charts show statistics by default 67
Displaying a summary statistic 68
Requesting specific statistics 68
Statistic request options 69

Turning off all horizontal bar chart statistics 69
Displaying statistics on vertical bar charts 70
Controlling statistics text appearance 71
More Information 72

Chapter 13 - Changing the Order of Bars 73

What determines the default bar order? 73
Controlling bar order with the MIDPOINTS= option: character variables 74
Controlling bar order with the MIDPOINTS= option: numeric variables 75
How does the AXIS ORDER= option differ from the MIDPOINTS= option? 76
Displaying bars by length 77
Controlling the order of bar groups 78
More Information 79

Chapter 14 - Changing Bar Width and Spacing 81

Changing bar width 81
Changing bar spacing 83
Controlling space between bar groups 84
More Information 86

Chapter 15 - Charting with Numeric Variables 87

Default handling of numeric variables 87
Charting all values of a numeric variable 89
Specifying the number of midpoint levels 90
Specifying midpoint values 91
More Information 92

Chapter 16 - Using Value Ranges in Charts 95

Creating your own value ranges 95
Using ranges with numeric charting variables 95
Using ranges with character charting variables 97
More Information 98

Chapter 17 - Controlling Bar Fill Patterns 99

What the PATTERN statement does 99
Using the default bar patterns 100
Overriding the default bar patterns 101
Controlling pattern assignments 101
Assigning a different pattern to each bar 103
Assigning patterns to BY groups 104
Assigning patterns to bar groups 105
More Information 106

Part 3 - Working with Plots

Chapter 18 - Creating Scatter Plots 109

Creating a plot with the default settings 109
Changing the plot symbol 111
Changing the plot symbol color 112
More Information 113

Chapter 19 - Creating a Line Plot 115
Connecting data points 115
Adding data points to a line plot 116
How to fix the zigzag line problem 117
Changing the plot line type 119
Changing the plot line thickness 120
More Information 121

Chapter 20 - Smoothing Plot Lines 123
Using line smoothing options 123
How to plot a regression line 124
Adding confidence limits to regression plots 125
More Information 126

Chapter 21 - Adding a Second Axis 127
Adding a second axis with the PLOT2 statement 127
How to identify each plot 128
Why isn't the SYMBOL2 statement being used? 130
More Information 131

Chapter 22 - Plotting Multiple Sets of Points 133
Using a third variable to generate multiple plots in a single set of axes 133
Controlling the number of plots when using a third variable 135
Using multiple plot requests and overlays 136
More Information 138

Chapter 23 - Filling an Area under a Line 139
Filling under a line 139
Filling under multiple lines 140
More Information 142

Chapter 24 - Creating a Cumulative Area Plot 143
What is a cumulative area plot? 143
Data for the cumulative plot 144
Creating the plot 144
More Information 147

Chapter 25 - Using Plot Appearance Options 149
Drawing reference lines 149
Filling in the plot frame 150
Setting the axes origin to zero 151
More Information 153

Part 4 - Working with Maps

Chapter 26 - Understanding Map Data Sets 157
What are map data sets? 157
How are map data used? 158
Projecting map data sets 159
More Information 161

Chapter 27 - Creating a Map 163

What types of maps are available? 163
Mapping numeric data 163
How to specify midpoints 165
Specifying the number of midpoints 166
Mapping with character variables 167
How to create an empty map 168
More Information 169

Chapter 28 - Using Value Ranges in Maps 171

Creating your own value ranges for maps 171
More Information 172

Chapter 29 - Handling Empty Areas 173

Default handling of empty areas 173
Displaying empty areas 174
More Information 175

Chapter 30 - Selecting Map Colors and Fills 177

Controlling fill patterns 177
Changing color and assigning an empty pattern 179
How user-defined and default patterns are selected 180
More Information 181

Part 5 - Working with Pie Charts

Chapter 31 - Creating a Pie Chart.............................. 185

Using PROC GCHART to create pie charts 185
Charting a numeric variable 186
Controlling the number of slices with numeric variables 187
Selecting your own midpoints 188
Showing all slices with a numeric variable 189
Making slices represent sums 190
More Information 191

Chapter 32 - Labeling Pie Slices 193

Specifying a value to display and its location 193
Displaying only percentage values 195
Using arrow leaders and the INSIDE location value 196
More Information 197

Chapter 33 - Creating Multiple Pie Charts per Page 199

Creating multiple charts with the GROUP= option 199
Controlling page layout 200
More Information 201

Chapter 34 - Controlling Pie Chart Appearance 203

Adding exploded slices 203
Outlining slices 204

Making a slice invisible 205
Matching text and slice color 206
Turning off the chart type heading 207
Changing the location of the first slice 208
Controlling slice order 209
More Information 210

Chapter 35 - Selecting Pie Chart Colors and Fills 211
Controlling fill patterns 211
Varying the fill pattern 212
Varying fill color 213
Controlling color and fill 214
More Information 215

Part 6 - Fine-Tuning Your Graph

Chapter 36 - Controlling Titles and Footnotes 219
Controlling title font, color, and size 219
Adding titles and footnotes 221
Changing text orientation 222
Changing text within a line 224
More Information 225

Chapter 37 - Adding Dollar Signs and Decimal Places... 227
Controlling decimal places 227
Using formats 228
Displaying dollar signs 229
More Information 231

Chapter 38 - Displaying Dates with Plots and Charts 233
Placing dates on a plot axis 233
Controlling the date format 234
Formatted dates in charts 235
More Information 237

Chapter 39 - Controlling Axes on Plots and Charts 239
Using the AXIS statement 239
Defining axis label text 239
How to define plot tick marks 241
Controlling tick mark labels and minor tick marks 242
Changing bar chart axis labels 243
More Information 244

Chapter 40 - Controlling Legends 247
Using the LEGEND statement 247
How to define legends for plots 248
Setting legend labels 249
Controlling the size of point markers 250

Defining bar chart legends 251
Defining legends on maps 252
More Information 253

Chapter 41 - Creating Multiple Graphs from a Single Data Set 255
Using BY groups 255
How to create multiple graphs with BY groups 255
Suppressing the BY line 257
More Information 258

Chapter 42 - Saving and Reviewing Graphs 259
Why save graphs? 259
How to save graphs in a SAS catalog 259
Replaying cataloged graphs 263
Listing cataloged graphs 264
More Information 265

Data Used in Examples 267
LIB1.ALLFUEL 267
LIB1.DEER 268
LIB1.FUEL2 268
LIB1.JOBREV 268
LIB1.JOBSITES 269
LIB1.LAKES 269
LIB1.MEETINGS 270
LIB1.MONTHLY 271
LIB1.REVENUES 271
LIB1.SALESQ1 272
LIB1.SALESREP 272
LIB1.TYPEFUEL 272
LIB1.UTILITY 273
LIB1.UTILYEAR 273

About This Book

In This Chapter

- This book is for you
- What's covered in this book?
- In each chapter
- What you should know before using this book
- About the author

This book is for you

The How-To Book for SAS/GRAPH Software is for SAS/GRAPH software users who need quick working solutions for common graphics problems. If you are a new or occasional user of SAS/GRAPH software, this book provides the information you need to get started on your graphics project. More advanced users will find valuable information on graphics programming techniques and subject-oriented documentation references for SAS/GRAPH features.

What's covered in this book?

The How-To Book for SAS/GRAPH Software covers commonly used SAS/GRAPH procedures and methods. Topics include:

- Using graphics devices
- Organizing data for use with graphics procedures
- Bar charts
- Pie charts
- Maps
- Plots
- Controlling the appearance of graphs and text
- Saving and reviewing graphs

SAS/GRAPH procedures covered:

- PROC GCHART
- PROC GMAP
- PROC GPLOT
- PROC GREPLAY
- PROC GOPTIONS
- PROC GDEVICE

In each chapter

Each chapter covers a single topic. Annotated SAS programs and output illustrate the topic. Subtopics are covered under separate sections within each chapter.

At the beginning of each chapter is the "In This Chapter" card. All section headings are listed in the card. This allows you to see at a glance the topics covered.

> **In This Chapter**
>
> • This book is for you
> • What's covered in this book?
> • In each chapter
> • What you should know before using this book
> • About the author

At the end of each chapter is the "More Information" section headed with:

More Information

More Information lists items covered in the chapter and tells you where to find related SAS Institute documentation. Use the "More Information" references to find syntax documentation, technical overviews, and more examples.

Many chapters contain Closer Look text identified by the Closer Look icon:

"Closer Look" sections discuss issues, alternatives, or technical details related to the chapter topic.

What you should know before using this book

It is assumed that you know how to write SAS programs and run the SAS System at your site or on your computer. It is also assumed that you are familiar with the following SAS system components and concepts:

- SAS libraries and assigning librefs
- SAS data sets
- SAS variables
- SAS observations
- DATA steps, procedure steps, and global statements

About the author

Thomas Miron is an information systems consultant and trainer with more than ten years of experience with SAS software. *The How-To Book for SAS/GRAPH Software* is the result of working with hundreds of end-users to help them get the most from SAS/GRAPH software.

Part 1
Up and Running

Chapter 1 - Overview of SAS/GRAPH® Software
Chapter 2 - Using Graphics Displays
Chapter 3 - Using Graphics Hardcopy Devices
Chapter 4 - Previewing Hardcopy
Chapter 5 - Choosing an Output Device Driver
Chapter 6 - How to Structure Data for Graphs
Chapter 7 - Using Graphics Options

Overview of SAS/GRAPH® Software

┌─ In This Chapter ───┐

- How SAS/GRAPH software relates to the SAS System
- Components of SAS/GRAPH software
- What you need to run SAS/GRAPH software
- SAS/GRAPH checklist

└───┘

How SAS/GRAPH software relates to the SAS System

SAS/GRAPH software is a separately priced product within the SAS System that is similar to SAS Institute products such as SAS/ETS, SAS/STAT, or SAS/EIS software. Base SAS software is required to run SAS/GRAPH.

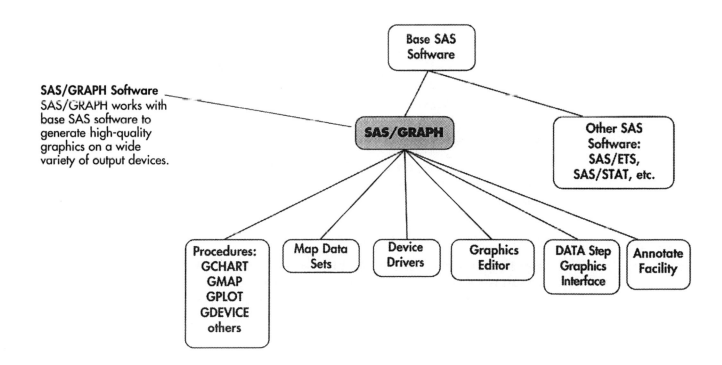

SAS/GRAPH Software
SAS/GRAPH works with base SAS software to generate high-quality graphics on a wide variety of output devices.

Components of SAS/GRAPH software

SAS/GRAPH software has several components:

- **Graphics procedures** generate charts, plots, maps, and other graphs. Some graphics procedures provide utility functions to help you manage graphics output and map data sets.

- **Map data sets** contain geographic outlines and other information for generating high-quality maps.

- **Device drivers** serve as the interface between graphics procedures and output devices such as plotters, displays, printers, film recorders, or output files.

- The **Graphics Editor** allows you to interactively edit or create graphics output.

- The **DATA Step Graphics Interface** allows you to create graphs from within a DATA step program.

- The **Annotate Facility** allows you to customize graphs with data held in SAS data sets.

The Graphics Editor, DATA Step Interface, and Annotate Facility are not covered in this book.

What you need to run SAS/GRAPH software

Base SAS software must be installed on your computer to run SAS/GRAPH. Any computer system capable of running base SAS should be able to run SAS/GRAPH software.

In addition to base SAS and SAS/GRAPH software, you need devices capable of handling graphics output. Typical devices include a graphics display device so you can view your graphs on screen and a hardcopy device for output on paper or film. Most commercially available display and hardcopy devices are supported by SAS/GRAPH software. See Chapters 2 and 3 for more on using display and hardcopy devices.

To create maps you must install SAS map data sets which are supplied with SAS/GRAPH. If you use the map data sets you need to consider disk storage requirements. These requirements are discussed in your SAS/GRAPH installation documentation. Installation of the map data sets is optional. You need only install the maps you plan to use.

You should have access to SAS Institute documentation for the features of the system you plan to use. The basic documentation is *SAS/GRAPH Software: Reference, Version 6, First Edition, Volumes 1 and 2*. Additional documentation is listed under "More Information" at the end of this chapter.

SAS/GRAPH checklist

The following are required to run SAS/GRAPH:

✔ base SAS software

✔ SAS/GRAPH software

✔ adequate disk storage space for software and maps

✔ graphics display device

✔ graphics hardcopy output device

✔ SAS/GRAPH documentation

More Information

using displays, overview

"Using Direct Display to Monitors", in Chapter 3 "Graphics Output", *SAS/GRAPH Software: Reference, Version 6, First Edition, Volume 1*, p. 50

using hardcopy devices, overview

"Sending Graphics Output to a Hardcopy Device", in Chapter 3 "Graphics Output", *SAS/GRAPH Software: Reference, Volume 1*, p. 50

using the Graphics Editor

"Prerequisites", in "Using This Book", *SAS/GRAPH Software: Graphics Editor, Version 6, First Edition*, pp. xiii-xiv

Annotate Facility, reference

"Part 4, The Annotate Facility", *SAS/GRAPH Software: Reference*, pp. 465-595

system-specific requirements

See one of the following guides for your computer system:

SAS/GRAPH Software: Using Graphics Devices in the CMS Environment, Version 6, First Edition

SAS/GRAPH Software: Using Graphics Devices in the MVS Environment, Version 6, First Edition

SAS/GRAPH Software: Using Graphics Devices in the UNIX Environment and Derivatives, Version 6, First Edition

SAS/GRAPH Software: Using Graphics Devices in the VMS Environment, Version 6, First Edition

Using Graphics Displays

- What is a graphics display?
- Can I use my display with SAS/GRAPH software?
- Checking the display device driver
- Using GRAPH windows and the GWINDOW option

What is a graphics display?

A graphics display is a screen or monitor that can reproduce graphics output. Most graphics displays can reproduce colors or shades of gray. Graphics displays vary in their capabilities. Some displays can show only a limited set of colors or gray shades; others display "millions of colors."

Graphics displays are often not the final destination of your graphics output. But, they are very useful for previewing output that will ultimately be printed, plotted, or otherwise reproduced on a piece of paper or film with a hardcopy device.

Can I use my display with SAS/GRAPH software?

If your computer system is running a graphical operating system such as Windows or OS/2 you should be able to display SAS/GRAPH output on your monitor. On other systems you may have to install special hardware and software to display graphs. If your workstation is connected to the computer system through a network, there may be additional network hardware and software requirements. For information on network connections and other system-specific considerations, see the documentation listed in "More Information."

Checking the display device driver

Output from SAS/GRAPH procedures is passed through software called a device driver that translates it for a specific display or output device. Many device drivers are supplied with SAS/GRAPH software. You must select the one that is appropriate for your display.

Display Output

To find the name of the default or current device driver, run the GTESTIT procedure:

```
00001  proc gtestit;
00002  run;
```

If the current or default device driver is correct for your display, you should see the PROC GTESTIT output on the screen. If no output is displayed, check the SAS log. PROC GTESTIT writes several pieces of information to the log, including the name of the current device driver. You must be sure that this driver is appropriate for your display. See Chapter 5 for more on selecting device drivers.

PROC GTESTIT log output —
D= names the current
device driver. In this case
the device driver is WIN.

```
D=WIN          B=1200     R= 32 C= 89 P=256
H= 18 W= 11 MAX=*** D=C000000000000000
RF=C210800000000000  S=0000000000000000
OPTS=D592644040000000 NCOLORS= 11
Background color = BLACK
Color 1 = WHITE
Color 2 = RED
Color 3 = GREEN
Color 4 = BLUE
Color 5 = CYAN
Color 6 = MAGENTA
Color 7 = YELLOW
Color 8 = GRAY
Color 9 = PINK
Color 10 = ORANGE
Color 11 = BROWN
Ratio = 0.58836
Hsize = 8.15833
Vsize =     4.8
F=1

NOTE: The PROCEDURE GTESTIT used 30.42 seconds.
```

Using GRAPH windows and the GWINDOW option

Graphics output can be sent directly to the display screen. Output can also be sent to a GRAPH window. The GRAPH window is a resizable, scrollable window in the SAS Display Manager system that allows you to view current output or output from previous graphics procedures. You can send graphs to output devices directly from the GRAPH window with the PRINT command. Many graphics displays support the use of the GRAPH window.

GRAPH windows are turned on or off with the GWINDOW option. When the GWINDOW option is set, graphs are displayed in a GRAPH window. When the NOGWINDOW option is in effect, graphs are sent directly to the display screen. Use an OPTIONS statement to set the GWINDOW option:

GWINDOW option
Submit this statement to enable GRAPH windows.

```
00001    options gwindow;

00001    options nogwindow;
```

NOGWINDOW option
Submit this statement to disable GRAPH windows.

When the NOGWINDOW option is in effect, the graph fills the entire screen. Press the mouse button or the ENTER key (or another key, depending on your computer system) to view the next graph or return to display manager.

The GRAPH window is normally enabled on systems that support a graphical interface such as Windows or OS/2. Because you can review graphs generated earlier in your session, GRAPH windows add flexibility when developing graphics programs.

GRAPH window
The GRAPH window is part of the SAS Display Manager System.

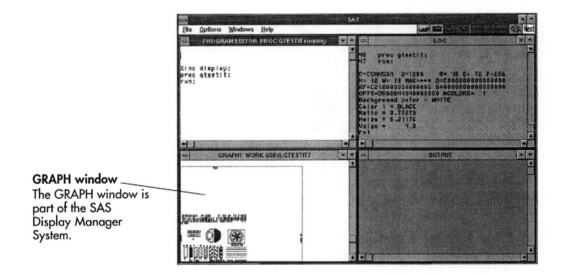

More Information

using the GWINDOW option, enabling GRAPH windows

"Using Direct Display to Monitors", in Chapter 3, "Graphics Output", *SAS/GRAPH Software: Reference, Version 6, First Edition, Volume 1*, p. 50

"Making GRAPH Windows Available" and "Suppressing GRAPH Windows", in Chapter 3, "Graphics Output", *SAS/GRAPH Software: Reference, Volume 1*, pp. 52-53

GRAPH windows, general reference

"The GRAPH Windows", in Chapter 3, "Graphics Output", *SAS/GRAPH Software: Reference, Volume 1*, pp. 51-61

PROC GTESTIT, general reference

Chapter 38, "The GTESTIT Procedure", *SAS/GRAPH Software: Reference, Volume 2*, pp. 1269-1277

system-specific display information can be found in the following:

See one of the following guides for your computer system:

SAS/GRAPH Software: Using Graphics Devices in the CMS Environment, Version 6, First Edition

SAS/GRAPH Software: Using Graphics Devices in the MVS Environment, Version 6, First Edition

SAS/GRAPH Software: Using Graphics Devices in the UNIX Environment and Derivatives, Version 6, First Edition

SAS/GRAPH Software: Using Graphics Devices in the VMS Environment, Version 6, First Edition

Using Graphics Hardcopy Devices

In This Chapter

- What is a hardcopy device?
- What do graphics device drivers do?
- Testing your hardcopy device
- Hardcopy device checklist

What is a hardcopy device?

A hardcopy device prints, plots, or otherwise reproduces your graphs on some medium, such as paper, film, or transparencies. SAS/GRAPH software supports most graphics hardcopy devices. If your computer can be connected to a graphics capable device, SAS/GRAPH software will probably work with it.

What do graphics device drivers do?

Output from SAS/GRAPH procedures is passed through software called a device driver. The device driver translates the output for a specific graphics device. Device drivers are supplied by SAS Institute and are part of the SAS/GRAPH product. See Chapter 5 for more on how to select a device driver.

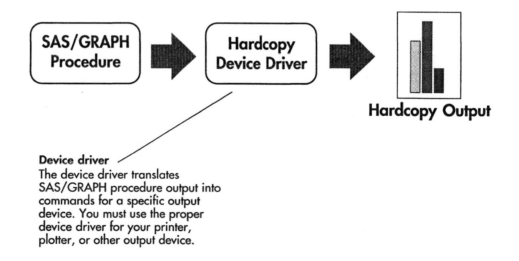

Device driver
The device driver translates SAS/GRAPH procedure output into commands for a specific output device. You must use the proper device driver for your printer, plotter, or other output device.

Testing your hardcopy device

You can test the device driver and the connection to your hardcopy device with the GOPTIONS statement and GTESTIT procedure as shown below. If your workstation or terminal is connected to a host computer through a network, there may be special network hardware and software requirements to consider. See the documentation listed under "More Information" for details on system-specific connections.

Name the output device
The DEVICE= option assigns the current output device driver. Here the HPLJS3 driver (HP LaserJet III printer) is assigned.

```
00001    goptions device=hpljs3;
00002
00003    proc gtestit;
00004    run;
```

PROC GTESTIT step
The GTESTIT procedure exercises the output device.

PROC GTESTIT output
PROC GTESTIT generates three pages of output to test various device features and output quality. GTESTIT output for the HPLJS3 driver is shown.

GTESTIT output in the log
The driver name follows "D=."

```
D=HPLJS3      B=1200      R= 60 C= 80 P=256
H=   9 W=  12 MAX=*** D=C000000000000000
RF=C210800000000000 S=0000000000000000
OPTS=D492644040000000 NCOLORS=   1
Background color = WHITE
Color 1 = BLACK
Ratio =     1.25
Hsize =     3.84
Vsize =     4.8
F=1

NOTE: The PROCEDURE GTESTIT used 20.92 seconds.
```

If you use the correct device driver but the GTESTIT procedure does not generate graphics output, you may have a problem with how the connection to your device is defined. There are several SAS graphics options that must be set to correspond to how the hardcopy device is actually connected to your computer. With some systems, notably mainframe computers, several other graphics options must be correctly set in order to direct output to your hardcopy device. In these cases, you may need help from technical support staff to find the proper graphics options settings. See the references listed in "More Information" for your computer system and the device-driver information displayed when you use the HELP DEVICES display manager command.

Hardcopy device checklist

Hardcopy devices vary widely in quality of output and features. You should consider the following when choosing a device:

✔ Can the device be connected to my computer system?

✔ Is there a SAS/GRAPH device driver for the device? (See Chapter 5.)

✔ Is color supported?

✔ Does the device require manual intervention (plotter pens, special paper trays, film loading, etc.)?

✔ How fast is the device?

✔ Can the device handle the anticipated volume of output?

✔ Can the device handle the medium required (transparencies, coated paper, plain paper, etc.)?

✔ Is output quality satisfactory (resolution, ink durability, color quality)?

📖 More Information

hardcopy output, overview

"Sending Graphics Output to a Hardcopy Device" in Chapter 3, "Graphics Output", *SAS/GRAPH Software: Reference, Volume 1*, Version 6, First Edition, pp. 50-51

PROC GTESTIT, general reference

Chapter 38, "The GTESTIT Procedure", *SAS/GRAPH Software: Reference, Volume 2*, pp. 1269-1277

system-specific display information can be found in the following:

See one of the following guides for your computer system:

SAS/GRAPH Software: Using Graphics Devices in the CMS Environment, Version 6, First Edition

SAS/GRAPH Software: Using Graphics Devices in the MVS Environment, Version 6, First Edition

SAS/GRAPH Software: Using Graphics Devices in the UNIX Environment and Derivatives, Version 6, First Edition

SAS/GRAPH Software: Using Graphics Devices in the VMS Environment, Version 6, First Edition

Previewing Hardcopy

In This Chapter

- Why preview?
- How to preview
- When ready for final output
- What if you don't know which display device driver to use?

Why preview?

SAS/GRAPH software allows you to preview graphics output on a display device as it would appear on a hardcopy device. This feature is useful when you are developing a graph and want to see what the final hardcopy will look like, but don't want to waste time and paper sending it to a printer or plotter each time you make a change.

How to preview

To preview output on your screen as it would appear on a hardcopy device, use a GOPTIONS statement with the TARGETDEVICE= and DEVICE= options. The DEVICE= option names the current display device. The TARGETDEVICE= option names the intended hardcopy device. SAS/GRAPH software will display a graph on your display screen as it would appear on the target hardcopy device.

The following example shows you how to use SAS program comments and the GOPTIONS statement to switch between a graphics display and a hardcopy device.

Target-device emulation is not always perfect. Some target-device colors may not be available on the display. Colors are notoriously hard to match between devices. "Red" on a display and "red" on a plotter are not necessarily the same.

GOPTIONS statement
Name the driver for the current display in the DEVICE= option. Here the current device is the Windows operating system display: WIN.

Comments
Statements that begin with an asterisk (*) are comments. A commented GOPTIONS statement makes it easy to switch to your final output device. (See below.)

TARGETDEVICE= option
Name the device you want to emulate with the TARGETDEVICE= option. The HP7440 device driver is for the Hewlett-Packard 7440 plotter.

```
00001   goptions device=win
00002           targetdevice=hp7440;
00003
00004   *goptions device=hp7440;
00005            targetdevice=;
00006
00007   pattern1 value=solid color=black;
00008   pattern2 value=empty color=black;
00009
00010   title height=8 pct font=swiss 'Previewing Hardcopy';
00011
00012   proc gchart data=howto.sample1;
00013     vbar month /
00014       subgroup=type
00015         sumvar=amount
00016   ;
00017   run;
00018   quit;
```

When ready for final output

When you are ready to send your graph to the final output device, comment the GOPTIONS statement with the TARGETDEVICE= setting and uncomment the final destination GOPTIONS statement. Like all global options, TARGETDEVICE= remains in effect until you change it, or your SAS session ends. For final output, no target device is necessary, so program line 5 resets the TARGETDEVICE= option to null.

Comment the display GOPTIONS statement
Use an asterisk (*) to comment the GOPTIONS statement that sends output to the display screen.

Uncomment the hardcopy GOPTIONS statement
Remove the asterisk (*) from the GOPTIONS statement for the hardcopy output device.

Reset TARGETDEVICE
The TARGETDEVICE= option is reset to null.

```
00001   *goptions device=win
00002            targetdevice=hp7440;
00003
00004   goptions device=hp7440
00005            targetdevice=;
00006
00007   pattern1 value=solid color=black;
00008   pattern2 value=empty color=black;
00009
00010   title height=8 pct font=swiss 'Previewing Hardcopy';
00011
00012   proc gchart data=howto.sample1;
00013     vbar month /
00014       subgroup=type
00015         sumvar=amount
00016   ;
00017   run;
00018   quit;
```

What if you don't know which display device driver to use?

If you don't know the name of your graphics display device, you can still switch between previewing on the display and directing output to hardcopy. Use the DEVICE= option with no device specified to refer to the default graphics display. Most SAS/GRAPH installations have a default graphics display device. As shown in the previous example, use commenting to switch between preview and final copy. Note that this will only work when the default graphics device corresponds to the display you are actually using.

```
00001  goptions device=
00002          targetdevice=hp7440;
00003
00004  *goptions device=hp7440
00005          targetdevice=;
00006
00007  pattern1 value=solid color=black;
00008  pattern2 value=empty color=black;
00009
00010  title height=8 pct font=swiss 'Previewing Hardcopy';
00011
00012  proc gchart data=howto.sample1;
00013     vbar month /
00014        subgroup=type
00015        sumvar=amount
00016     ;
00017  run;
00018  quit;
```

 ## More Information

TARGETDEVICE= option, syntax and general reference

"TARGETDEVICE" in Chapter 5, "Graphics Options and Device Parameters Dictionary", *SAS/GRAPH Software: Reference, Volume 1, Version 6, First Edition*, p. 147

TARGETDEVICE= option, usage and examples

"Previewing Hardcopies" in Chapter 44, "Producing Graphics Output", *SAS/GRAPH Software: Usage, Version 6, First Edition*, pp. 603-604

"Previewing Graphics Output on a Different Output Device" in Chapter 12, "The GOPTIONS Statement", *SAS/GRAPH Software: Reference, Volume 1*, pp. 301-302

"Device-Independent Catalog Entries" in Chapter 3, "Graphics Output", *SAS/GRAPH Software: Reference, Volume 1*, p. 64

GOPTIONS statement, general reference

Chapter 12, "The GOPTIONS Statement", *SAS/GRAPH Software: Reference, Volume 1*, pp. 291-302

Which device driver name should I use?

Chapter 5, "Choosing an Output Device", in this book

"Selecting a Device Driver", in Chapter 4, "Device Drivers", *SAS/GRAPH Software: Reference, Volume 1*, pp. 75-78

Also see the *SAS/GRAPH Software: Using Graphics Devices* book for your computer system. Each book gives you system-specific information relating to graphics devices. A complete list of available books appears on page 12.

What about previewing colors?

"Device Capabilities", in Chapter 7, "SAS/GRAPH Colors", *SAS/GRAPH Software: Reference, Volume 1*, pp. 194-197

comments in SAS programs

"Comment", in Chapter 9, "SAS Language Statements", *SAS Language: Reference, Version 6, First Edition*, p. 318

5 Choosing an Output Device Driver

┌─ *In This Chapter* ─────────────────────────────┐

- What is a device driver?
- What device drivers are available?
- Getting more information on device drivers
- Naming a device driver in your SAS program
- Overriding driver settings

└──┘

What is a device driver?

Each graphics output device requires specific commands and connections. In order to accommodate the many graphics devices available, software device drivers handle device-specific requirements. Output from SAS/GRAPH procedures is passed through a device driver which, in turn, sends commands to the final output device. The driver translates the procedure output into commands appropriate for the device. When you change output devices, you do not have to change your SAS/GRAPH program. You only need to name a different device driver. SAS/GRAPH software includes drivers for most common graphics devices.

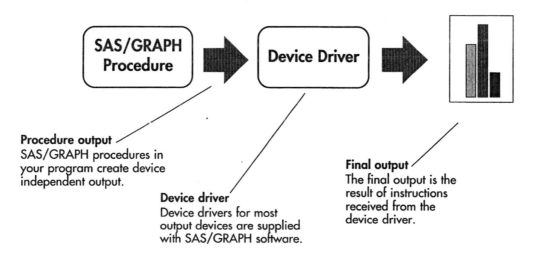

Procedure output
SAS/GRAPH procedures in your program create device independent output.

Device driver
Device drivers for most output devices are supplied with SAS/GRAPH software.

Final output
The final output is the result of instructions received from the device driver.

What device drivers are available?

You can get a list of available device drivers by executing the following program from the SAS Display Manager. The device list will be displayed in the GDEVICE window. (See the display below.)

Display manager

```
proc gdevice;
run;
quit;
```

If you are running in batch or non-interactive mode, run the program below. The device list will be sent to the standard SAS print destination.

Batch processing

```
proc gdevice;
   list _all_;
run;
```

Getting more information on device drivers

When using the display manager, you can get more information on a specific driver by selecting the driver from the GDEVICE window (see above.) The driver information is displayed in a series of screens. To move to the next screen, enter NEXTSCR on the command line, or use the function key assigned to the NEXTSCR command.

Display manager

GDEVICE window
To see a series of screens with device driver details, select a driver with an "s" in the line command field.

GDEVICE
GDEVICE: DIRECTORY SASHELP.DEVICES (B)

	Name	Type	Description	Updated
L	APLPLUS	DEV	Apple Laserwriter Plus (PostScript)	10/05/93
_	APPLELW	DEV	Apple Laserwriter (PostScript)	10/05/93
_	APPLELWM	DEV	Apple Laserwriter A4 paper	03/04/94
_	CAL81	DEV	CalComp 81 plotter	10/05/93
_	CAL84	DEV	CalComp 84 plotter	10/05/93
_	CGM	DEV	CGM generator--binary output	10/05/93
_	CGM35	DEV	CGM binary for BPS 35mm EXPRESS	10/05/93
_	CGMAUTO	DEV	CGM for Autografix System	10/05/93
S	CGMBQA	DEV	CGM color for BORLAND QUATTRO 3.0	10/05/93
_	CGMC	DEV	CGM generator w/colors--binary output	10/05/93
_	CGMCHAR	DEV	CGM generator--character format	10/05/93
_	CGMCLEAR	DEV	CGM generator--Clear text format	10/05/93
_	CGMCRT	DEV	CGM for CRTs--binary format	10/05/93
_	CGMCRTCH	DEV	CGM for CRTs--character format	10/05/93
_	CGMCRTCL	DEV	CGM for CRTs--clear text format	10/05/93
_	CGMDP	DEV	CGM for Draw Perfect System	10/05/93
_	CGMDPA	DEV	CGM Draw Perfect with Hardware Fonts	10/05/93
_	CGMFL	DEV	CGM binary for Lotus Freelance rel 3.0	10/05/93
_	CGMFLALJ	DEV	CGM Lotus Freelance - Laserjet, EGA	10/05/93
_	CGMFLAPL	DEV	CGM Lotus Freelance - Apple Laserwriter	10/05/93
_	CGMFLAPT	DEV	CGM Lotus Freelance - HP7475A Plotter	10/05/93
_	CGMFLM	DEV	CGM binary monochrome - Lotus Freelance	10/05/93
_	CGMFLWA	DEV	CGM Lotus Freelance - Windows	10/05/93
_	CGMGG	DEV	CGM driver for H-P Graphics Gallery 3.0	10/05/93
_	CGMHG	DEV	CGM color for Harvard Graphics 2.12	10/05/93
_	CGMHG3A	DEV	CGM color for Harvard Graphics 3.0 FONT	10/05/93
_	CGMHGM	DEV	CGM mono for Harvard Graphics 2.12	10/05/93
_	CGMHGWA	DEV	CGM for Harvard Graphics Windows	10/05/93

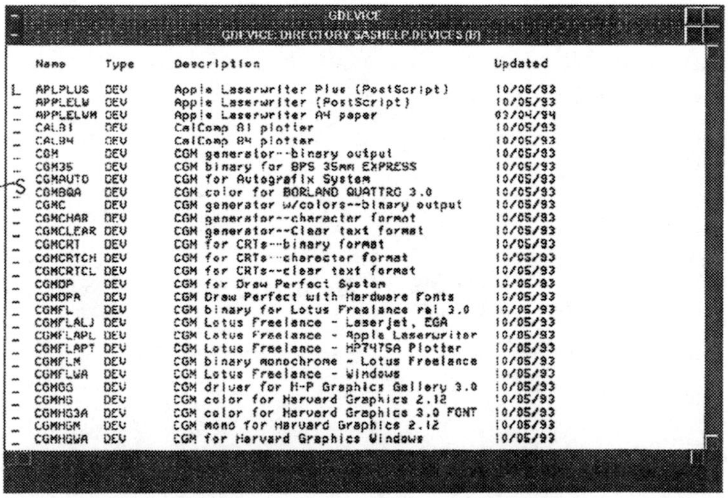

To see device driver details in batch mode, run PROC GDEVICE. Name the driver in the LIST statement.

Batch processing

```
proc gdevice;
   list hpljs3;
run;
```

Driver name
Driver details will be listed for the HPLJS3 driver.

Some of the settings for the HPLJS3 (HP LaserJet III) device driver are shown in the output below. All settings except "Orig. Driver" can be modified. Many settings are technical and need to be changed only in unusual circumstances.

Driver detail listing

```
                         GDEVICE procedure
               Listing from SASHELP.DEVICES - Entry HPLJS3

Orig Driver: HPLJS3              Module:  SASGDHPJ  Model:   3018
Description: HP LaserJet Series III (1 meg)--300 DPI     Type: PRINTER
*** Institute-supplied ***
Lrows:    0 Xmax:    8.500 IN   Hsize:    8.000 IN  Xpixels:  2550
Lcols:    0 Ymax:   11.000 IN   Vsize:   10.000 IN  Ypixels:  3300
Prows:   66                     Horigin:  0.250 IN
Pcols:   85                     Vorigin:  0.500 IN
Aspect:   0.000                 Rotate:
Driver query: Y                 Queued messages: N
                                Paperfeed:   0.000 IN


OPTIONS
Erase:                  Autofeed:              Chartype:    0
Swap:                   Cell:                  Maxcolors:   2
Autocopy:               Characters:            Repaint:     0
Handshake:     HARDWARE Circlearc:             Gcopies:     1
                        Dash:                  Gsize:       0
Prompt - startup:       Fill:                  Speed:       0
         end graph:     Piefill:               Fillinc:     1
         mount pen:     Polyfill:              Maxpoly:     0
         chg paper:     Symbol:                Lfactor:     0
                        Pensort:        N
Devopts:        '1402100100000000'X
UCC:        '000001000001'X

Cback:     WHITE                 Colortbl:
Color list:

   BLACK
```

Naming a device driver in your SAS program

If you do not explicitly name a device driver, a default driver will be used. In most cases, the default driver will send output to your workstation display. To specify a different output device use the DEVICE= option in a GOPTIONS (or OPTIONS) statement.

DEVICE= option
In this example the GOPTIONS statement with the DEVICE= option sets the graphics device driver to HPLJS3.

```
00001   goptions device=hpljs3;
```

DEVICE= is a global option. This means that once it is defined in your SAS session it is in effect until you change it or the session ends.

Follow these steps to name a specific output device driver:

1. Run PROC GDEVICE to get a list of available device drivers.

2. Locate your device from the description in the PROC GDEVICE listing.

3. Note the driver name associated with the device description.

4. Execute a GOPTIONS statement with the DEVICE= option naming the driver. The GOPTIONS statement must be submitted before your SAS/GRAPH procedure.

Overriding driver settings

For common graphics output devices attached directly to your computer, settings in Institute-supplied device drivers will probably work without modification. If you have special requirements or are on a network-attached terminal or workstation, you may have to modify some device driver settings.

There are four methods to override standard settings:

1. Use a GOPTIONS statement to temporarily override a setting.

2. Create your own modified copy of the device driver in an alternate catalog.

3. Create your own modified copy of the device driver in the standard driver catalog SASHELP.DEVICES. (Recommended only if method 1 or 2 cannot be used.)

4. Modify the Institute-supplied driver. (This is possible, but not recommended.)

The following examples show how methods 1, 2, and 3 work to override the default HSIZE= setting for the HP7470 device driver. In the examples, HSIZE= is set to 4 inches.

Method 1

The temporary override method is used in the following program. With this method, a GOPTIONS statement with the HSIZE=4 IN option must be specified in each SAS session or batch job.

GOPTIONS statement
The HSIZE=4 IN option is set in a GOPTIONS statement. The setting is only in effect for the current SAS session or batch job.

```
00001  goptions hsize=4 in
00002           device=hp7470
00003  ;
00004
00005  proc gtestit;
00006  run;
```

Graphics procedure
Subsequent graphics procedures (here PROC GTESTIT) will use the HSIZE=4 IN setting.

Method 2

The next example shows how to create a modified device driver in an alternate driver catalog.

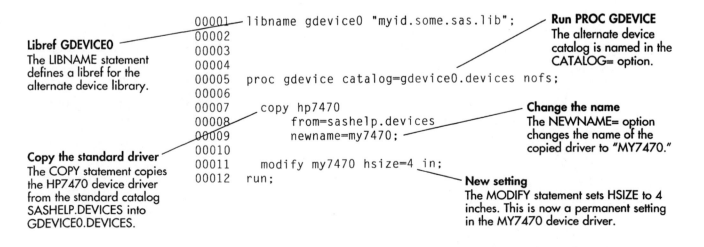

Libref GDEVICE0
The LIBNAME statement defines a libref for the alternate device library.

Copy the standard driver
The COPY statement copies the HP7470 device driver from the standard catalog SASHELP.DEVICES into GDEVICE0.DEVICES.

```
00001  libname gdevice0 "myid.some.sas.lib";
00002
00003
00004
00005  proc gdevice catalog=gdevice0.devices nofs;
00006
00007    copy hp7470
00008      from=sashelp.devices
00009      newname=my7470;
00010
00011    modify my7470 hsize=4 in;
00012  run;
```

Run PROC GDEVICE
The alternate device catalog is named in the CATALOG= option.

Change the name
The NEWNAME= option changes the name of the copied driver to "MY7470."

New setting
The MODIFY statement sets HSIZE to 4 inches. This is now a permanent setting in the MY7470 device driver.

The modified driver needs to be created only once. It will be available to any SAS/GRAPH procedure as long as the GDEVICE0 library has been established in the SAS program or session. To use the modified device driver, establish the GDEVICE0 libref; then, name the driver in a GOPTIONS statement.

```
00001    libname gdevice0 "myid.some.sas.lib";        Establish the
00002                                                  GDEVICE0 libref
00003    goptions device=my7470;
00004                                    Name the new driver
00005    proc gtestit;
00006    run;
```

Alternate catalogs must reside in a library with the libref GDEVICE*n*, where *n* is 0 to 9. When a device driver is specified in your program, libraries beginning with GDEVICE0 are searched first. The search sequence is GDEVICE0, GDEVICE1, GDEVICE2, etc. The last library searched is SASHELP, which contains the standard device catalog. It is rarely necessary to have more than one or two alternate device catalog libraries. See "More Information" for references on modifying device driver entries and creating alternate driver catalogs.

Method 3

The final example shows how to make a modified copy of the HP7470 driver incorporating the HSIZE=4 IN setting. The modified driver is called MY7470 and is stored in the Institute-supplied device catalog: SASHELP.DEVICES.

Copy the standard driver
The standard driver HP7470 is copied to MY7470 within the SASHELP.DEVICES catalog.

```
00001    proc gdevice catalog=sashelp.devices nofs;
00002       copy hp7470 newname=my7470;
00003       modify my7470 hsize=4 in;          Modify the copy
00004    run;                                   The HSIZE= option is set to 4
                                                inches in the MY7470 device
                                                driver.
```

To use the modified device driver, name it in a GOPTIONS statement. No LIBNAME statement is necessary. The SASHELP library is automatically available to your session or job.

```
00001    goptions device=my7470;
00002                                    Name the new driver
00003    proc gtestit;
00004    run;
```

There are two things to consider when you use method 3. First is your authority to modify the default SAS device-driver catalog library SASHELP. Unless you are working on a single-user computer, SASHELP is commonly protected by access rules that allow only a SAS system administrator to modify it. Second, if you do store your modified device driver in SASHELP.DEVICES, you must ensure that your modified driver is not deleted when a new version of SAS software is installed and the old SASHELP library is replaced by the new version.

More Information

creating and using alternate driver catalogs

"Search Order of Catalogs for a Device Driver", in Chapter 25, "The GDEVICE Procedure", *SAS/GRAPH Software: Reference, Volume 2, Version 6, First Edition*, pp. 893-894

"Selecting a Device Driver", in Chapter 4, "Device Drivers", *SAS/GRAPH Software: Reference, Volume 1*, pp. 75-78

device drivers, overview

Chapter 4, "Device Drivers", *SAS/GRAPH Software: Reference, Volume 1*, pp. 73-83

device driver settings, list and reference

Chapter 5, "Graphics Options and Device Parameters Dictionary", *SAS/GRAPH Software: Reference, Volume 1*, pp. 85-153

HOSTSPEC= graphics option

"HOSTSPEC" in Chapter 1, "The SAS/GRAPH Environment", *SAS Technical Report P-215, SAS/GRAPH Software: Changes and Enhancements, Release 6.07*, p. 6

GDEVICE procedure, general reference

Chapter 25, "The GDEVICE Procedure", *SAS/GRAPH Software: Reference, Volume 2*, pp. 889-932

GOPTIONS procedure, general reference

Chapter 30, "The GOPTIONS Procedure", *SAS/GRAPH Software: Reference, Volume 2*, pp. 1063-1071

How to Structure Data for Graphs

In This Chapter

- What is data structure?
- Data for bar and pie charts
- Data for maps
- Data for plots
- Restructuring data for graphs

What is data structure?

Data structure refers to the way your SAS data set is organized into observations (rows) and variables (columns). Data can be structured in many ways. For example, the SAS data set CARS1 holds information on the cars owned by three people: Tom, Maria, and Dave.

CARS1 data set

```
OBS    TOMCAR    MARIACAR    DAVECAR

 1      FORD       ACURA      NISSAN
```

CARS1 has one observation and three variables: TOMCAR, MARIACAR, and DAVECAR. The person who owns the car is identified in the variable name. The same information can be restructured as shown in the data set CARS2.

CARS2 data set

```
OBS    NAME    CAR

 1     TOM     FORD
 2     MARIA   ACURA
 3     DAVE    NISSAN
```

CARS2 has three observations and two variables: NAME and CAR. The person who owns the car is identified by the value of the variable NAME.
SAS/GRAPH procedures require data that is structured like the CARS2 data set, where each observation contains information about a single entity, in this case, a person. The information held about each person is the name and the kind of car owned. In contrast, CARS1 holds data about all three people in a single observation.

There are some guidelines you can use to make sure your data are structured properly for SAS/GRAPH procedures. The following examples show data sets structured correctly for the types of graphs discussed in this book.

Data for bar and pie charts

Bar and pie charts created with PROC GCHART show a quantity associated with each value of a chart variable. There is one bar or slice for each value or range of values of the chart variable. Additional variables can be used to show sums, segments, and groups of bars or pies. The following examples show how these variables are used to create bar and pie charts. The SAS data set CHARTIT, shown on the next page, is used in both examples. The first example shows a bar chart of utility costs.

Summary variable
When a summary variable is used, the bar height represents its sum or mean. Here, the bars show the sum of the variable AMOUNT. If no summary variable is used, the chart represents frequency (count) instead of sum or mean.

Chart variable
The chart variable is the only required variable. A bar is generated for each value of the chart variable QUARTER.

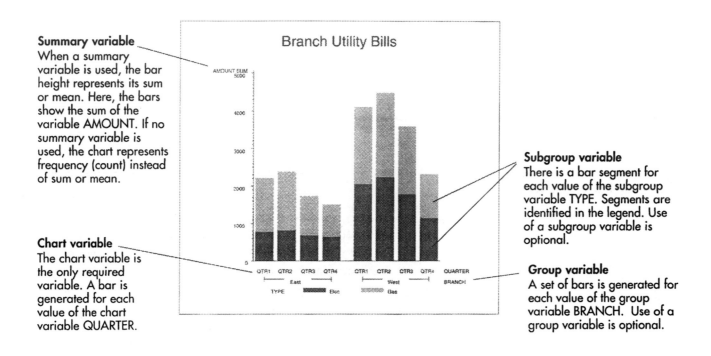

Subgroup variable
There is a bar segment for each value of the subgroup variable TYPE. Segments are identified in the legend. Use of a subgroup variable is optional.

Group variable
A set of bars is generated for each value of the group variable BRANCH. Use of a group variable is optional.

The following program uses variables from the CHARTIT data set to generate the bar chart shown above.

Chart variable
The chart variable QUARTER is named in the VBAR statement.

Subgroup variable
The subgroup variable TYPE is named in the SUBGROUP= option.

```
00001    title "Branch Utility Bills";
00002
00003    proc gchart data=chartit;
00004      vbar quarter /
00005        sumvar=amount
00006        group=branch
00007        subgroup=type
00008      ;
00009    run;
00010    quit;
```

Summary variable
The summary variable AMOUNT is named in the SUMVAR= option.

Group variable
The group variable BRANCH is named in the GROUP= option.

The PIE statement SUBGROUP= option is not shown here, but SAS Release 6.10 and beyond allows you to use a subgroup variable with pie charts. The PIE statement SUBGROUP= option generates concentric pies, with one pie for each value of the subgroup variable.

Chart variable
QUARTER identifies each quarter of the year. QUARTER is the chart variable.

```
                        CHARTIT

OBS    QUARTER    TYPE    BRANCH    AMOUNT

  1     QTR1      Gas     East       1433
  2     QTR1      Elec    East        780
  3     QTR1      Gas     West       2052
  4     QTR1      Elec    West       2052
  5     QTR2      Gas     East       1555
  6     QTR2      Elec    East        821
  7     QTR2      Gas     West       2239
  8     QTR2      Elec    West       2239
  9     QTR3      Gas     East       1051
 10     QTR3      Elec    East        682
 11     QTR3      Gas     West       1789
 12     QTR3      Elec    West       1789
 13     QTR4      Gas     East        850
 14     QTR4      Elec    East        652
 15     QTR4      Gas     West       1154
 16     QTR4      Elec    West       1154
```

Summary variable
The summary variable is summed (or averaged) for each value of the chart variable AMOUNT.

Subgroup variable
If you want to break bars or pies into segments (subgroups), you need a separate subgroup variable. Here the subgroup variable is TYPE.

Group variable
A separate pie or bar group is generated for each value of the group variable. BRANCH is the group variable.

The following pie chart is generated from the CHARTIT data set using the program below.

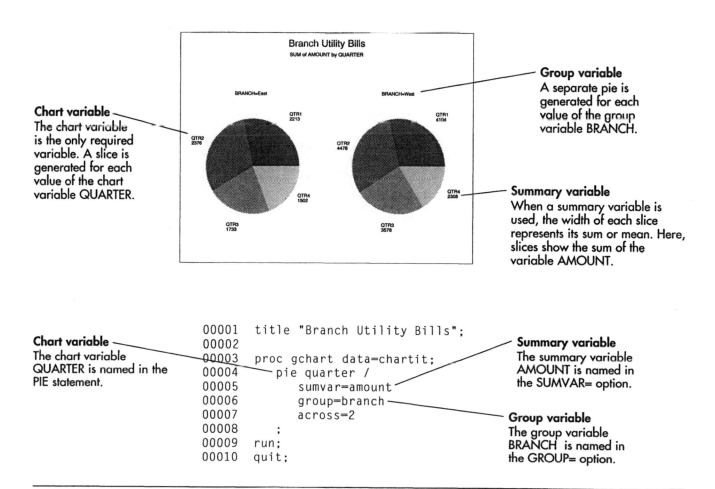

Group variable
A separate pie is generated for each value of the group variable BRANCH.

Chart variable
The chart variable is the only required variable. A slice is generated for each value of the chart variable QUARTER.

Summary variable
When a summary variable is used, the width of each slice represents its sum or mean. Here, slices show the sum of the variable AMOUNT.

Chart variable
The chart variable QUARTER is named in the PIE statement.

```
00001    title "Branch Utility Bills";
00002
00003    proc gchart data=chartit;
00004       pie quarter /
00005          sumvar=amount
00006          group=branch
00007          across=2
00008       ;
00009    run;
00010    quit;
```

Summary variable
The summary variable AMOUNT is named in the SUMVAR= option.

Group variable
The group variable BRANCH is named in the GROUP= option.

The following tables describe the SAS data set variables used in bar and pie charts. See "Part 2" for more on bar charts and "Part 7" for more on pie charts.

Bar Chart Variables

	Variable Description	Variable Name In Example	SAS Code In Example	Required For This Procedure?
Chart variable	There is a bar for each value (or range of values) of this variable	QUARTER	VBAR QUARTER line 4	Yes. This is the minimum requirement to create a bar chart.
Summary variable	The height of each bar represents the sum or mean of this variable.	AMOUNT	SUMVAR=AMOUNT line 5	No. If no SUMVAR= variable is specified, each bar represents frequency.
Subgroup variable	There is a bar segment for each value of this variable.	TYPE	SUBGROUP=TYPE line 7	No
Group variable	A side-by-side group of bars is generated for each value of this variable.	BRANCH	GROUP=BRANCH line 6	No

Pie Chart Variables

	Variable Description	Variable Name In Example	SAS Code In Example	Required For This Procedure?
Chart variable	There is a slice for each value (or range of values) of this variable	QUARTER	PIE QUARTER line 4	Yes. This is the minimum requirement to create a pie chart.
Summary variable	The width of each slice represents the sum or mean of this variable.	AMOUNT	SUMVAR=AMOUNT line 5	No. If no SUMVAR= variable is specified, the width of each slice represents frequency.
Subgroup variable	There is a concentric pie for each value of this variable.	not shown	not shown	No
Group variable	A separate pie is generated for each value of this variable.	BRANCH	GROUP=BRANCH line 6	No

Data for maps

The GMAP procedure requires two data sets: the map data set and the response data set. The SAS data set containing response data must have at least two variables. The response variable represents some attribute of a geographic area, such as the number of job sites per state as shown in the example below. The second required variable is an ID variable that identifies each geographic area. In the example, STATE is the ID variable.

Normally, you will be using Institute-supplied map data sets or maps derived from these data sets. You should not have to worry about the structure of these map data sets, but you must know the names of the ID variable (or variables) in the map data set. The ID variable in your response data set must match the name, type, and length of the ID variable in the map data set. If you are unsure, use PROC CONTENTS to compare the structure of your response data set and the map data set. See "Part 4" for more on maps.

The following example uses the SAS data set JOBSITES, shown on the next page. JOBSITES contains information about the number of job sites in each state. States are identified by FIPS code (Federal Information Processing Standards) in the data set JOBSITES and in the map data set MAPS.US. The resulting map is shown below.

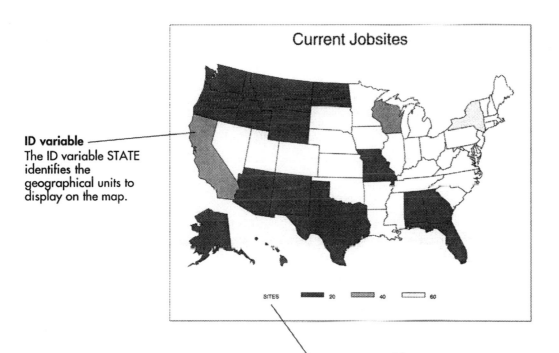

ID variable
The ID variable STATE identifies the geographical units to display on the map.

Response variable
Response variable values are represented by patterns in the map. In this map, the response variable SITES is grouped into three ranges by the LEVELS=3 option.

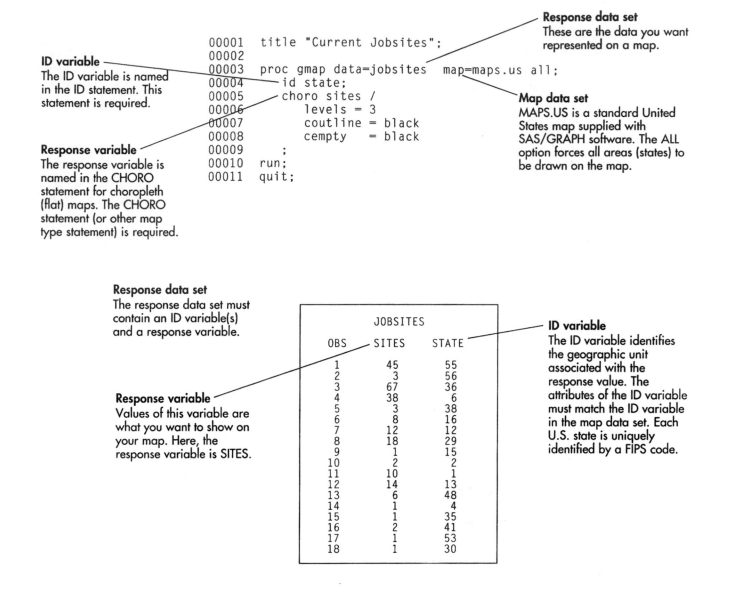

Response data set
These are the data you want represented on a map.

ID variable
The ID variable is named in the ID statement. This statement is required.

Map data set
MAPS.US is a standard United States map supplied with SAS/GRAPH software. The ALL option forces all areas (states) to be drawn on the map.

Response variable
The response variable is named in the CHORO statement for choropleth (flat) maps. The CHORO statement (or other map type statement) is required.

```
00001   title "Current Jobsites";
00002
00003   proc gmap data=jobsites   map=maps.us all;
00004     id state;
00005     choro sites /
00006         levels = 3
00007         coutline = black
00008         cempty   = black
00009      ;
00010   run;
00011   quit;
```

Response data set
The response data set must contain an ID variable(s) and a response variable.

Response variable
Values of this variable are what you want to show on your map. Here, the response variable is SITES.

```
              JOBSITES

OBS      SITES      STATE

  1        45         55
  2         3         56
  3        67         36
  4        38          6
  5         3         38
  6         8         16
  7        12         12
  8        18         29
  9         1         15
 10         2          2
 11        10          1
 12        14         13
 13         6         48
 14         1          4
 15         1         35
 16         2         41
 17         1         53
 18         1         30
```

ID variable
The ID variable identifies the geographic unit associated with the response value. The attributes of the ID variable must match the ID variable in the map data set. Each U.S. state is uniquely identified by a FIPS code.

The following table describes the response data set variables used with PROC GMAP.

Map Variables

	Variable Description	Variable Name In Example	SAS Code In Example	Required For This Procedure?
Response variable	Each value or range of values of this variable is displayed with a distinct pattern.	SITES	CHORO SITES line 5	Yes
ID variable	The values of this variable identify geographic areas. The ID variable must match the name, type, and length of the map data set ID variable.	STATE	ID STATE line 4	Yes

Data for plots

Plots show the relationship between two variables, so you need a minimum of two variables in your data set. These are referred to as the *x* and *y*, independent and dependent, or horizontal and vertical axis variables. You can create many plots in a PROC GPLOT step and your plotting data set may contain several pairs of *x* and *y* variables. You may also have a third variable, or classification variable, as shown in the example below. PROC GPLOT generates a separate line or set of points relating the *x* and *y* variables for each value of the classification variable.

The following example uses the REVENUES data set, shown on the next page, to generate the plot below.

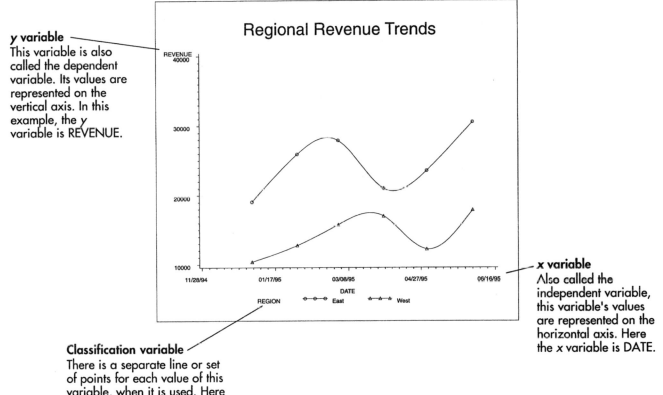

y variable
This variable is also called the dependent variable. Its values are represented on the vertical axis. In this example, the *y* variable is REVENUE.

x variable
Also called the independent variable, this variable's values are represented on the horizontal axis. Here the *x* variable is DATE.

Classification variable
There is a separate line or set of points for each value of this variable, when it is used. Here the classification variable is REGION.

The GPLOT program below uses the REVENUES data set to create the plot shown on the previous page.

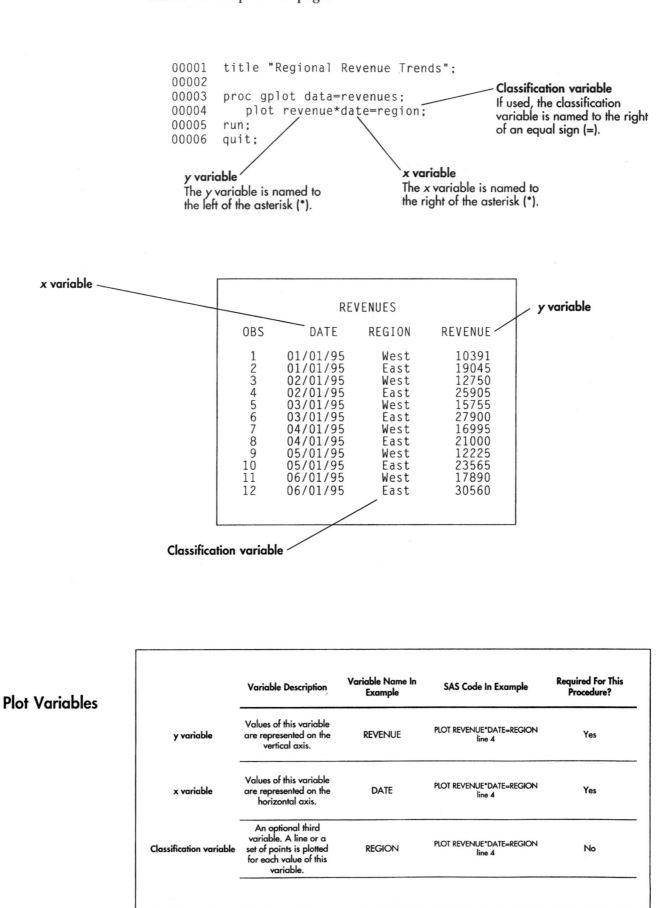

```
00001   title "Regional Revenue Trends";
00002
00003   proc gplot data=revenues;
00004      plot revenue*date=region;
00005   run;
00006   quit;
```

Classification variable
If used, the classification variable is named to the right of an equal sign (=).

y variable
The y variable is named to the left of the asterisk (*).

x variable
The x variable is named to the right of the asterisk (*).

x variable

y variable

REVENUES

OBS	DATE	REGION	REVENUE
1	01/01/95	West	10391
2	01/01/95	East	19045
3	02/01/95	West	12750
4	02/01/95	East	25905
5	03/01/95	West	15755
6	03/01/95	East	27900
7	04/01/95	West	16995
8	04/01/95	East	21000
9	05/01/95	West	12225
10	05/01/95	East	23565
11	06/01/95	West	17890
12	06/01/95	East	30560

Classification variable

Plot Variables

	Variable Description	Variable Name In Example	SAS Code In Example	Required For This Procedure?
y variable	Values of this variable are represented on the vertical axis.	REVENUE	PLOT REVENUE*DATE=REGION line 4	Yes
x variable	Values of this variable are represented on the horizontal axis.	DATE	PLOT REVENUE*DATE=REGION line 4	Yes
Classification variable	An optional third variable. A line or a set of points is plotted for each value of this variable.	REGION	PLOT REVENUE*DATE=REGION line 4	No

Restructuring data for graphs

If your data are not structured properly, you can usually run a SAS DATA step to build a restructured SAS data set for use with a SAS/GRAPH procedure. The example below represents a common data structure problem: utility costs are recorded in an observation for each quarter of the year with four types of cost included in each observation. The different types of cost are distinguished by variable names such as EBGAS for the east branch gas cost and WBGAS for the west branch gas cost. To use this data with PROC GCHART, each observation must hold a single cost, not four.

The program below restructures the utility cost data. The information in each of the original observations is written to the temporary SAS data set CHARTIT, as four observations. Instead of distinguishing the type of cost with a separate variable (EBGAS, EBELEC, WBGAS, or WBELEC), it is distinguished by the values of the variables TYPE (Gas or Elec) and BRANCH (East or West).

Original data set
Each observation holds utility costs for a quarter of the year. Four types of cost are held in each observation.

		UTILITY			
OBS	QUARTER	EBGAS	EBELEC	WBGAS	WBELEC
1	QTR1	1433	780	2052	1148
2	QTR2	1555	821	2239	1246
3	QTR3	1051	682	1789	1017
4	QTR4	850	652	1154	908

Restructured data set
A temporary SAS data set named CHARTIT will be built from the original data.

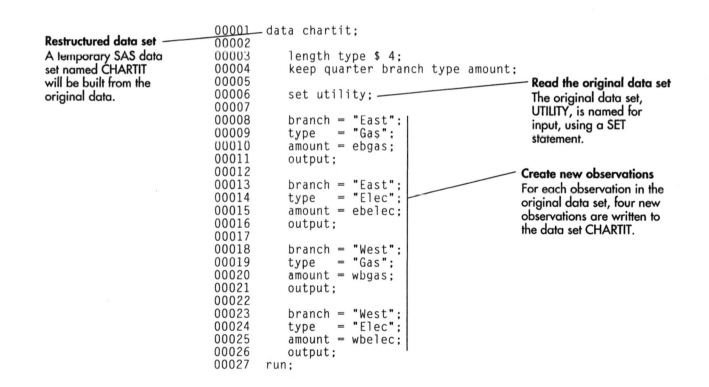

```
00001  data chartit;
00002
00003     length type $ 4;
00004     keep quarter branch type amount;
00005
00006     set utility;
00007
00008     branch = "East";
00009     type   = "Gas";
00010     amount = ebgas;
00011     output;
00012
00013     branch = "East";
00014     type   = "Elec";
00015     amount = ebelec;
00016     output;
00017
00018     branch = "West";
00019     type   = "Gas";
00020     amount = wbgas;
00021     output;
00022
00023     branch = "West";
00024     type   = "Elec";
00025     amount = wbelec;
00026     output;
00027  run;
```

Read the original data set
The original data set, UTILITY, is named for input, using a SET statement.

Create new observations
For each observation in the original data set, four new observations are written to the data set CHARTIT.

Restructured data
In the new data set, the values of the variables TYPE, QUARTER, and BRANCH distinguish each amount.

```
                          CHARTIT

    OBS     TYPE     QUARTER     BRANCH     AMOUNT
     1      Gas      QTR1        East       1433
     2      Elec     QTR1        East        780
     3      Gas      QTR1        West       2052
     4      Elec     QTR1        West       2052
     5      Gas      QTR2        East       1555
     6      Elec     QTR2        East        821
     7      Gas      QTR2        West       2239
     8      Elec     QTR2        West       2239
     9      Gas      QTR3        East       1051
    10      Elec     QTR3        East        682
    11      Gas      QTR3        West       1789
    12      Elec     QTR3        West       1789
    13      Gas      QTR4        East        850
    14      Elec     QTR4        East        652
    15      Gas      QTR4        West       1154
    16      Elec     QTR4        West       1154
```

TYPE
The values of TYPE determine whether AMOUNT is for gas or electricity.

QUARTER
The values of QUARTER determine which quarter the cost is for.

BRANCH
The values of BRANCH determine which branch office the cost is for.

AMOUNT
This is the cost for each item.

Chart variable QUARTER

Subgroup variable TYPE

```
00001     title "Branch Utility Bills";
00002
00003     proc gchart data=chartit;
00004       vbar quarter /
00005           sumvar=amount
00006           group=branch
00007           subgroup=type
00008       ;
00009     run;
00010     quit;
```

Summary variable AMOUNT

Group variable BRANCH

Utility cost chart
Once the quarter, type of bill, branch, and amount are all held in separate variables, they can be used with the various PROC GCHART options to create a chart showing the relationships among the various utility cost factors.

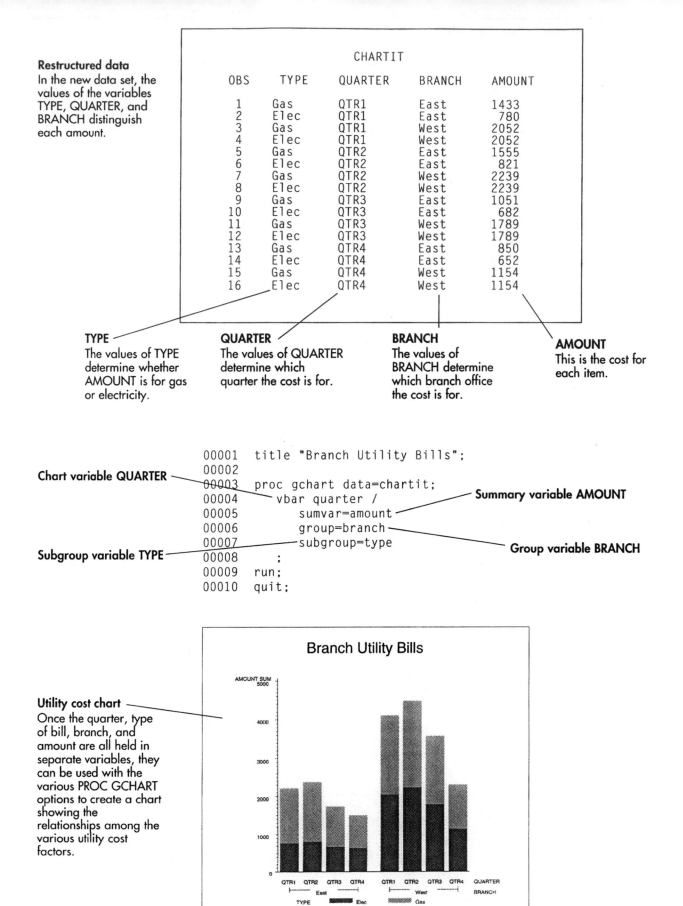

More Information

restructuring data for graphics, discussion and example

"Structuring Data to Produce a Classification Variable", in Chapter 21, "Producing Plots with Legends", *SAS/GRAPH Software: Usage, Version 6, First Edition*, pp. 296-300

PROC GCHART, chart variables

"Data Considerations" in Chapter 23, "The GCHART Procedure", *SAS/GRAPH Software: Reference, Volume 2, Version 6, First Edition*, pp. 760-763

PROC GMAP map data sets

"Map Data Sets" in Chapter 29, "The GMAP Procedure", *SAS/GRAPH Software: Reference, Volume 2*, pp. 1007-1012

PROC GMAP response data sets (your data)

"Response Data Sets" in Chapter 29, "The GMAP Procedure", *SAS/GRAPH Software: Reference, Volume 2*, pp. 1013-1014

PROC GPLOT, data sets for plotting

"Data Considerations" in Chapter 31, "The GPLOT Procedure", *SAS/GRAPH Software: Reference, Volume 2*, pp. 1080-1081

DATA step programming, overview

Chapter 2, "The DATA Step", *SAS Language: Reference, Version 6, First Edition*, pp. 13-42

OUTPUT statement, reference

"OUTPUT" in Chapter 9, "SAS Language Statements", *SAS Language: Reference*, pp. 447-448

7 Using Graphics Options

In This Chapter

- What are graphics options?
- Using graphics options
- When to use global versus statement options
- What can graphics options do?

What are graphics options?

Graphics options are similar to standard SAS system options like LINESIZE=, PAGESIZE=, or NOSOURCE. Like standard system options, graphics options are global: they remain in effect until you change them or your SAS session or job ends.

Graphics options
Graphics options are independent of individual steps in your program. Graphics option settings are available to all SAS/GRAPH procedures.

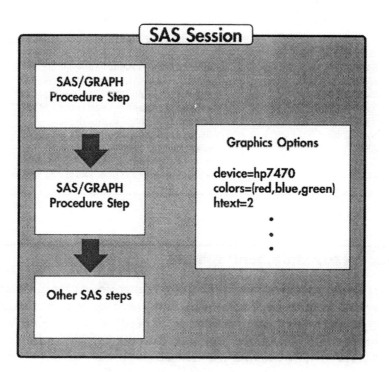

SAS Session

SAS/GRAPH Procedure Step

SAS/GRAPH Procedure Step

Other SAS steps

Graphics Options

device=hp7470
colors=(red,blue,green)
htext=2

Using graphics options

Most graphics options have default settings. You can change these settings with the GOPTIONS statement. Any number of options can be set in a single GOPTIONS statement. The following GOPTIONS statement sets the DEVICE= option to HP7470 and the ROTATE= option to LANDSCAPE.

Set specific options

```
00001   goptions device=hp7470 rotate=landscape;
```

You can reset all options to their defaults by executing the following statement.

Reset all options

```
00001   goptions reset=all;
```

To list the current graphics options use PROC GOPTIONS. When you execute the following step, the options list will appear in the SAS log.

List option settings

```
00001   proc goptions;
00002   run;
```

You can redirect the list from the log to the OUTPUT window or standard print destination with the NOLOG option.

List options in the the standard print destination

```
00001   proc goptions nolog;
00002   run;
```

Following is a partial PROC GOPTIONS output.

PROC GOPTIONS output

```
                    SAS/GRAPH software options and parameters

     NOADMGDF              GDDM driver output an ADMGDF file
     ASPECT=               Aspect ratio (width/height) for software characters
     NOAUTOCOPY            Automatic hardcopy after display
     NOAUTOFEED            Automatic paper feed after plot
     BAUD=                 Communications line speed
     NOBORDER              Draw a border around display or plot
     CBACK=                Background color
     CBY=                  BY line color
     CELL                  Hardware characters must be on cell boundaries
```

When to use global versus statement options

In some cases you have a choice of controlling a graphics element with a global graphics option or with a statement option. For example, if you want to change the first title-line font to CENTBE (Century bold, empty), you could set the FTITLE= global option or use the FONT= option in your TITLE statement. The method you use affects the scope of the setting. Remember that graphics options are global, so they affect all following graphics output. If you want the first title line for *all* procedure output displayed in the CENTBE font, then use the FTITLE= option. If you want just one title displayed in CENTBE, use the FONT= option in the TITLE statement.

What can graphics options do?

Graphics options control many aspects of the graphics environment, for example, the output device, fonts, colors, and output size. Following is a list of graphics options grouped by category. Some options appear in more than one category. Some rarely used options are not listed. Commonly used options are marked with ✔. For complete documentation on an option, see the references listed under "More Information."

Color

CBACK=	Background color
CBY=	BY line color
✔ COLORS=	Default color list
CPATTERN=	Default pattern color
CSYMBOL=	Default symbol color
CTEXT=	Default text color
CTITLE=	Default title, footnote, and note color

Display Control

DISPLAY	Display graph on device
GWAIT=	Time delay between graphs being displayed
KEYMAP=	Selects the keyboard map to use
SWAP	Reverses black and white in graphics output
✔ TARGETDEVICE=	Intended hardcopy device

Fonts

CHARACTERS	Use hardware characters
CHARTYPE=	Select hardware font
FBY=	BY line font
✔ FTEXT=	Default text font
FTITLE=	Default font for first title
HBY=	BY line height
✔ HTEXT=	Default text height
HTITLE=	Default height of first TITLE line
KEYMAP=	Selects the keyboard map to use
SIMFONT=	Software font to use as simulated hardware font

Graphics Catalog Control

GOUTMODE=	GOUT catalog mode: APPEND or REPLACE
PCLIP	Stores clipped polygons with the graph

Mainframe Computers

ADMGDF	Specifies whether to write an ADMGDF file
DEVADDR=	IBM Device address or node name
GACCESS=	Output format for graphics stream
GCLASS=	IBM3287 sysout class
GDDMCOPY=	GDDM driver hardcopy type
GDDMNICKNAME=	GDDM nickname
GDDMTOKEN=	GDDM token
GDEST=	IBM3287 sysout destination
GFORMS=	IBM3287 sysout forms code
GPROTOCOL=	Sets output stream format for protocol converters
GRAPHRC	SAS/GRAPH is to issue step condition codes at exit
GWRITER=	IBM3287 sysout writer name
TRANTAB=	Terminal translate table

Output Device Control

	AUTOCOPY	Generates hardcopy automatically
	AUTOFEED	Feeds paper automatically
	BAUD=	Communications line speed
	CELL	Hardware characters must be on cell boundaries
	CHARACTERS	Use hardware characters
	CHARTYPE=	Select hardware font
	CIRCLEARC	Use hardware circle/arc generator
✔	COLORS=	Default color list
	DASH	Use hardware dashed-line generator
✔	DEVICE=	Default device driver
	DEVMAP=	Specifies the device map for hardware fonts
	FILL	Use hardware rectangle fill generator
	FILLINC=	Moves a number of pixels before drawing a line in software fill
	GCOPIES=	Number of output copies
	GEND=	Buffer termination string
	GEPILOG=	Device termination string
	GPROLOG=	Device initialization string
	GSTART=	Buffer initialization string
	HANDSHAKE=	ASCII device handshake protocol
	HORIGIN=	Horizontal offset to graph origin
	HPOS=	Character cells per line
	HSIZE=	Horizontal plot size in inches
	LFACTOR=	Hardware line-thickness factor
	PAPERFEED=	Amount of paper to feed on drum plotters
	PAPERLIMIT=	Physical width of the plotting paper
	PENMOUNTS=	Number of pens/colors to be used
	PENSORT	Sort plotter colors
	PIEFILL	Use hardware pie fill generator
	POLYGONCLIP	Allows polygons with a device-dependent pattern to be clipped
	POLYGONFILL	Use hardware polygon fill generator
	PROMPT	Allow/disallow user prompting by device driver
	PROMPTCHARS=	Terminal prompt characters
✔	ROTATE=	Controls page orientation
	SIMFONT=	Software font to use as simulated hardware font
	SPEED=	Pen speed
	SWAP	Reverses black and white in graphics output
	SYMBOL	Use hardware symbol generator
	VORIGIN=	Vertical offset to graph origin
	VPOS=	Character cells per column
	VSIZE=	Vertical plot size in inches
	V5COMP	Allows programs developed under Version 5 to run under Version 6

Output Graphics Stream File Control

GACCESS=	Output format for graphics stream
GSFLEN=	Length of Graphics Stream File records
GSFMODE=	Graphics Stream File access mode
GSFNAME=	Graphics Stream File name
GSFPROMPT	Writes prompt messages to the graphics stream file

Size, Shape, Appearance

✔	ASPECT=	Aspect ratio (width/height) for graphics elements
	BORDER	Draws a border around the graphics output area
	FILLINC=	Moves a number of pixels before drawing a line in software fill
	GUNIT=	Default text units
	HORIGIN=	Horizontal offset to graph origin
	HPOS=	Character cells per line
	HSIZE=	Horizontal plot size in inches
	INTERPOL=	Default symbol interpolation
	LFACTOR=	Hardware line-thickness factor
✔	OFFSHADOW=	X, Y offset for dropshadows
✔	ROTATE=	Controls page orientation
	TARGETDEVICE=	Intended hardcopy device
	VORIGIN=	Vertical offset to graph origin
	VPOS=	Character cells per column
	VSIZE=	Vertical plot size in inches

More Information

graphics options, reference

Chapter 5, "Graphics Options and Device Parameters Dictionary", *SAS/GRAPH Software: Reference, Volume 1, Version 6, First Edition*, pp. 85-153

GOPTIONS statement, reference and examples

Chapter 12, "The GOPTIONS Statement", *SAS/GRAPH Software: Reference, Volume 1*, pp. 291-302

graphics options, categorized (alternative to categories herein)

"Syntax" in Chapter 12, "The GOPTIONS Statement", *SAS/GRAPH Software: Reference, Volume 1*, pp. 291-294

graphics options, updates and additions

See the SAS Technical Reports covering changes and enhancements for your current release of SAS software. For example:

SAS Technical Report P-215, SAS/GRAPH Software: Changes and Enhancements, Release 6.07 and *SAS Technical Report P-242, SAS Software: Changes and Enhancements, Release 6.08*

GOPTIONS procedure, general reference

Chapter 30, "The GOPTIONS Procedure", *SAS/GRAPH Software: Reference, Volume 2*, pp. 1063-1071

Part 2
Working with
Bar Charts

Chapter 8 - Charting Counts

Chapter 9 - Charting Sums

Chapter 10 - Charting Averages

Chapter 11 - Charting Percentages

Chapter 12 - Displaying Statistics

Chapter 13 - Changing the Order of Bars

Chapter 14 - Changing Bar Width and Spacing

Chapter 15 - Charting with Numeric Variables

Chapter 16 - Using Value Ranges in Charts

Chapter 17 - Controlling Bar Fill Patterns

Charting Counts

In This Chapter

- Bar charts show counts by default
- Charting counts with numeric variables
- Making each observation count more than once
- Showing subgroup contributions to the total count
- Comparing data groups side-by-side

Bar charts show counts by default

Horizontal and vertical bar charts can represent frequency (count), sums, means, or percents. The default chart type is frequency.

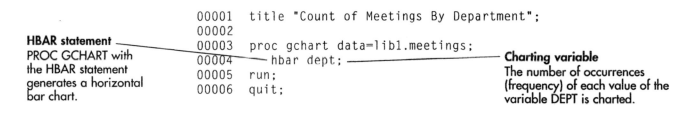

HBAR statement
PROC GCHART with the HBAR statement generates a horizontal bar chart.

```
00001    title "Count of Meetings By Department";
00002
00003    proc gchart data=lib1.meetings;
00004        hbar dept;
00005    run;
00006    quit;
```

Charting variable
The number of occurrences (frequency) of each value of the variable DEPT is charted.

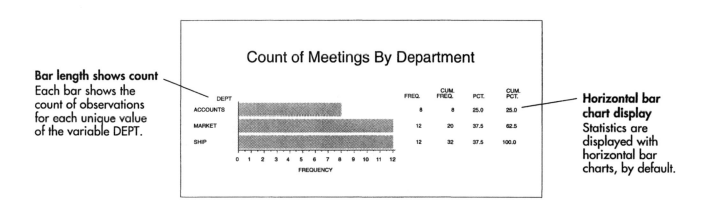

Bar length shows count
Each bar shows the count of observations for each unique value of the variable DEPT.

Count of Meetings By Department

DEPT	FREQ.	CUM. FREQ.	PCT.	CUM. PCT.
ACCOUNTS	8	8	25.0	25.0
MARKET	12	20	37.5	62.5
SHIP	12	32	37.5	100.0

FREQUENCY

Horizontal bar chart display
Statistics are displayed with horizontal bar charts, by default.

Closer Look

Count is also referred to as frequency. Normally, each observation is counted once. In the example above, the bar for the accounting department has a length of eight. This means there were eight observations in the data set LIB1.MEETINGS where the value of the variable DEPT was ACCOUNTS. See "Data Used in Examples" at the end of this book for a listing of the input data set.

Charting counts with numeric variables

In addition to counting occurrences with character variables, you can chart with numeric variables. When charting numeric variables, PROC GCHART groups the numeric data around midpoints. Midpoints are selected based on the range of values in the data. The following example shows the default midpoints for the variable HOURS in the data set LIB1.MEETINGS. See Chapter 15 for more on charting numeric variables.

```
00001    title "Count of Meetings By Length";
00002
00003    proc gchart data=lib1.meetings;
00004       vbar hours;
00005    run;
00006    quit;
```

VBAR with a numeric variable
The VBAR statement generates a frequency chart for the variable HOURS. HOURS values are grouped into midpoints.

Frequency chart
The default chart type is frequency (count).

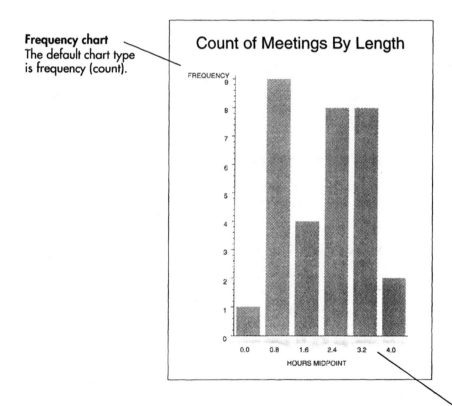

Bars at midpoints
Instead of a bar for each unique value of HOURS, there is a bar for each of the default midpoints generated by PROC GCHART.

Making each observation count more than once

Normally each observation in the charting data set is counted once. However, you can use the FREQ= option in the VBAR or HBAR statement to weight the contribution of each observation. In the following example, the numeric variable POP is used to weight each observation. The charting variable is REGION. Instead of each observation counting once towards the frequency of each value for REGION, it counts the value of the variable POP.

Input data
In this example, each observation will be weighted by the value of the variable POP.

```
                    LIB1.DEER

        OBS    REGION    TYPE    POP

         1     North     buck     57
         2     North     doe      89
         3     North     fawn     21
         4     Central   buck    107
         5     Central   doe     231
         6     Central   fawn     54
         7     South     buck     72
         8     South     doe     101
         9     South     fawn     15
```

```
00001   title "Deer Population Count";
00002
00003   proc gchart data=lib1.deer;
00004      vbar region /
00005          type=freq
00006          freq=pop
00007      ;
00008   run;
00009   quit;
```

TYPE= option
The TYPE= option specifies a frequency chart.

The FREQ= option
Each observation is weighted by the value of the variable POP.

Weighted frequency
With the FREQ= option, each bar shows the count of the variable REGION weighted by the variable POP.

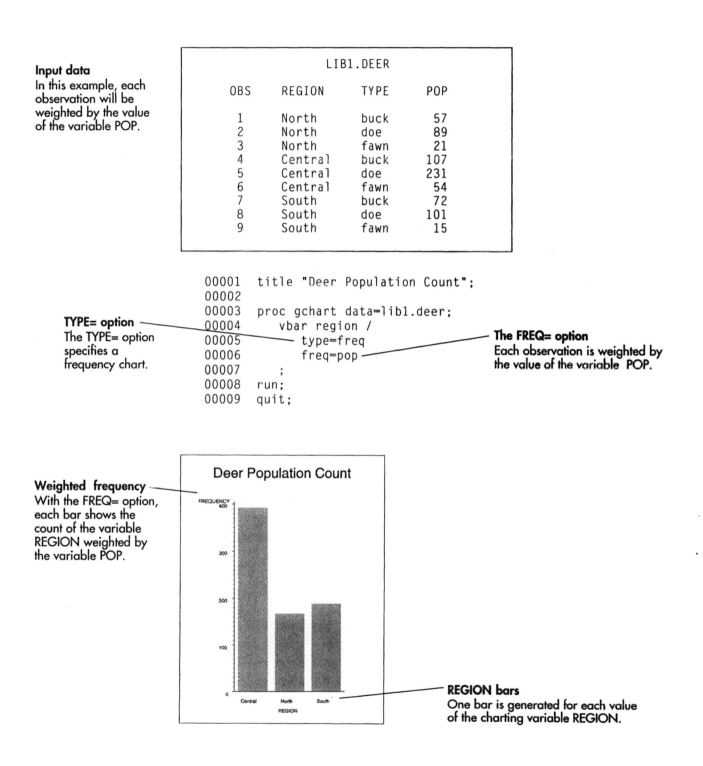

Deer Population Count

REGION bars
One bar is generated for each value of the charting variable REGION.

Showing subgroup contributions to the total count

With the SUBGROUP= option, you can create segmented bars that show how subgroups of data contribute to the total count, which is represented by the height of each bar.

```
00001   title "Count of Meetings";
00002
00003   proc gchart data=lib1.meetings;
00004      vbar room /
00005           subgroup=dept
00006   ;
00007   run;
00008   quit;
```

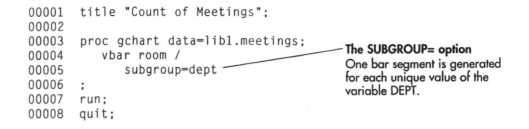

The SUBGROUP= option
One bar segment is generated for each unique value of the variable DEPT.

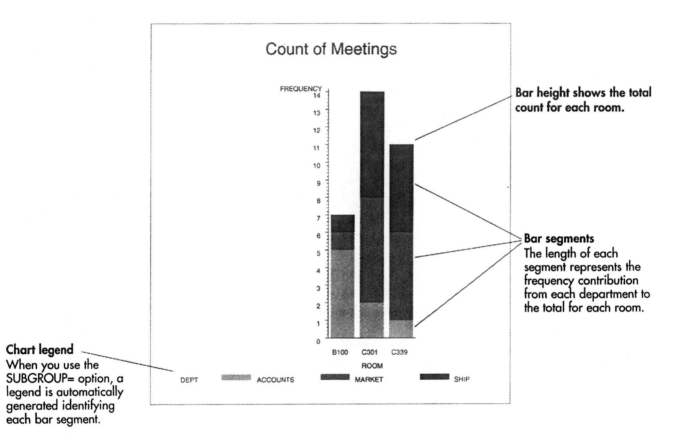

Bar height shows the total count for each room.

Bar segments
The length of each segment represents the frequency contribution from each department to the total for each room.

Chart legend
When you use the SUBGROUP= option, a legend is automatically generated identifying each bar segment.

The FREQ= option (see example on the previous page) uses only the integer portion of the frequency weight variable. If the value of the weighting variable for a given observation is 9.75, a weight of 9 will be given to that observation. There is no rounding.

Do not confuse the FREQ= option with the TYPE=FREQ option. The TYPE= option names the statistic represented by the height of the bars. TYPE=FREQ means the height of each bar represents frequency. TYPE=FREQ is the default if the TYPE= option is not used, as shown in the example above.

Comparing data groups side-by-side

You can name a group variable with the GROUP= option. Observations for each value of the group variable are represented in a bar group. Bar groups are displayed side-by-side, on a single set of axes.

```
00001   title "Count of Meetings";
00002
00003   proc gchart data=lib1.meetings;
00004      vbar room /
00005         group=dept
00006   ;
00007   run;
00008   quit;
```

GROUP= option
The GROUP= option specifies that the count for each department be charted side-by-side.

Meeting count
Within each department group, the height of each bar represents the number of meetings in each room.

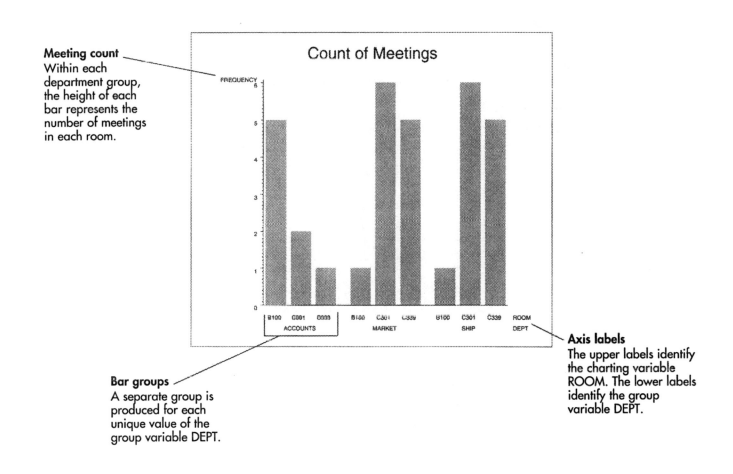

Bar groups
A separate group is produced for each unique value of the group variable DEPT.

Axis labels
The upper labels identify the charting variable ROOM. The lower labels identify the group variable DEPT.

 Closer Look When you use the GROUP= option, the total number of bars is the number of unique values of the group variable (DEPT, in the example) multiplied by the number of bars for the charting variable (ROOM, in the example.) To avoid a cluttered chart, use grouping variables with a small number of unique values.

More Information

frequency chart, examples and discussion

Chapter 3, "Bar Charts", *SAS/GRAPH Software: Introduction, Version 6, First Edition,* pp. 20-26

Chapter 4, "Introduction to Bar Charts", *SAS/GRAPH Software: Usage, Version 6, First Edition,* pp. 28-34

PROC GCHART, general reference

Chapter 23, "The GCHART Procedure", *SAS/GRAPH Software: Reference, Volume 2,* pp. 751-766, pp. 782-809 (HBAR), pp. 842-865 (VBAR)

GROUP= option, reference

Chapter 23, *SAS/GRAPH Software: Reference, Volume 2,* p. 788 (HBAR), pp. 848-849 (VBAR)

SUBGROUP= option, reference

Chapter 23, *SAS/GRAPH Software: Reference, Volume 2,* p. 793 (HBAR), p. 854 (VBAR)

FREQ= option, reference

Chapter 23, *SAS/GRAPH Software: Reference, Volume 2,* p. 788 (HBAR), p. 848 (VBAR)

TYPE= option, reference

Chapter 23, *SAS/GRAPH Software: Reference, Volume 2,* p. 794 (HBAR), p. 854 (VBAR)

Charting Sums

In This Chapter

- **Using the TYPE=SUM and SUMVAR= options to chart sums**
- **Showing subgroup bar segments**
- **Showing bar groups**

Using the TYPE=SUM and SUMVAR= options to chart sums

When you want the height of each bar to represent a sum, use the TYPE=SUM and SUMVAR= options in the VBAR or HBAR statement in the GCHART procedure.

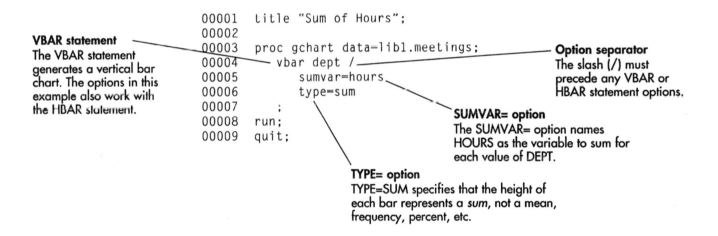

VBAR statement
The VBAR statement generates a vertical bar chart. The options in this example also work with the HBAR statement.

```
00001   title "Sum of Hours";
00002
00003   proc gchart data=lib1.meetings;
00004      vbar dept /
00005         sumvar=hours
00006         type=sum
00007      ;
00008   run;
00009   quit;
```

Option separator
The slash (/) must precede any VBAR or HBAR statement options.

SUMVAR= option
The SUMVAR= option names HOURS as the variable to sum for each value of DEPT.

TYPE= option
TYPE=SUM specifies that the height of each bar represents a *sum*, not a mean, frequency, percent, etc.

When you use the SUMVAR= option, the TYPE= option defaults to SUM; so it is not strictly necessary to add the TYPE= option to produce a sum chart. Using TYPE=SUM makes it clear to someone reading your program that you want a sum chart, not a means chart. See Chapter 10 for TYPE=MEAN examples.

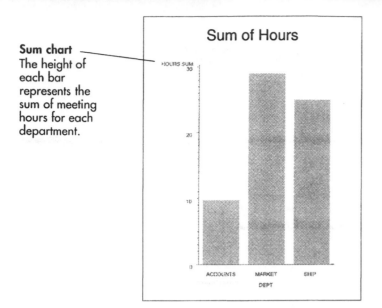

Sum chart
The height of each bar represents the sum of meeting hours for each department.

Showing subgroup bar segments

You can show how subgroups contribute to a sum by using the SUBGROUP= option. Here, SUBGROUP=ROOM is added to the program shown in the previous example. There is one bar for each department. The bars are broken into segments for each meeting room.

SUMVAR= option
The SUMVAR= option names the variable to sum.

TYPE= option
TYPE=SUM specifies that the height of each bar represents a sum.

```
00001    title "Sum of Hours";
00002
00003    proc gchart data=lib1.meetings;
00004      vbar dept /
00005        sumvar=hours
00006        type=sum
00007        subgroup=room
00008      ;
00009    run;
00010    quit;
```

SUBGROUP= option
The SUBGROUP= option generates segmented bars. There is one segment for each value of the variable ROOM.

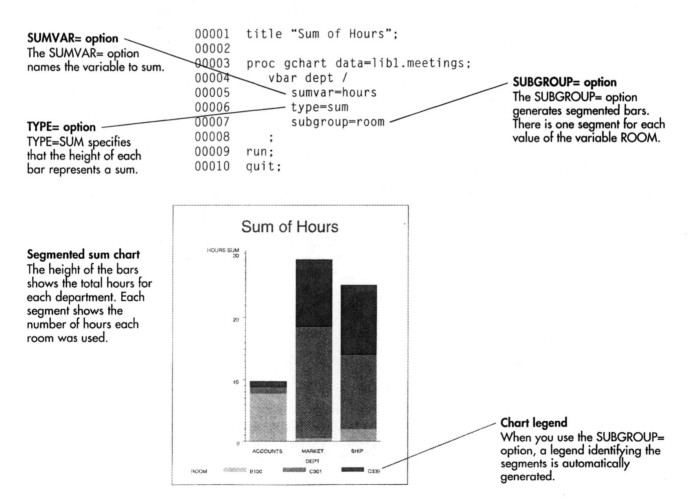

Segmented sum chart
The height of the bars shows the total hours for each department. Each segment shows the number of hours each room was used.

Chart legend
When you use the SUBGROUP= option, a legend identifying the segments is automatically generated.

Showing bar groups

To show sums with groups charted side-by-side, use the GROUP= option with the VBAR (or HBAR) statement. In this example, a group is generated for each room. Compare this with the previous example to judge whether your data are best represented with the SUBGROUP= or GROUP= option.

SUMVAR= option
The SUMVAR= option names the variable to sum to determine the height of the bar.

TYPE= option
TYPE=SUM specifies that the height of each bar represents a sum.

GROUP= option
GROUP=ROOM generates a group of bars for each room.

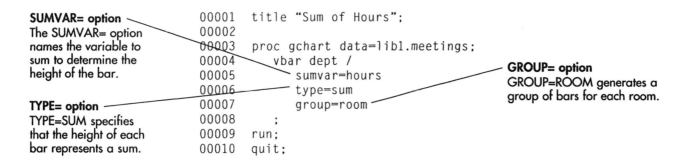

```
00001    title "Sum of Hours";
00002
00003    proc gchart data=lib1.meetings;
00004        vbar dept /
00005            sumvar=hours
00006            type=sum
00007            group=room
00008        ;
00009    run;
00010    quit;
```

Group bar chart
The height of each bar represents the total hours each room was used by each department.

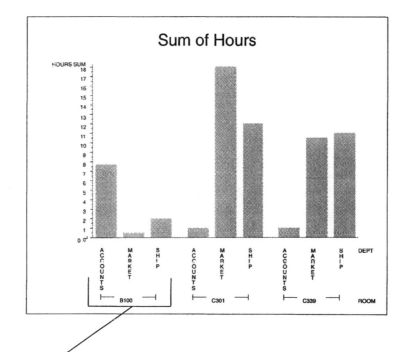

Side-by-side groups
A group is created for each meeting room. Note that grouping generates several bars and can quickly crowd the graphics display area.

You can use the SUBGROUP= and GROUP= options together to create a grouped chart with segmented bars.

More Information

sum chart with subgroups, example

Chapter 3, "Bar Charts", *SAS/GRAPH Software: Introduction, Version 6, First Edition*, pp. 27-28

TYPE=SUM, reference

Chapter 23, "The GCHART Procedure", *SAS/GRAPH Software: Reference, Volume 2*, pp. 794-795 (HBAR), pp. 854-855 (VBAR)

GROUP= option, reference

Chapter 23, *SAS/GRAPH Software: Reference, Volume 2*, p. 788 (HBAR), pp. 848-849 (VBAR)

SUBGROUP= option, reference

Chapter 23, *SAS/GRAPH Software: Reference, Volume 2*, pp. 793-794 (HBAR), p. 854 (VBAR)

Charting Averages

In This Chapter

- Use TYPE=MEAN with the SUMVAR= option to chart averages
- Showing means within groups

Use TYPE=MEAN with the SUMVAR= option to chart averages

When you want the height of each bar to show an average, or mean, use the TYPE=MEAN and SUMVAR= options.

HBAR statement
The HBAR statement creates a horizontal bar chart. All options shown also work with the VBAR statement for vertical bar charts.

```
00001    title "Mean of Hours";
00002
00003    proc gchart data=lib1.meetings;
00004        hbar dept /
00005            sumvar=hours
00006            type=mean
00007        ;
00008    run;
00009    quit;
```

Option separator
The slash (/) must precede any VBAR or HBAR statement options.

SUMVAR= option
The SUMVAR= option names the variable that is averaged and represented by the height of each bar.

TYPE=MEAN
TYPE=MEAN specifies that the bars show the mean of the SUMVAR= variable HOURS.

Means chart
The length of each bar represents the mean number of hours spent on meetings for each department.

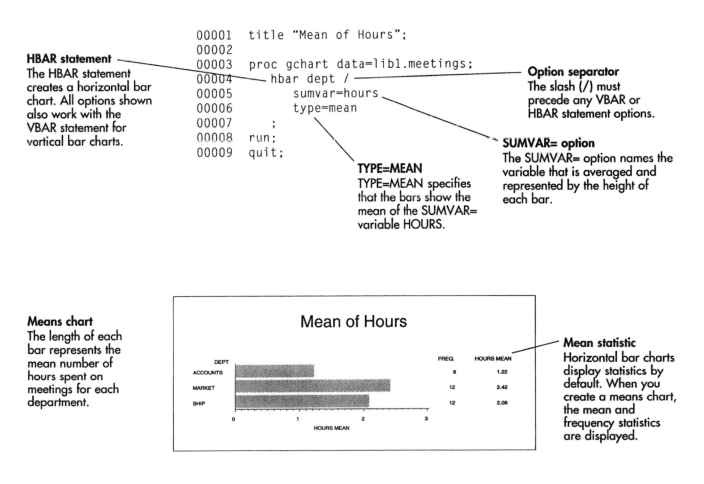

Mean of Hours

DEPT	FREQ.	HOURS MEAN
ACCOUNTS	8	1.22
MARKET	12	2.42
SHIP	12	2.08

HOURS MEAN

Mean statistic
Horizontal bar charts display statistics by default. When you create a means chart, the mean and frequency statistics are displayed.

Showing means within groups

Use the GROUP= option to produce a side-by-side chart showing means within data groups. Note that the mean represented is within the group only, not overall.

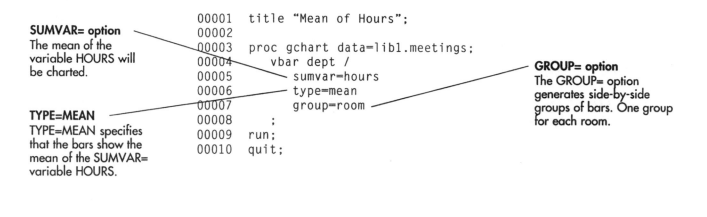

SUMVAR= option
The mean of the variable HOURS will be charted.

TYPE=MEAN
TYPE=MEAN specifies that the bars show the mean of the SUMVAR= variable HOURS.

```
00001    title "Mean of Hours";
00002
00003    proc gchart data=lib1.meetings;
00004      vbar dept /
00005        sumvar=hours
00006        type=mean
00007        group=room
00008      ;
00009    run;
00010    quit;
```

GROUP= option
The GROUP= option generates side-by-side groups of bars. One group for each room.

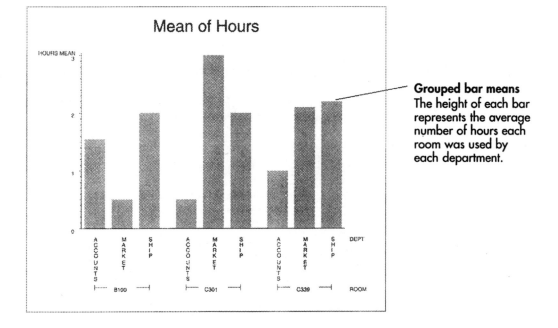

Grouped means chart
A separate bar group is generated for each room.

Grouped bar means
The height of each bar represents the average number of hours each room was used by each department.

As shown in other chapters, you can use the SUBGROUP= option to produce segmented bars. When you use SUBGROUP= with TYPE=MEAN, each segment represents the sum of the SUMVAR= variable for the subgroup divided by the frequency of the charting variable value for that bar. The segment length does not represent the average for each subgroup. If this were the case, the total height of the bar would not represent the overall mean for the charting variable. Ordinarily, the SUBGROUP= option with TYPE=MEAN is not useful. To show the mean within a data group, use the GROUP= option as described above.

More Information

means chart, example

Chapter 6, "Producing Vertical Bar Charts", *SAS/GRAPH Software: Usage*, pp. 64-66

TYPE=MEAN, reference

Chapter 23, "The GCHART Procedure", *SAS/GRAPH Software: Reference, Volume 2*, pp. 794-795 (HBAR), pp. 854-855 (VBAR)

GROUP= option, reference

Chapter 23, *SAS/GRAPH Software: Reference, Volume 2*, p. 788 (HBAR), pp. 848-849 (VBAR)

SUBGROUP= option, reference

Chapter 23, *SAS/GRAPH Software: Reference, Volume 2*, pp. 793-794 (HBAR), p. 854 (VBAR)

Charting Percentages

In This Chapter

- Showing the percentage of a count
- Showing the percentage of a sum
- Showing percentages with grouped bars
- Showing percentage within a data group
- Subgroup percentages with segmented bars

Showing the percentage of a count

When you want to create a bar chart where each bar shows the percentage of a count, use the TYPE=PERCENT option with the HBAR or VBAR statement. The example below uses the SAS data set LIB1.MEETINGS shown in "Data Used in Examples" at the end of this book. The resulting chart shows what percentage of all meetings is accounted for by each department.

VBAR statement
PROC GCHART with the VBAR statement generates a vertical bar chart with one bar for each department.

```
00001   title "Percent of All Meetings";
00002
00003   proc gchart data=lib1.meetings;
00004       vbar dept /
00005           type=percent
00006       ;
00007   run;
00008   quit;
```

TYPE=PERCENT
The TYPE=PERCENT option generates a percentage chart.

Percentage chart
The height of each bar represents the percentage of meetings scheduled by each department. The sum of all bars is 100 percent.

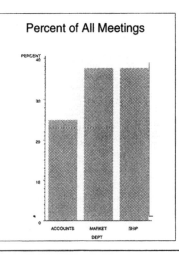

Showing the percentage of a sum

There is no direct way of requesting a chart that shows the percentage of a sum. But you can achieve the same result by combining the TYPE=PERCENT and FREQ= options. When you use the FREQ= option, each observation is counted not once but by the value of the FREQ= variable. This has the effect of summing the FREQ= variable, then calculating the percentage based on that sum.

Only the integer portion of the frequency variable is used, for example, 0.99 counts as 0 (zero) and 3.1 as 3. Unless you know that the variable you want summed holds only whole numbers, you will need to use a DATA step to multiply the FREQ= variable by some power of 10 so that the resulting whole number will be precise enough to accurately reflect your data. The magnitude of the result does not matter since your chart shows percentages, not actual sums.

Create a new variable
The variable HOURS is multiplied by 10 to move significant digits to the left of the decimal place. The result is stored in a new variable called HOURS10.

Create a temporary data set
The original data, in LIB1.MEETINGS, are read and modified. The new data are written to a temporary data set named CHART_IT.

```
00001   data chart_it;
00002     set lib1.meetings;
00003     hours10 = hours * 10;
00004   run;
00005
00006   title "Percent of Meeting Hours";
00007
00008   proc gchart data=chart_it;
00009     vbar dept /
00010        type=percent
00011        freq=hours10
00012     ;
00013   run;
00014   quit;
```

Chart the temporary data set
The data set CHART_IT is used as input to PROC GCHART instead of the original data set LIB1.MEETINGS.

TYPE=PERCENT
The TYPE=PERCENT option generates the percentage chart.

Use the FREQ= option
Instead of counting each observation once, each observation is counted by the value of HOURS10.

Percentage chart
The height of each bar shows the percentage of all meeting hours accounted for by each department. The sum of all bars is 100 percent.

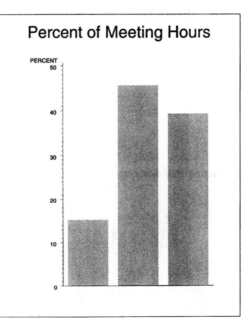

Showing percentages with grouped bars

Use the GROUP= option to show side-by-side groups based on the GROUP= variable. When you use GROUP=, the sum of all bars is 100 percent. The height of each bar represents the overall percentage, not the percentage within the group.

```
00001   title "Percent of Meetings In Each Room";
00002
00003   proc gchart data=lib1.meetings;
00004     vbar dept /
00005       type=percent
00006       group=room
00007     ;
00008   run;
00009   quit;
```

GROUP= option
The GROUP= option generates a chart with bars grouped by room.

TYPE=PERCENT
The TYPE=PERCENT option requests a percentage chart.

Grouped percentage bars
Note that the height of each bar represents the overall percentage for each department/room combination. The sum of all bars is 100 percent.

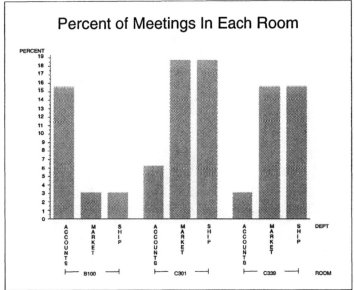

The example on the previous page uses the FREQ= option. Because it considers only the integer portion of a value, the FREQ= option differs from the WEIGHT statement used with the SAS procedures FREQ, MEANS, and others. Unless you are absolutely sure that the frequency variable is always a whole number, you should multiply it by some power of 10 to remove the fractional part of the number. Subtle errors can result when this is not done. Your chart may look reasonable, but it will not be accurate.

Showing percentage within a data group

The previous example shows how to create a grouped percentage chart where each bar shows the overall percentage. To show the percentage *within* each data group, use the GROUP= option with the G100 option. When you use G100, the bars within each group sum to 100 percent.

```
00001    title "Percent of Meetings In Each Room";
00002
00003    proc gchart data=lib1.meetings;
00004       vbar dept /
00005          type=percent
00006          group=room
00007          g100
00008          ;
00009    run;
00010    quit;
```

GROUP= option
The GROUP= option generates a chart with bars grouped by room.

TYPE=PERCENT
TYPE=PERCENT calls for a percentage chart.

G100 option
The G100 option generates a grouped chart with bars showing percentage within a group, not overall.

G100 chart
Bars within each group add up to 100 percent and show percentage within the group only, not overall.

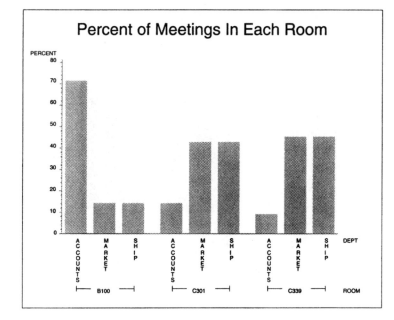

64   Part 2 - Working with Bar Charts

Subgroup percentages with segmented bars

To show how data subgroups contribute to the bar height, use the SUBGROUP= option. The length of each segment shows the overall percentage for that subgroup. The sum of all bars is 100 percent.

TYPE= option
The TYPE=PERCENT option calls for a percentage chart.

```
00001    title "Percent of Meetings";
00002
00003    proc gchart data=lib1.meetings;
00004       vbar dept /
00005          type=percent
00006          subgroup=room
00007       ;
00008    run;
00009    quit;
```

SUBGROUP= option
SUBGROUP= option generates a segmented bar chart.

Subgroup percentage chart
Each segment shows the percentage accounted for by each room/department combination. The overall bar height represents the percentage accounted for by the department.

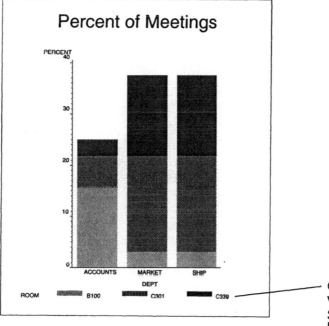

Chart legend
When you use the SUBGROUP= option, a legend identifying the segments is automatically generated.

More Information

percentage chart, example

Chapter 5, "Producing Horizontal Bar Charts", *SAS/GRAPH Software: Usage, Version 6, First Edition*, p. 47-48

TYPE=PERCENT, description

Chapter 23, "The GCHART Procedure", *SAS/GRAPH Software: Reference, Volume 2*, pp. 794-795 (HBAR), pp. 854-855 (VBAR)

GROUP= option, description

Chapter 23, *SAS/GRAPH Software: Reference, Volume 2*, p. 788 (HBAR), pp. 848-849 (VBAR)

SUBGROUP= option, description

Chapter 23, *SAS/GRAPH Software: Reference, Volume 2*, pp. 793-794 (HBAR), p. 854 (VBAR)

G100 option, description

Chapter 23, *SAS/GRAPH Software: Reference, Volume 2*, p. 788 (HBAR), p. 848 (VBAR)

Displaying Statistics

In This Chapter

- Horizontal bar charts show statistics by default
- Displaying a summary statistic
- Requesting specific statistics
- Statistic request options
- Turning off all horizontal bar chart statistics
- Displaying statistics on vertical bar charts
- Controlling statistics text appearance

Horizontal bar charts show statistics by default

In SAS/GRAPH software the numbers displayed with charts are referred to as statistics. Statistic values are automatically displayed to the right of the chart on horizontal bar charts.

HBAR statement
PROC GCHART with the HBAR statement generates a horizontal bar chart.

```
00001    title height=6 pct 'First Quarter Sales';
00002    proc gchart data=lib1.salesql;
00003      hbar month /
00004        midpoints='JAN' 'FEB' 'MAR'
00005      ;
00006    run;
00007    quit;
```

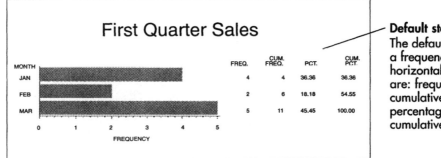

Default statistics
The default statistics for a frequency type horizontal bar chart are: frequency, cumulative frequency, percentage, and cumulative percentage.

Displaying a summary statistic

When you use the SUMVAR= option in the HBAR statement, frequency and a summary statistic are displayed. The summary statistic can be either the sum or the mean of the SUMVAR= variable, depending on the setting of the TYPE= option. When the TYPE= option is absent, as shown below, the default statistic is sum. If you use the TYPE=MEAN option, the mean statistic is displayed. See Chapters 9, 10, and 11 for more on the TYPE= option.

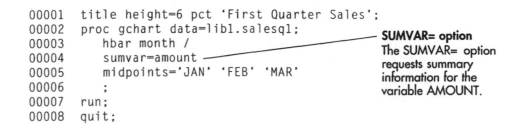

```
00001    title height=6 pct 'First Quarter Sales';
00002    proc gchart data=lib1.salesq1;
00003       hbar month /
00004       sumvar=amount
00005       midpoints='JAN' 'FEB' 'MAR'
00006       ;
00007    run;
00008    quit;
```

SUMVAR= option
The SUMVAR= option requests summary information for the variable AMOUNT.

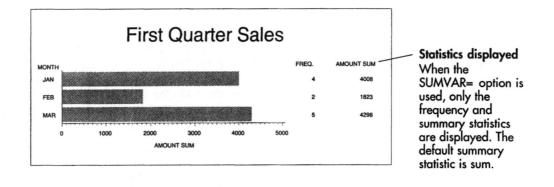

Statistics displayed
When the SUMVAR= option is used, only the frequency and summary statistics are displayed. The default summary statistic is sum.

Requesting specific statistics

Use statistic request options in the HBAR statement to display specific statistics. You can request one or more statistics. Only those you request are displayed; all others are suppressed. Note that statistic requests apply only to the values displayed on the chart, not to the values represented by the bars.

Statistic requests
The SUM and MEAN options request the display of the sum and mean statistics.

```
00001    title height=6 pct 'First Quarter Sales';
00002    proc gchart data=lib1.salesq1;
00003       hbar month /
00004       sumvar=amount
00005       sum mean
00006       midpoints='JAN' 'FEB' 'MAR'
00007       ;
00008    run;
00009    quit;
```

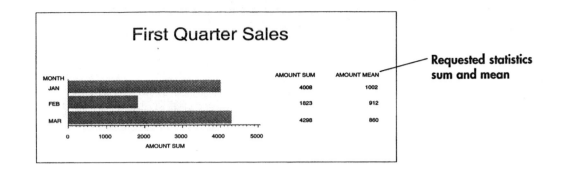

First Quarter Sales

Requested statistics sum and mean

Statistic request options

Statistic request options can be used in both the VBAR (vertical bar) and HBAR (horizontal bar) statements. See the next page for a vertical bar chart example.

Statistic Request Option	Statistic Displayed	Is the SUMVAR= option required?
SUM	Sum of the SUMVAR= variable	Yes
MEAN	Mean (average) of the SUMVAR= variable	Yes
FREQ	Frequency. The count of observations contributing to the bar	No
CFREQ	Cumulative frequency	No
PERCENT	Percentage of all observations accounted for by observations contributing to the bar	No
CPERCENT	Cumulative percentage	No

Turning off all horizontal bar chart statistics

You can suppress all horizontal bar chart statistics with the NOSTATS option.

NOSTATS option

```
00001 title height=6 pct 'First Quarter Sales';
00002 proc gchart data=lib1.salesq1;
00003    hbar month /
00004       nostats
00005       sumvar=amount
00006       midpoints= 'JAN' 'FEB' 'MAR'
00007 ;
00008 run;
00009 quit;
```

Displaying statistics on vertical bar charts

Statistics are not displayed on vertical bar charts unless you ask for them with a statistic request option. Use the statistic request options shown in the table on the previous page. If there is not enough room to fit the numbers above the bars, the statistic request is ignored and a warning message is displayed in the SAS log. Unlike horizontal bar charts, only a single statistic can be displayed on vertical bar charts.

VBAR statement
The VBAR statement generates a vertical bar chart. By default, vertical bar charts do not display statistics.

```
00001   title height=6 pct 'First Quarter Sales';
00002   proc gchart data=lib1.salesq1;
00003     vbar month /
00004       mean
00005       sumvar=amount
00006       midpoints='JAN' 'FEB' 'MAR'
00007       ;
00008   run;
00009   quit;
```

Statistic request
The MEAN option displays the mean statistic for the SUMVAR= variable AMOUNT.

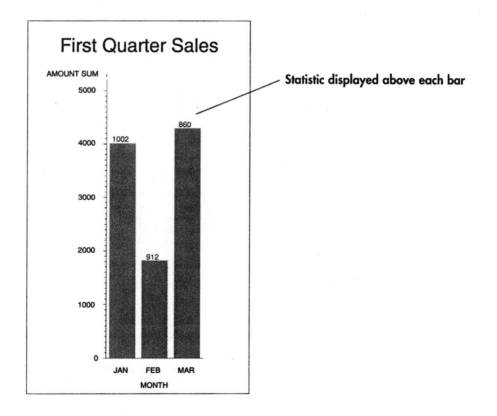

Statistic displayed above each bar

In the example above, the height of each bar represents the *sum* of the SUMVAR= variable AMOUNT even though the statistic request option is MEAN. Statistic request options apply only to the number displayed, not to the bar itself. Use the TYPE= option to control the value represented by the height of the bar. When the TYPE= option is absent, the height of the bar represents the sum of the SUMVAR= variable.

Controlling statistics text appearance

You cannot explicitly set the font, size, or color of statistics text, but you can set attribute defaults for *all* text, including statistics text. The FTEXT= option sets the font for all text on your graph. The HTEXT= option sets the default size (height) for all text. The CTEXT= option sets the default text color for all text. Use the GOPTIONS statement to set these options. Keep in mind that these options set the default for all text. However, you can use options in other statements to override the defaults for titles, footnotes, notes, axes labels, and legends.

Use the FORMAT statement to apply a format to numbers displayed on the chart. The DOLLAR format displays numbers with dollar signs and commas.

Defaults for all text
In the GOPTIONS statement, the font is set to TRIPLEX and the height is set to two percent of the graphics display area for all text on the graph.

```
00001   goptions ftext=triplex htext=2 pct;
00002
00003   title height=6 pct font=swiss
00004        'First Quarter Sales';
00005
00006   proc gchart data=lib1.salesql;
00007      format amount dollar6.;
00008      vbar month /
00009      mean
00010      sumvar=amount
00011      midpoints='JAN' 'FEB' 'MAR'
00012      ;
00013   run;
00014   quit;
```

Font and height overrides
The FONT= and HEIGHT= option settings for the title override the FTEXT= and HTEXT= default options set in the GOPTIONS statement (line 1).

Add dollar signs
The FORMAT statement displays the variable AMOUNT with dollar signs and commas.

Title text override
The TITLE statement font and height settings override the FTEXT= and HTEXT= option settings for the title.

Default text display
Graph text is displayed in the font and height set with the FTEXT= and HTEXT= options in the GOPTIONS statement.

Formatted AMOUNT values

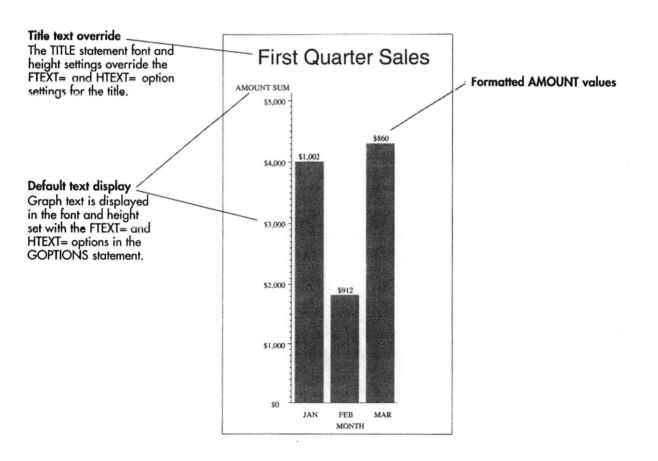

More Information

CTEXT= graphics option, description

Chapter 5, "Graphics Options and Device Parameters", *SAS/GRAPH Software: Reference, Version 6, Volume 1, First Edition*, p. 96

FTEXT= graphics option, description

Chapter 5, "Graphics Options and Device Parameters", *SAS/GRAPH Software: Reference, Volume 1*, p. 106

HTEXT= graphics option, description

Chapter 5, *SAS/GRAPH Software: Reference, Volume 1*, pp. 124-125

HTEXT= and FTEXT= graphics options, examples

Chapter 51, "Modifying Axes", *SAS/GRAPH Software: Usage*, pp. 697-698

HBAR statement, general reference

Chapter 23, "The GCHART Procedure", *SAS/GRAPH Software: Reference, Volume 2*, pp. 782-809

MEAN option, description

Chapter 23, *SAS/GRAPH Software: Reference, Volume 2*, p. 789 (HBAR) and p. 850 (VBAR)

MEAN option, example

Chapter 6, "Producing Vertical Bar Charts", *SAS/GRAPH Software: Usage*, p. 72

NOSTATS option, description

Chapter 23, *SAS/GRAPH Software: Reference, Volume 2*, p. 791

overview of statistic display options and the effect of the TYPE= option

Chapter 6, *SAS/GRAPH Software: Usage*, pp. 70-72

Chapter 23, *SAS/GRAPH Software: Reference, Volume 2*, p. 798-799

PROC GCHART, general reference

Chapter 23, *SAS/GRAPH Software: Reference, Volume 2, Version 6, First Edition*, pp. 751-866

SUM option, description

Chapter 23, *SAS/GRAPH Software: Reference, Volume 2*, p. 794 (HBAR) and p. 854 (VBAR)

SUM option, example with the VBAR statement

Chapter 51, "Modifying Axes", *SAS/GRAPH Software: Usage, Version 6, First Edition*, p. 702

SUMVAR= and TYPE= options, descriptions, relationship to each other

Chapter 23, *SAS/GRAPH Software: Reference, Volume 2*, pp. 794-795 (HBAR) and pp. 854-855 (VBAR)

FORMAT statement, example

Chapter 3, "Bar Charts", *SAS/GRAPH: Introduction, Version 6, First Edition*, pp. 27-28

Chapter 23, "The GCHART Procedure", *SAS/GRAPH Software: Reference, Volume 2*, pp. 860-861

SAS formats, general reference

Chapter 14, "SAS Formats", *SAS Language: Reference, Version 6, First Edition*, pp. 673-713

SAS formats, list and descriptions

Chapter 3, "Components of the SAS Language", *SAS Language: Reference*, pp. 64-69

Changing the Order of Bars

In This Chapter

- **What determines the default bar order?**
- **Controlling bar order with the MIDPOINTS= option: character variables**
- **Controlling bar order with the MIDPOINTS= option: numeric variables**
- **How does the AXIS ORDER= option differ from the MIDPOINTS= option?**
- **Displaying bars by length**
- **Controlling the order of bar groups**

What determines the default bar order?

When you use PROC GCHART with the HBAR or VBAR statement, the default bar arrangement is by ascending order of the chart variable values, top-to-bottom for horizontal bar charts and left-to-right for vertical bar charts.

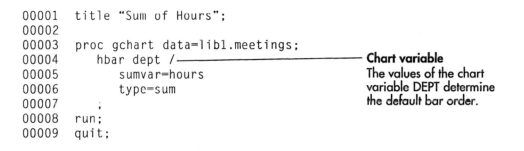

```
00001    title "Sum of Hours";
00002
00003    proc gchart data=lib1.meetings;
00004       hbar dept /——————————————————  Chart variable
00005          sumvar=hours                The values of the chart
00006          type=sum                    variable DEPT determine
00007          ;                           the default bar order.
00008    run;
00009    quit;
```

Default bar order
Bars are displayed in top-to-bottom ascending alphabetic order of the chart variable DEPT.

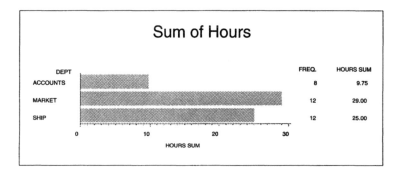

Controlling bar order with the MIDPOINTS= option: character variables

The MIDPOINTS= option allows you to explicitly order the bars displayed on the chart. List the chart variable values or midpoints in the order you want them to appear. Use one or more spaces to separate values. Character values must be in quotes. Note that the values must be listed in the same case and spelling as they appear in the data.

```
00001    title "Sum of Hours";
00002
00003    proc gchart data=lib1.meetings;
00004       vbar dept /
00005          sumvar=hours
00006          type=sum
00007          midpoints = "MARKET" "SHIP" "ACCOUNTS"
00008       ;
00009    run;
00010    quit;
```

MIDPOINTS= option
List the midpoints you want, in the order you want them.

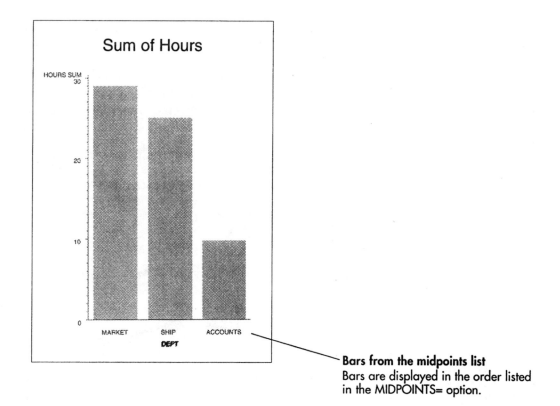

Bars from the midpoints list
Bars are displayed in the order listed in the MIDPOINTS= option.

 When you use the MIDPOINTS= option, you do not have to list all possible values of the chart variable. For example, if you change line 7 in the program above to:

```
midpoints= "MARKET" "SHIP";
```

only the marketing and shipping department bars will be displayed. For more on midpoints and charting with numeric variables see Chapter 15.

Controlling bar order with the MIDPOINTS= option: numeric variables

You can list values for a numeric chart variable with the MIDPOINTS= option. If the intervals you choose are not evenly spaced or they are out of numeric order, the resulting chart may be misleading and you will receive a warning message in the SAS log. You can list numeric values separately or, to guarantee even spacing, specify start, end, and increment values. See Chapter 15 for more on numeric midpoints.

```
00001   title "Length of Meetings";
00002
00003   proc gchart data=lib1.meetings;
00004      vbar hours /
00005         midpoints = 4 to 2 by -0.5
00006      ;
00007   run;
00008   quit;
```

MIDPOINTS= option
Numeric midpoints are listed with values for start, end, and increment. Here the start value is greater than the end value and the increment value is negative.

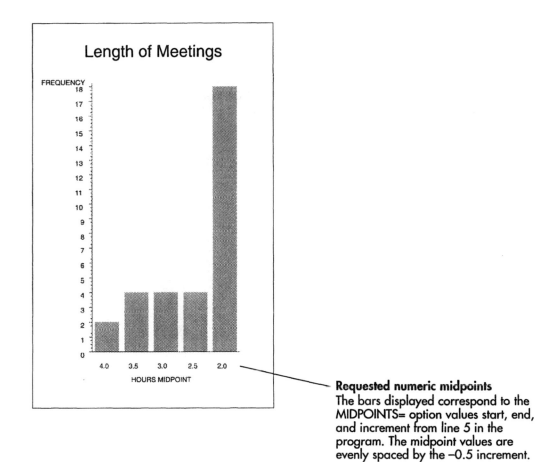

Requested numeric midpoints
The bars displayed correspond to the MIDPOINTS= option values start, end, and increment from line 5 in the program. The midpoint values are evenly spaced by the −0.5 increment.

How does the AXIS ORDER= option differ from the MIDPOINTS= option?

It's easy to confuse the tick mark specifications in the AXIS statement ORDER= option and the midpoints specified with the MIDPOINTS= option. Keep in mind that the AXIS statement defines tick marks only. It is your responsibility to ensure that data exist that correspond to those tick marks.

In the following example an AXIS statement with the ORDER= option defines tick marks, but only one of the midpoints generated by PROC GCHART actually corresponds to these ticks. As a result only one bar is displayed.

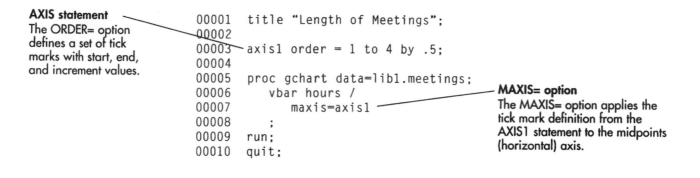

AXIS statement
The ORDER= option defines a set of tick marks with start, end, and increment values.

```
00001    title "Length of Meetings";
00002
00003    axis1 order = 1 to 4 by .5;
00004
00005    proc gchart data=lib1.meetings;
00006        vbar hours /
00007            maxis=axis1
00008        ;
00009    run;
00010    quit;
```

MAXIS= option
The MAXIS= option applies the tick mark definition from the AXIS1 statement to the midpoints (horizontal) axis.

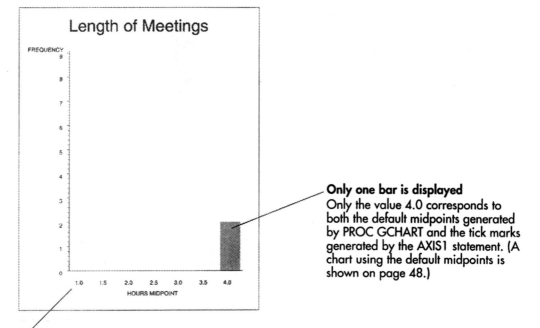

Only one bar is displayed
Only the value 4.0 corresponds to both the default midpoints generated by PROC GCHART and the tick marks generated by the AXIS1 statement. (A chart using the default midpoints is shown on page 48.)

AXIS statement tick marks
The midpoints axis (horizontal) tick marks are shown as defined by the AXIS statement ORDER= option.

Displaying bars by length

The ASCENDING and DESCENDING options force the bars to be displayed in height order. From smallest-to-largest (ASCENDING) or largest-to-smallest (DESCENDING). This is useful for showing a ranking relationship. The ASCENDING option is used in the example below. If the DESCENDING option were used, the bar order would be reversed.

```
00001   title "Total Meeting Hours";
00002
00003   proc gchart data=lib1.meetings;
00004     vbar dept /
00005        sumvar=hours
00006        type=sum
00007        ascending
00008      ;
00009   run;
00010   quit;
```

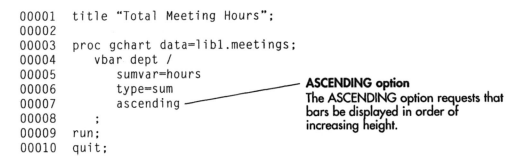

ASCENDING option
The ASCENDING option requests that bars be displayed in order of increasing height.

Bars in ascending height
Bars are displayed in order of increasing height regardless of the midpoint values.

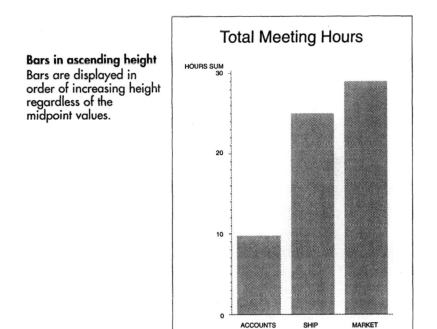

Controlling the order of bar groups

You can control the order of the bar groups generated with the GROUP= option. Create an axis definition with an AXIS statement and assign it to the group axis with the GAXIS= option. The values listed in the AXIS statement ORDER= option must match the grouping variable values exactly, including case.

AXIS statement
The AXIS statement with the ORDER= option defines a set of tick marks.

GROUP= option
The GROUP= option generates a bar chart grouped by the variable ROOM.

GAXIS= option
The GAXIS= option applies the AXIS1 tick mark definition to the group axis.

```
00001    title "Total Meeting Hours";
00002    axis1 order= "C301" "C339" "B100";
00003
00004    proc gchart data=lib1.meetings;
00005       vbar dept /
00006          sumvar=hours
00007          type=sum
00008          group=room
00009          gaxis=axis1
00010          ;
00011    run;
00012    quit;
```

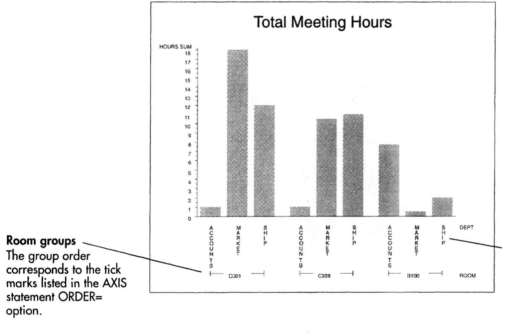

Room groups
The group order corresponds to the tick marks listed in the AXIS statement ORDER= option.

Bar order within groups
Since no other ordering options are specified in the program, bars within each group are in the default order, that is, ascending values of the chart variable DEPT.

You can't use the GAXIS= option with the DESCENDING, ASCENDING, or NOZERO options. If you do, the GAXIS= option is ignored and a note is displayed in the SAS log. You can use GAXIS= with the MIDPOINTS= option.

More Information

PROC GCHART, general reference

Chapter 23, "The GCHART Procedure", *SAS/GRAPH Software: Reference, Volume 2, Version 6, First Edition*, pp. 751-866

reordering midpoints (bars), examples and discussion

Chapter 4, "Introduction to Bar Charts", *SAS/GRAPH Software: Usage, Version 6, First Edition*, pp. 35-36

AXIS statement, ORDER= option

Chapter 9, "The AXIS Statement", *SAS/GRAPH Software: Reference, Volume 1, Version 6, First Edition*, pp. 224-226

AXIS statement, ORDER= option, examples

Chapter 7, "Grouping and Subgrouping", *SAS/GRAPH Software: Usage, Version 6, First Edition*, pp. 86-88

MIDPOINTS= option, description

Chapter 23, "The GCHART Procedure", *SAS/GRAPH Software: Reference, Volume 2*, pp. 850-851 (VBAR) and pp. 790-791 (HBAR)

grouped bars, arranging bars within groups, example

Chapter 23, "The GCHART Procedure", *SAS/GRAPH Software: Reference, Volume 2*, pp. 804-805

midpoints, definition and discussion

Chapter 23, "The GCHART Procedure", *SAS/GRAPH Software: Reference, Volume 2*, pp. 760-761

listing specific midpoints, examples

Chapter 23, "The GCHART Procedure", *SAS/GRAPH Software: Reference, Volume 2*, pp. 800-801 (HBAR), 860-861 (VBAR)

ASCENDING option, description

Chapter 23, "The GCHART Procedure", *SAS/GRAPH Software: Reference, Volume 2*, pp. 785 (HBAR), 815 (VBAR)

DESCENDING option, description

Chapter 23, "The GCHART Procedure", *SAS/GRAPH Software: Reference, Volume 2*, pp. 787 (HBAR), 847 (VBAR)

DESCENDING option, example

Chapter 7, "Grouping and Subgrouping", *SAS/GRAPH Software: Usage*, pp. 85-86

Changing Bar Width and Spacing

In This Chapter

- Changing bar width
- Changing bar spacing
- Controlling space between bar groups

Changing bar width

Default bar width is based on the number of bars in your chart and the space available to display them. The program below generates a chart with the default bar width. Alternatively, you can use the WIDTH= option in the HBAR or VBAR statement to override the default width. An example is shown in the program on the next page. When you use the WIDTH= option, the value you specify must be greater than zero. This value may be a fractional number.

```
00001    title "Count of Meetings By Department";
00002
00003    proc gchart data=lib1.meetings;
00004       hbar dept /
00005          nostats
00006       ;
00007    run;
00008    quit;
```

Default bar width
Compare this chart with the chart on the next page.

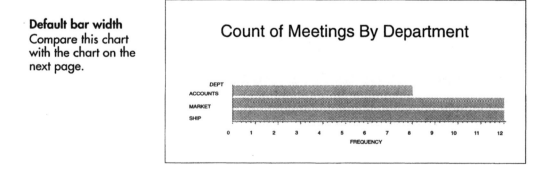

```
00001    title "Count of Meetings By Department";
00002
00003    proc gchart data=lib1.meetings;
00004       hbar dept /
00005          nostats
00006          width=6 ──────────────────
00007       ;
00008    run;
00009    quit;
```

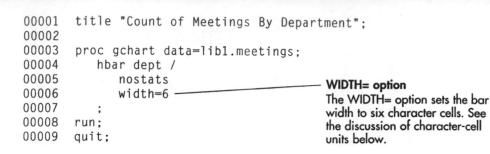

WIDTH= option
The WIDTH= option sets the bar width to six character cells. See the discussion of character-cell units below.

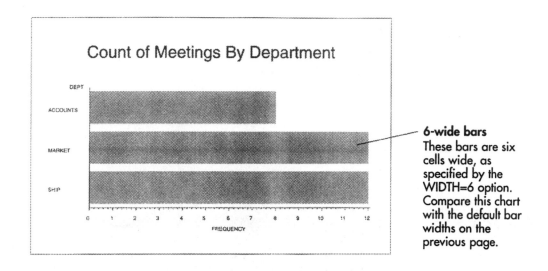

6-wide bars
These bars are six cells wide, as specified by the WIDTH=6 option. Compare this chart with the default bar widths on the previous page.

The units used for the WIDTH= option are character cells. In theory, you could determine the width of a character cell and use that to calculate the exact width you want. In practice, it's usually faster to use trial-and-error and preview the graph on a monitor screen. When you preview your graph, make sure the TARGETDEVICE= graphics option names the final output device so the relative character-cell size on the display will match that on the final output device. See Chapter 4 for more on previewing.

When the WIDTH= option is not used, PROC GCHART automatically adjusts the width of bars according to the available graphics display area. If your chart has many bars, the width of each bar will be narrow. If your chart has few bars, each bar will be wider. When you use the WIDTH= option, the width you specify will be used no matter how many bars are in the chart. If the number of bars increases, your chart may no longer fit in the graphics display area. In this case, no chart is produced and a warning message is displayed in the SAS log.

Changing bar spacing

The first program below generates a chart with default bar spacing. The SPACE= option in the VBAR or HBAR statement controls the amount of space between bars. The SPACE= option is added in the second program; and the resulting chart is shown on the next page.

Like the WIDTH= option discussed above, the units used for the SPACE= option are character cells. The best way to arrive at the spacing you want is to use trial-and-error and preview your chart on a monitor screen. Make sure the TARGETDEVICE= graphics option names your final output device so the relative spacing on the display will match that on the final output device. See Chapter 4 for more on previewing.

```
00001   title "Count of Meetings By Department";
00002
00003   proc gchart data=lib1.meetings;
00004      vbar dept;
00005   run;
00006   quit;
```

Chart with default bar spacing

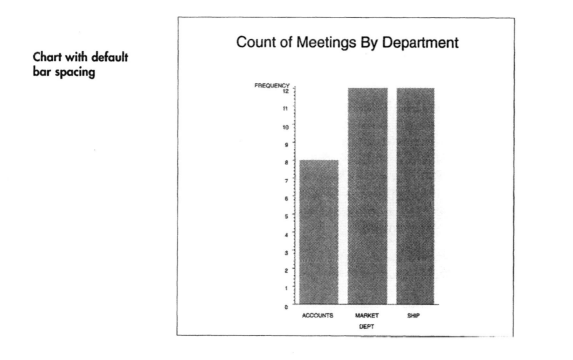

```
00001   title "Count of Meetings By Department";
00002
00003   proc gchart data=lib1.meetings;
00004      vbar dept /
00005         space=8
00006      ;
00007   run;
00008   quit;
```

SPACE= option
Use the SPACE= option to change the default space between bars. The width is specified in character cells. See the chart on the next page.

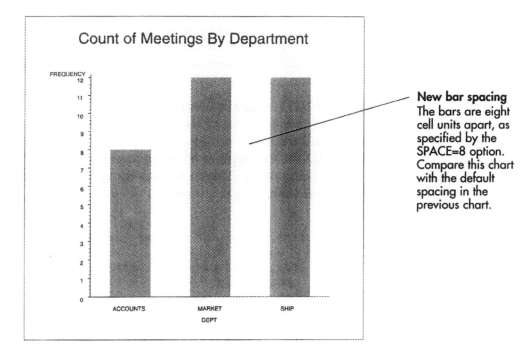

New bar spacing
The bars are eight cell units apart, as specified by the SPACE=8 option. Compare this chart with the default spacing in the previous chart.

Controlling space between bar groups

In addition to the space between bars, you can control the space between bar groups generated with the GROUP= option. The program below generates the first chart on the next page, using the default spacing between bar groups. In the second program, the GSPACE= option is added to change the group spacing. The GSPACE= option specifies the space between groups. The units specified with GSPACE= are character cells. The actual space between groups is the SPACE= setting plus the GSPACE= setting. You can use both the SPACE= and GSPACE= options, if appropriate. See the previous section for more on the SPACE= option.

```
00001    title "Count of Meetings By Department";
00002
00003    proc gchart data=lib1.meetings;
00004       vbar dept /                         GROUP= option
00005          group=room                       The GROUP= option
00006       ;                                    creates a grouped
00007    run;                                    bar chart.
00008    quit;
```

 The settings for the WIDTH=, SPACE=, and GSPACE= options are in character cells. Each device has a default number of vertical and horizontal character cells in its graphics output area. The exact size of these cells can vary depending on the values of other options such as the HPOS= and VPOS= options. Changing these interrelated settings can require some experimentation. In most cases, you don't have to worry about the exact size of a character cell and it is rarely necessary to change the character-cell sizing options. See "More Information" for references on character cells.

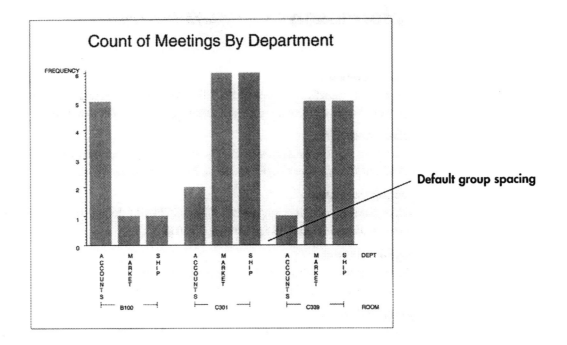

Count of Meetings By Department

Default group spacing

```
00001   title "Count of Meetings By Department";
00002
00003   proc gchart data=lib1.meetings;
00004      vbar dept /
00005         group=room
00006         gspace=8
00007      ;
00008   run;
00009   quit;
```

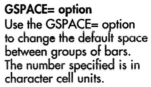

GSPACE= option
Use the GSPACE= option
to change the default space
between groups of bars.
The number specified is in
character cell units.

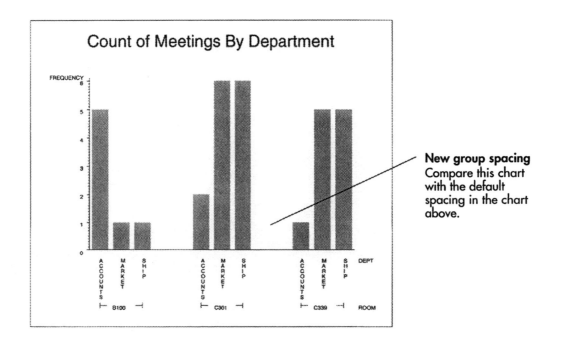

Count of Meetings By Department

New group spacing
Compare this chart
with the default
spacing in the chart
above.

More Information

SPACE= option, reference

"VBAR Statement", in Chapter 23, "The GCHART Procedure", SAS/*GRAPH Software: Reference, Volume 2, Version 6, First Edition*, p. 853 (p. 793 for HBAR)

SPACE= option, example

"Changing the Space between the Bars", in Chapter 6 "Producing Vertical Bar Charts", *SAS/GRAPH Software: Usage, Version 6, First Edition*, pp. 67-68

GSPACE= option, reference

"VBAR Statement", in Chapter 23, "The GCHART Procedure", SAS/*GRAPH Software: Reference, Volume 2*, p. 849 (p. 789 for HBAR)

GSPACE= option, example

"Changing the Spacing between Groups of Bars", in Chapter 7 "Grouping and Subgrouping", *SAS/GRAPH Software: Usage*, pp. 84-85

WIDTH= option, reference

"VBAR Statement", in Chapter 23, "The GCHART Procedure", SAS/*GRAPH Software: Reference, Volume 2*, p. 855 (p. 795 for HBAR)

WIDTH= option, example

"Removing an Axis", in Chapter 51 "Modifying Axes", *SAS/GRAPH Software: Usage*, p. 702

character cells, discussion

"Defining the Graphics Output Area", in Chapter 2, "Running SAS/GRAPH Programs", *SAS/GRAPH Software: Reference, Volume 1*, pp. 25-26

Charting with Numeric Variables

In This Chapter

- Default handling of numeric variables
- Charting all values of a numeric variable
- Specifying the number of midpoint levels
- Specifying midpoint values

Default handling of numeric variables

PROC GCHART calculates a number of midpoints based on the range of values of the variable when charting a numeric variable. A bar is generated for each of these midpoints, not for each unique value of the numeric variable. The midpoint represents the median of a range of values. All values that lie on either side of the midpoint, up to the halfway point of the next midpoint, are counted as part of the midpoint.

Midpoints are used because the number of unique values of a numeric variable is potentially very large. If a value is measured with a precision of 0.001 there are 1000 unique values between 1.000 and 2.000. Charting many irregularly or closely spaced values is usually not useful.

Numeric variable midpoints are illustrated in the following examples. These examples use the SAS data set LIB1.MEETINGS shown on the next page. HOURS is the charting variable, so PROC GCHART calculates midpoints based on its range of values.

```
                       LIB1.MEETINGS

        OBS     HOURS    DEPT      ROOM     DATE

         1      0.25    ACCOUNTS   B100    21MAR95
         2      0.50    ACCOUNTS   B100    24JAN95
         3      0.50    ACCOUNTS   B100    08MAR95
         4      0.50    ACCOUNTS   C301    29MAR95
         5      0.50    SHIP       C339    12APR95
         6      0.50    MARKET     B100    02MAY95
         7      0.50    MARKET     C339    12JUL95
         8      0.50    ACCOUNTS   C301    28SEP95
         9      1.00    ACCOUNTS   C339    10JAN95
        10      1.00    MARKET     C339    15NOV95
        11      1.50    SHIP       C301    27MAR95
        12      1.50    MARKET     C301    25APR95
        13      1.50    SHIP       C339    28AUG95
        14      1.50    SHIP       C301    01NOV95
        15      2.00    SHIP       C339    30JAN95
        16      2.00    SHIP       C301    01JUN95
        17      2.00    SHIP       C301    14JUN95
        18      2.00    SHIP       B100    21NOV95
        19      2.50    SHIP       C301    12MAY95
        20      2.50    SHIP       C301    14AUG95
        21      2.50    MARKET     C339    05DEC95
        22      2.50    MARKET     C301    21DEC95
        23      3.00    SHIP       C339    07JUN95
        24      3.00    ACCOUNTS   B100    03AUG95
        25      3.00    MARKET     C339    15SEP95
        26      3.00    MARKET     C301    11OCT95
        27      3.50    MARKET     C301    24FEB95
        28      3.50    ACCOUNTS   B100    03MAR95
        29      3.50    MARKET     C301    25MAY95
        30      3.50    MARKET     C339    22NOV95
        31      4.00    SHIP       C339    28FEB95
        32      4.00    MARKET     C301    01MAR95
```

The program below uses the data set LIB1.MEETINGS to produce a vertical bar chart. The numeric variable HOURS is used as the charting variable. The default chart, shown on the next page, shows midpoints based on the actual values of HOURS.

```
00001   title "Length of Meetings";
00002
00003   proc gchart data=lib1.meetings;
00004      vbar hours;
00005   run;
00006   quit;
```

Charting a numeric variable
The numeric variable HOURS is charted. By default, the values of HOURS will be grouped around internally calculated midpoints.

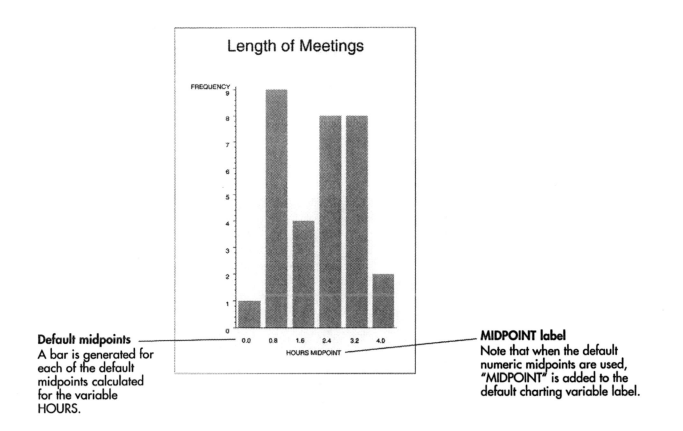

Default midpoints
A bar is generated for each of the default midpoints calculated for the variable HOURS.

MIDPOINT label
Note that when the default numeric midpoints are used, "MIDPOINT" is added to the default charting variable label.

Charting all values of a numeric variable

Use the DISCRETE option to force PROC CHART to use all the values of a numeric charting variable instead of grouping values around calculated midpoints.

```
00001   title "Length of Meetings";
00002
00003   proc gchart data=lib1.meetings;
00004      vbar hours /
00005         discrete
00006      ;
00007   run;
00008   quit;
```

DISCRETE option
The DISCRETE option overrides the default midpointing. The resulting chart is shown on the next page.

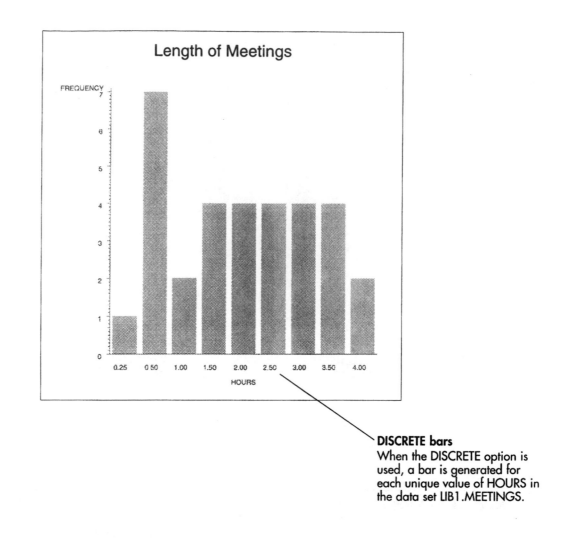

DISCRETE bars
When the DISCRETE option is used, a bar is generated for each unique value of HOURS in the data set LIB1.MEETINGS.

Specifying the number of midpoint levels

To specify the exact number of bars you want, use the LEVELS= option. The number you specify overrides the default, internally calculated, number of midpoint levels.

```
00001    title "Length of Meetings";
00002
00003    proc gchart data=lib1.meetings;
00004       vbar hours /
00005           levels=3
00006       ;
00007    run;
00008    quit;
```

LEVELS= option
The value specified in the LEVELS= option is the number of midpoints you want calculated. There is one bar for each midpoint.

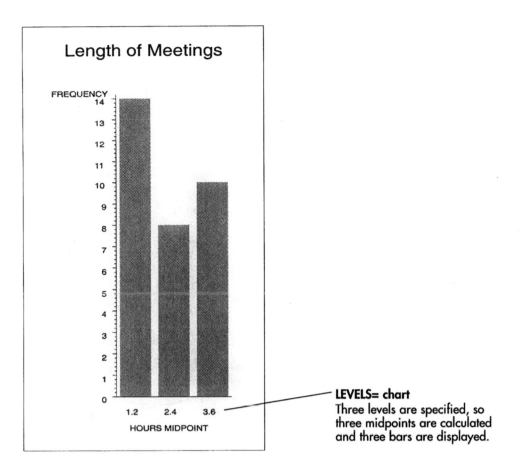

LEVELS= chart
Three levels are specified, so three midpoints are calculated and three bars are displayed.

Specifying midpoint values

You can specify the exact number *and* values for midpoints with the MIDPOINTS= option. If the midpoint values you specify are not spaced equally, a warning will be displayed in the SAS log.

In addition to listing exact values, you can name a start value, an end value, and an increment value. For more details about using start, end, and increment midpoints, see Chapter 13 and the reference for MIDPOINTS= in "More Information."

```
00001   title "Length of Meetings";
00002
00003   proc gchart data=lib1.meetings;
00004      vbar hours /
00005         midpoints = 0.5  1.0  1.5
00006      ;
00007   run;
00008   quit;
```

MIDPOINTS= option
In the MIDPOINTS= option, list the exact midpoints you want. Output is shown on the next page.

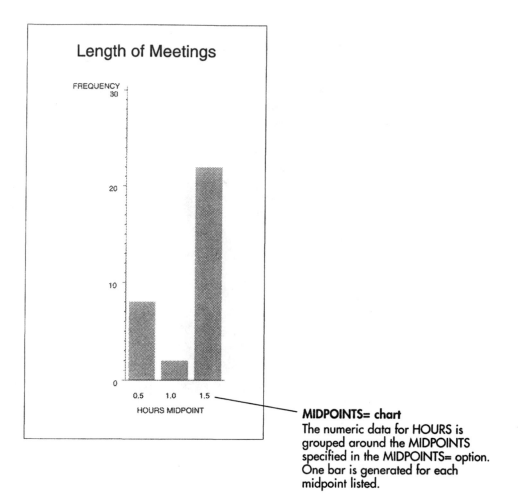

Length of Meetings

MIDPOINTS= chart
The numeric data for HOURS is grouped around the MIDPOINTS specified in the MIDPOINTS= option. One bar is generated for each midpoint listed.

 # More Information

MIDPOINTS= option, reference

"VBAR Statement", in Chapter 23, "The GCHART Procedure", *SAS/GRAPH Software: Reference, Volume 2, Version 6, First Edition*, pp. 850-851 (pp. 790-791 for HBAR)

MIDPOINTS discussion

"Chart Variables and Midpoint Selection", in Chapter 23, "The GCHART Procedure", *SAS/GRAPH Software: Reference, Volume 2*, pp. 760-763

controlling numeric variable midpoints, examples

"Manipulating Midpoints", in Chapter 4, "Introduction to Bar Charts", *SAS/GRAPH Software: Usage, Version 6, First Edition*, pp. 34-39

---

using PROC FORMAT to create custom midpoints, example

"Selecting the Values for Ranges by Using User-Written Formats", in Chapter 4, "Introduction to Bar Charts", *SAS/GRAPH Software: Usage,* pp. 39-41

LEVELS= option, reference

"VBAR Statement", in Chapter 23, "The GCHART Procedure", *SAS/GRAPH Software: Reference, Volume 2, Version 6, First Edition,* p. 849 (p. 789 for HBAR)

DISCRETE option, reference

"VBAR Statement", in Chapter 23, "The GCHART Procedure", *SAS/GRAPH Software: Reference, Volume 2, Version 6, First Edition,* p. 847 (p. 787 for HBAR)

PROC FORMAT, reference

Chapter 18, "The FORMAT Procedure", *SAS Procedures Guide, Version 6, Third Edition,* pp. 275-312

Using Value Ranges in Charts

In This Chapter

- Creating your own value ranges
- Using ranges with numeric charting variables
- Using ranges with character charting variables

Creating your own value ranges

You can create data ranges with the FORMAT procedure. Custom ranges or formats translate a single value or a range of values to a string of characters called a label. When you assign a custom format to the charting variable, PROC GCHART charts the label values instead of the actual or midpointed values. The following examples illustrate the use of custom formats with character and numeric charting variables.

Using ranges with numeric charting variables

When you use the FORMAT statement and the DISCRETE option with PROC GCHART, the formatted values of a numeric variable are charted instead of the midpoint values. Formatted values can represent ranges. Use PROC FORMAT to create your own range format; then use that format in a FORMAT statement within the GCHART procedure.

The ranges you create do not have to be evenly spaced, but if you use uneven ranges, as in the following example, you will receive a warning message in the SAS log.

PROC FORMAT step
The FORMAT procedure generates a format called SALEGRP. SALEGRP consists of four ranges. Any value that falls within one of the ranges is translated to the associated label text.

Range and label
This range includes the lowest value in the data up to, but not including, 500. Any value in this range returns the quoted label.

```
00001   proc format;
00002       value salegrp
00003           low-<500 = "less than $500"
00004           500-1000 = "$500 to $1000"
00005           1000<-1200 = "$1000 to $1200"
00006           1200<-high = "over $1200"
00007       ;
00008   run;
00009
00010   title "Sales By Amount Category";
00011
00012   proc gchart data=lib1.salesq1;
00013       format amount salegrp.;
00014       vbar amount /
00015           discrete;
00016   run;
00017   quit;
```

DISCRETE option
The DISCRETE option ensures that there will be one bar for each formatted value in the data. Otherwise, there would be a bar for each of the default midpoint values.

FORMAT statement
The FORMAT statement applies the SALEGRP format to the charting variable. The format name must end with a period.

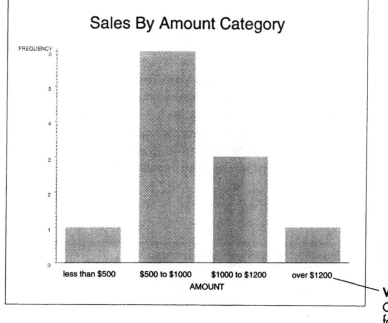

Value range bars
One bar is generated for each custom format value range.

The maximum length allowed for a format label is 200 characters, but PROC GCHART will only use the first 16 characters. When PROC GCHART truncates a label longer than 16 characters, a warning message is displayed in the SAS log.

Using ranges with character charting variables

You can use PROC FORMAT to create character value ranges. The custom format is applied with the FORMAT statement. In the following example, two character values, C301 and C339, are consolidated into one charting value, C Level. The DISCRETE option is not necessary when charting character variables.

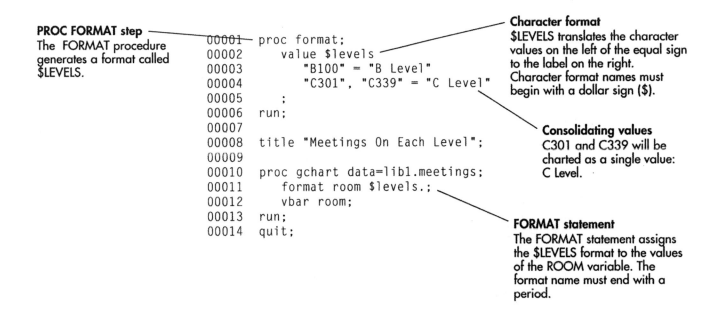

PROC FORMAT step
The FORMAT procedure generates a format called $LEVELS.

```
00001  proc format;
00002     value $levels
00003         "B100" = "B Level"
00004         "C301", "C339" = "C Level"
00005     ;
00006  run;
00007
00008  title "Meetings On Each Level";
00009
00010  proc gchart data=lib1.meetings;
00011     format room $levels.;
00012     vbar room;
00013  run;
00014  quit;
```

Character format
$LEVELS translates the character values on the left of the equal sign to the label on the right. Character format names must begin with a dollar sign ($).

Consolidating values
C301 and C339 will be charted as a single value: C Level.

FORMAT statement
The FORMAT statement assigns the $LEVELS format to the values of the ROOM variable. The format name must end with a period.

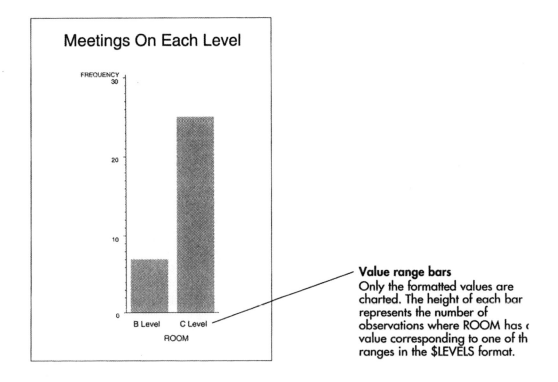

Value range bars
Only the formatted values are charted. The height of each bar represents the number of observations where ROOM has a value corresponding to one of the ranges in the $LEVELS format.

▣ More Information

FORMAT procedure, general reference

Chapter 18, "The FORMAT Procedure", *SAS Procedures Guide, Version 6, Third Edition*, pp. 275-312

specifying format ranges

"Details", in Chapter 18, "The FORMAT Procedure", *SAS Procedures Guide*, p. 294-295

creating a numeric format, example

"Categorizing Variable Values with Customized Formats", in Chapter 8, "Classifying Variables into Categories", *SAS Language and Procedures: Usage 2, Version 6, First Edition*, pp. 151-153

using a format with a bar chart, example

"Selecting the Values for Ranges by Using User-Written Formats", in Chapter 4 "Introduction to Bar Charts", *SAS/GRAPH Software: Usage, Version 6, First Edition*, pp. 39-41.

retrieving formats from SAS libraries

Chapter 26, "The FORMAT Procedure", *SAS Technical Report P-222, Changes and Enhancements to Base SAS Software, Release 6.07*, p. 208

DISCRETE option

"Options" in Chapter 23, "The GCHART Procedure", *SAS/GRAPH Software: Reference, Version 6, First Edition, Volume 2*, p. 787 (HBAR) or p. 847 (VBAR)

Controlling Bar Fill Patterns

In This Chapter

- What the PATTERN statement does
- Using the default bar patterns
- Overriding the default bar patterns
- Controlling pattern assignments
- Assigning a different pattern to each bar
- Assigning patterns to BY groups
- Assigning patterns to bar groups

What the PATTERN statement does

PATTERN statements define color and fill patterns for bar charts. Fill patterns can be crosshatches, angled lines, solid fill, or empty (no fill). Color can be any valid color for your output device. The PATTERN statement does not apply patterns to graphics elements; it only defines patterns that *may* be applied with certain charting options or through default pattern assignments.

Pattern statements are global. Once defined, a pattern remains available until you change it or your SAS session ends. Place PATTERN statements before or in the GCHART procedure that uses them. Example PATTERN statements are shown below.

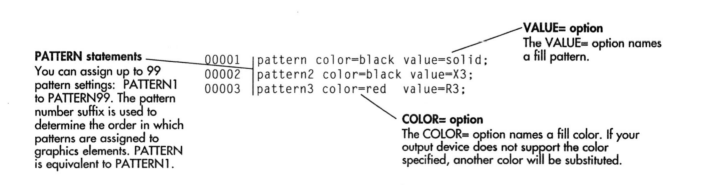

PATTERN statements
You can assign up to 99 pattern settings: PATTERN1 to PATTERN99. The pattern number suffix is used to determine the order in which patterns are assigned to graphics elements. PATTERN is equivalent to PATTERN1.

```
00001  pattern  color=black value=solid;
00002  pattern2 color=black value=X3;
00003  pattern3 color=red   value=R3;
```

VALUE= option
The VALUE= option names a fill pattern.

COLOR= option
The COLOR= option names a fill color. If your output device does not support the color specified, another color will be substituted.

Using the default bar patterns

If you do not define new pattern settings, SAS/GRAPH uses a series of default patterns to fill bars. To ensure that defaults will be used, you can reset all patterns with the RESET=PATTERN option, as shown below. The actual default fills and colors may vary depending on your output device and the setting of the CPATTERN= option. (See "Closer Look" below.)

```
00001    goptions reset=pattern;
00002
00003    title "Count of Meetings";
00004
00005    proc gchart data=lib1.meetings;
00006        vbar room /
00007            subgroup=dept
00008    ;
00009    run;
00010    quit;
```

Reset all patterns
The RESET=PATTERN option resets all patterns to the defaults.

PROC GCHART with subgroups
The GCHART procedure uses the default pattern settings to distinguish subgroups.

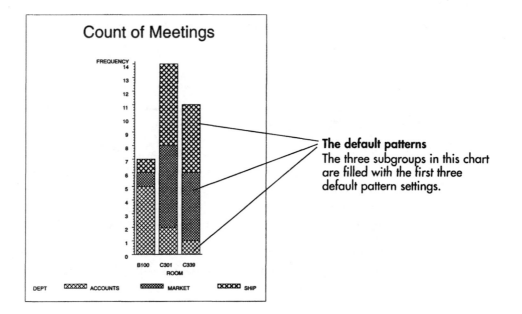

The default patterns
The three subgroups in this chart are filled with the first three default pattern settings.

PATTERN statements define combinations of color and fill. Default patterns are normally defined by combining each fill, in a series of default fills, with each available color. The first fill is combined with each color to generate a group of patterns. If more patterns are required, the next fill in the series is combined with each color. In this manner, default patterns vary by color first, then, if necessary, by fill. You can use the CPATTERN= option to force SAS/GRAPH to create default patterns using a single color while varying the fill. For example, the statement

```
goptions cpattern=black;
```

forces the default patterns to be combinations of each fill with the color black.

Overriding the default bar patterns

To override the default patterns, add a PATTERN statement with your own settings for color and fill.

Reset all patterns

```
00001  goptions reset=pattern;
00002
00003  pattern1 color=black value=solid;
00004
00005  title "Count of Meetings";
00006
00007  proc gchart data=lib1.meetings;
00008     vbar room /
00009         subgroup=dept
00010     ;
00011  run;
00012  quit;
```

Define a pattern
PATTERN1 is defined as a solid black fill.

Patterns assigned to subgroups
PROC GCHART assigns a different pattern to each subgroup.

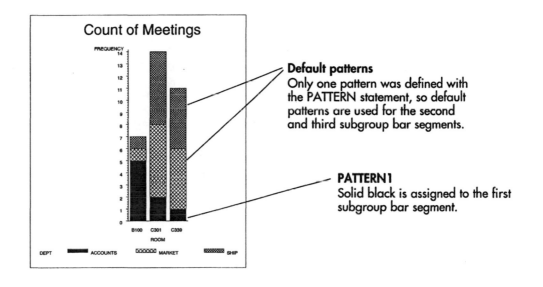

Default patterns
Only one pattern was defined with the PATTERN statement, so default patterns are used for the second and third subgroup bar segments.

PATTERN1
Solid black is assigned to the first subgroup bar segment.

Controlling pattern assignments

To completely control bar fill, you must define enough patterns for each filled element in your chart.

```
00001  pattern1 value=solid color=gray77;
00002  pattern2 value=solid color=graybb;
00003  pattern3 value=solid color=grayee;
00004
00005  title "Count of Meetings";
00006
00007  proc gchart data=lib1.meetings;
00008     vbar room /
00009         subgroup=dept
00010     ;
00011  run;
00012  quit;
```

Define three patterns
Enough patterns are defined to fill three subgroup segments.

SUBGROUP option
PROC GCHART assigns a pattern to each subgroup segment.

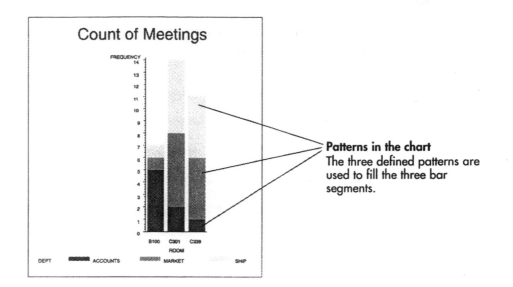

Count of Meetings

Patterns in the chart
The three defined patterns are used to fill the three bar segments.

By changing the PATTERN statement order you control how patterns are applied to your chart.

```
00001   pattern1 value=solid color=grayee;
00002   pattern2 value=solid color=graybb;
00003   pattern3 value=solid color=gray77;
00004
00005   title "Count of Meetings";
00006
00007   proc gchart data=lib1.meetings;
00008      vbar room /
00009         subgroup=dept
00010   ;
00011   run;
00012   quit;
```

Pattern order
The PATTERN statement order is reversed from the previous example.

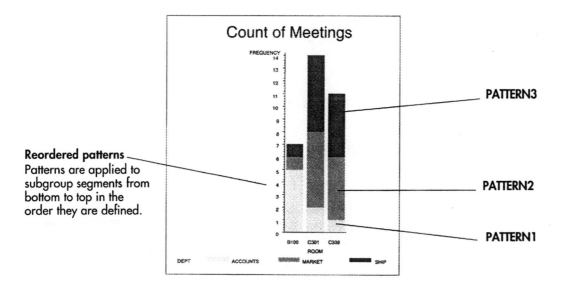

Count of Meetings

Reordered patterns
Patterns are applied to subgroup segments from bottom to top in the order they are defined.

PATTERN3

PATTERN2

PATTERN1

You can define a pattern without a color specification as in the PATTERN1 statement below.

```
pattern1 value=solid;
pattern2 value=x3 color=green;
```

In this case, patterns are assigned by using the solid fill combined with each available color *before* using the PATTERN2 definition. To avoid unexpected results, define patterns using both the VALUE= and COLOR= options.

Assigning a different pattern to each bar

If your chart does not use the SUBGROUP= option, you can apply patterns to each bar by using the PATTERNID=MIDPOINT option.

```
00001   pattern1 value=solid color=gray77;
00002   pattern2 value=solid color=graybb;
00003   pattern3 value=solid color=grayee;
00004
00005   title "Number of Meetings";
00006   title2 height=2 "In Each Room";
00007
00008   proc gchart data=lib1.meetings;
00009      vbar room /
00010          patternid=midpoint;
00011   run;
00012   quit;
```

Three patterns defined
In this example there are three bars on the chart.

PATTERNID=MIDPOINT option
The PATTERNID=MIDPOINT option uses patterns to distinguish each bar in the chart.

Each bar is assigned a different pattern.

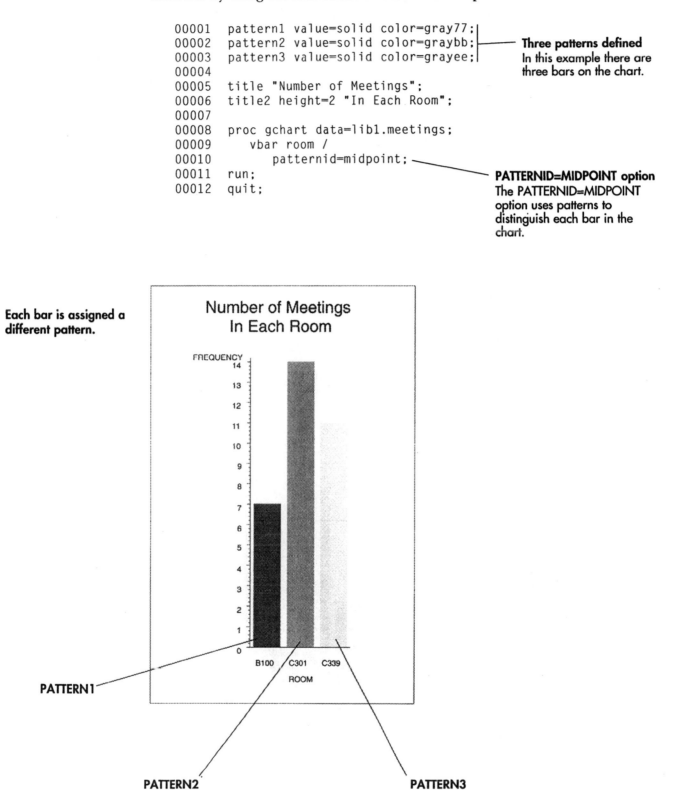

PATTERN1

PATTERN2

PATTERN3

Assigning patterns to BY groups

When you use a BY statement with PROC GCHART, a separate chart is generated for each BY group. To assign a different pattern to the bars in each BY group, use the PATTERNID=BY option. PATTERN1 is assigned to the first group, PATTERN2 to the second group, PATTERN3 to the third group, etc.

```
00001   pattern1 value=solid color=gray77;
00002   pattern2 value=solid color=graybb;
00003   pattern3 value=solid color=grayee;
00004
00005   title "Deer Count";
00006
00007   proc gchart data=lib1.deer;
00008      by region notsorted;
00009      vbar type /
00010         sumvar=pop
00011         patternid=by
00012      ;
00013   run;
00014   quit;
```

Three patterns defined
In this example there are three BY groups.

PATTERNID=BY option

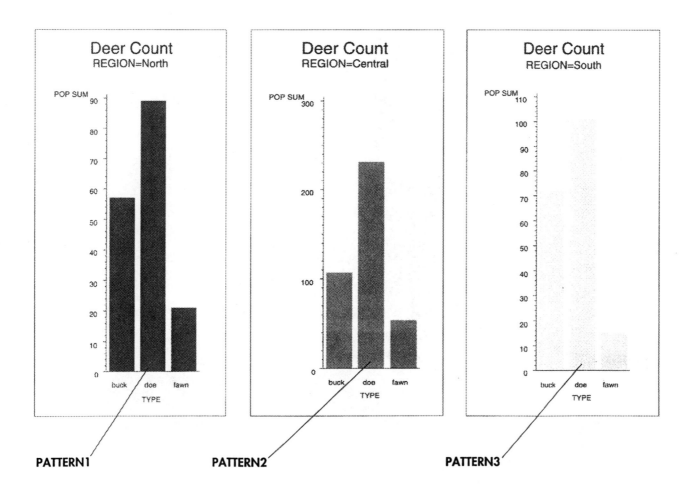

Assigning patterns to bar groups

Use the PATTERNID=GROUP option to assign a different pattern to each group in a grouped bar chart. In the example below, a separate bar group is generated for each of the three values of the group variable DEPT. PATTERN1 is assigned to the first group, PATTERN2 to the second, and PATTERN3 to the third.

```
00001    pattern1 value=solid color=gray77;
00002    pattern2 value=solid color=graybb;
00003    pattern3 value=solid color=grayee;
00004
00005    title "Count of Meetings";
00006
00007    proc gchart data=lib1.meetings;
00008       vbar room /
00009          group=dept
00010          patternid=group
00011    ;
00012    run;
00013    quit;
```

Three patterns defined
In this example there are three bar groups on the chart.

PATTERNID=GROUP option

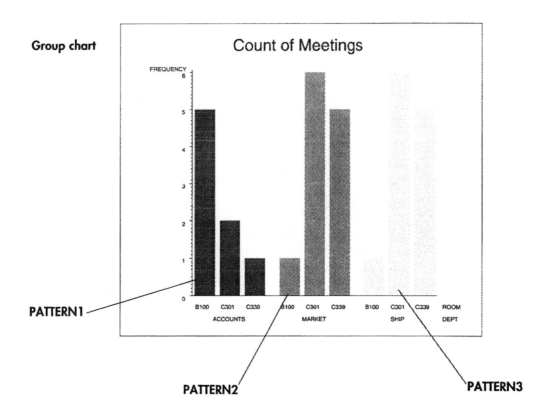

Group chart

PATTERN1

PATTERN2

PATTERN3

📖 More Information

PATTERN statement, general reference

Chapter 15, "The PATTERN Statement", *SAS/GRAPH Software: Reference, Volume 1, First Edition* pp. 365-398

bar chart fill patterns

"PATTERN Statement Options", in Chapter 15, "The PATTERN Statement", *SAS/GRAPH Software: Reference, Volume 1*, pp. 376-377

pattern sequences and defaults

"PATTERN Definitions" in Chapter 15, "The PATTERN Statement", *SAS/GRAPH Software: Reference, Volume 1*, pp. 369-373

using bar chart patterns, example

"Examples", in Chapter 15, "The PATTERN Statement", *SAS/GRAPH Software: Reference, Volume 1*, pp. 388-390

PATTERNID=MIDPOINT, horizontal bar chart, example

"Specifying How Patterns Are Assigned", in Chapter 5, "Producing Horizontal Bar Charts", *SAS/GRAPH Software: Usage*, Version 6, First Edition, pp. 50-52

PATTERNID=GROUP, horizontal bar chart, example

"Changing the Appearance of the Groups", in Chapter 7, "Grouping and Subgrouping", *SAS/GRAPH Software: Usage*, pp. 82-84

Part 3
Working with Plots

Chapter 18 - Creating Scatter Plots
Chapter 19 - Creating a Line Plot
Chapter 20 - Smoothing Plot Lines
Chapter 21 - Adding a Second Axis
Chapter 22 - Plotting Multiple Sets of Points
Chapter 23 - Filling an Area under a Line
Chapter 24 - Creating a Cumulative Area Plot
Chapter 25 - Using Plot Appearance Options

18 Creating Scatter Plots

Plots

In This Chapter

- Creating a plot with the default settings
- Changing the plot symbol
- Changing the plot symbol color

Creating a plot with the default settings

Use the PLOT statement in the GPLOT procedure to create plots relating the values of two variables. The default plot type in PROC GPLOT is a scatter plot. In a scatter plot, individual data points are displayed without connecting lines.

Examples in this and the following two chapters use the SAS data set LIB1.ALLFUEL, shown below. LIB1.ALLFUEL holds data relating miles per gallon fuel used (MPG) and total fuel used (TOTAL) to trip length (LENGTH).

SAS data set LIB1.ALLFUEL

```
                    LIB1.ALLFUEL

     OBS     LENGTH      TOTAL        MPG

      1         1       0.08035    13.7487
      2         2       0.15603    14.2366
      3         5       0.34026    15.9502
      4         8       0.54998    15.9710
      5        10       0.64835    17.0327
      6        15       0.99652    16.8029
      7        25       1.59152    17.2900
```

The PLOT statement names two plotting variables. You can use more than one PLOT statement in a single PROC GPLOT step. The *y* (vertical) axis variable is named to the left of the asterisk (*) and the *x* (horizontal) axis variable to the right of the asterisk.

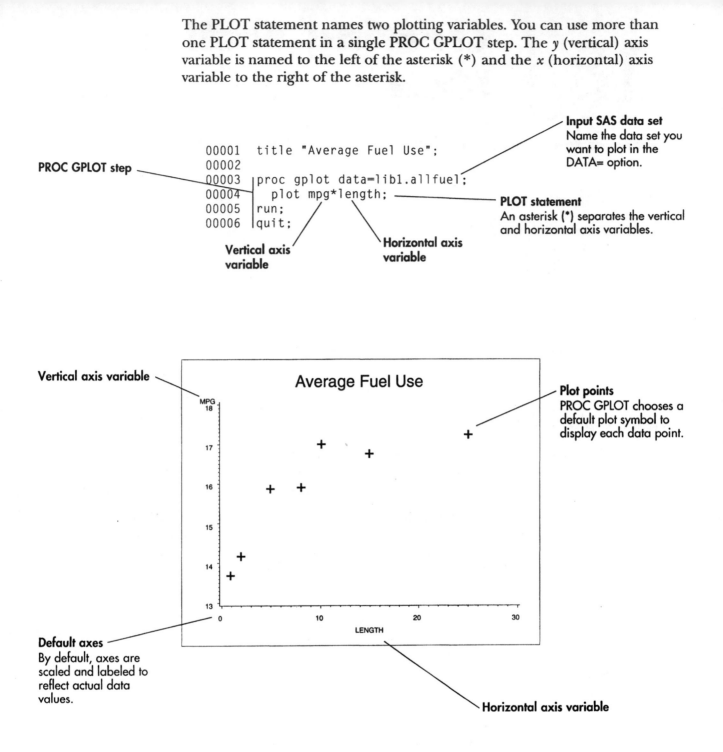

PROC GPLOT step

Input SAS data set
Name the data set you want to plot in the DATA= option.

```
00001   title "Average Fuel Use";
00002
00003   proc gplot data=lib1.allfuel;
00004     plot mpg*length;
00005   run;
00006   quit;
```

PLOT statement
An asterisk (*) separates the vertical and horizontal axis variables.

Vertical axis variable

Horizontal axis variable

Vertical axis variable

Plot points
PROC GPLOT chooses a default plot symbol to display each data point.

Average Fuel Use

Default axes
By default, axes are scaled and labeled to reflect actual data values.

Horizontal axis variable

Changing the plot symbol

Use the SYMBOL statement to control how data points are displayed. SYMBOL statements define symbol settings. These settings are automatically used by the GPLOT procedure to display points.

The VALUE= and HEIGHT= options specify the plot symbol character and size. The default height units are character cells. Any printable character can be used as the plotting symbol. In addition, there are several special symbols such as DOT, which is used in the program below. See Chapter 19 for more examples of plotting symbols.

SYMBOL statement

HEIGHT= option
The HEIGHT= option controls the size of the plot symbol. Units are character cells. The default height is 1.

```
00001   symbol1 color=black value=dot height=2;
00002
00003   title "Average Fuel Use";
00004
00005   proc gplot data=lib1.allfuel;
00006     plot mpg*length;
00007   run;
00008   quit;
```

VALUE= option
The VALUE= option names the plot point character. Here the special symbol DOT is used.

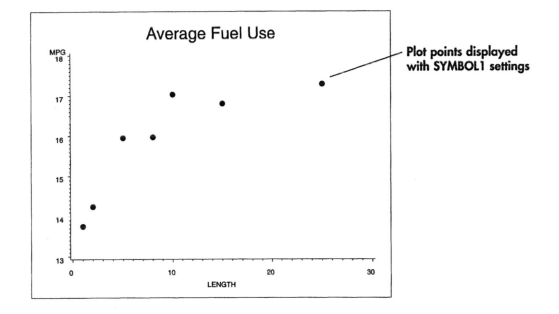

Plot points displayed with SYMBOL1 settings

 The VALUE= option names the plot symbol. In addition to special symbols such as DOT, you can use any printable character. For example, when you use

```
symbol1 value="H";
```

the letter H will be the plot symbol.

Changing the plot symbol color

Use the COLOR= option to control the color of plot symbols.

```
00001   symbol1 value=dot height=2 color=grayaa;
00002
00003   title "Average Fuel Use";
00004
00005   proc gplot data=lib1.allfuel;
00006     plot mpg*length;
00007   run;
00008   quit;
```

COLOR= option
The plotting symbol color is the grayscale color GRAYAA.

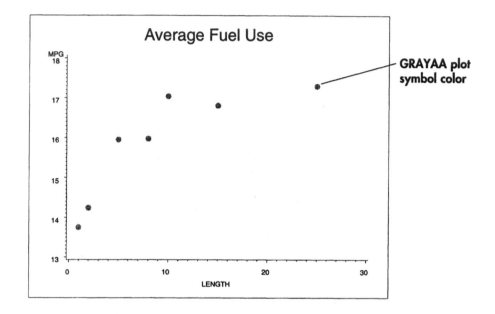

GRAYAA plot symbol color

The SYMBOL statement is the key to controlling the appearance of your plot. PROC GPLOT automatically uses the symbol definitions you set up with SYMBOL statements. The first symbol definition, assigned with the SYMBOL1 statement, is used for the first set of points plotted. Subsequent symbol definitions, SYMBOL2, SYMBOL3, SYMBOL4, etc., are assigned to subsequent plots when more than one plot is displayed in a set of axes.

When you define a symbol without using the COLOR= option as in SYMBOL1 below,

```
symbol1 value=dot;
symbol2 value=star color=red;
```

and more than one symbol is required for a plot, the SYMBOL1 value DOT will be used with all available colors *before* using the SYMBOL2 definition. To avoid unexpected results, always define symbols with both the VALUE= and COLOR= options.

More Information

PROC GPLOT, general reference

Chapter 31, "The GPLOT Procedure", *SAS/GRAPH Software: Reference, Volume 2, Version 6, First Edition*, pp. 1073-1130

PLOT statement, reference

"PLOT Statement" in Chapter 31, "The GPLOT Procedure", *SAS/GRAPH Software: Reference, Volume 2*, pp. 1100-1120

plot request formats in the PLOT statement, reference

"Syntax" in Chapter 31, "The GPLOT Procedure", *SAS/GRAPH Software: Reference, Volume 2*, pp. 1100-1101

plot request formats in the PLOT statement, discussion

"Using the PLOT statement" in Chapter 31, "The GPLOT Procedure", *SAS/GRAPH Software: Reference, Volume 2*, pp. 1108-1109

SYMBOL statement, general reference

Chapter 16, "The SYMBOL Statement", *SAS/GRAPH Software: Reference, Volume 1*, pp. 399-440

COLOR= option in the SYMBOL statement, syntax

"SYMBOL Statement Options" in Chapter 16, "The SYMBOL Statement", *SAS/GRAPH Software: Reference, Volume 1*, p. 409

HEIGHT= option in the SYMBOL statement, syntax

"SYMBOL Statement Options" in Chapter 16, "The SYMBOL Statement", *SAS/GRAPH Software: Reference, Volume 1*, p. 410

VALUE= option in the SYMBOL statement, syntax

"SYMBOL Statement Options" in Chapter 16, "The SYMBOL Statement", *SAS/GRAPH Software: Reference, Volume 1*, pp. 420-422

special plotting symbols, list of examples and names

"SYMBOL Statement Options" in Chapter 16, "The SYMBOL Statement", *SAS/GRAPH Software: Reference, Volume 1*, p. 421

scatter plot, example

"Producing a Simple Plot of Two Variables" in Chapter 19, "Introduction to Plots", *SAS/GRAPH Software: Usage, Version 6, First Edition*, pp. 231-233

using the SYMBOL statement, discussion

"Introduction to the SYMBOL Statement" in Chapter 19, "Introduction to Plots", *SAS/GRAPH Software: Usage*, pp. 233-235

19 Creating a Line Plot

In This Chapter

- **Connecting data points**
- **Adding data points to a line plot**
- **How to fix the zigzag line problem**
- **Changing the plot line type**
- **Changing the plot line thickness**

Connecting data points

Use the SYMBOL statement with the INTERPOL= option to connect the points in your plot. To connect each point with a straight line use INTERPOL=JOIN.

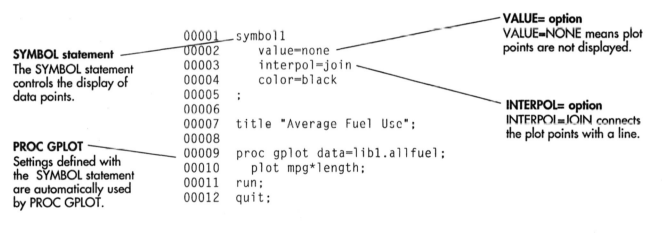

VALUE= option
VALUE=NONE means plot points are not displayed.

SYMBOL statement
The SYMBOL statement controls the display of data points.

INTERPOL= option
INTERPOL=JOIN connects the plot points with a line.

```
00001  symbol1
00002     value=none
00003     interpol=join
00004     color=black
00005  ;
00006
00007  title "Average Fuel Use";
00008
00009  proc gplot data=lib1.allfuel;
00010    plot mpg*length;
00011  run;
00012  quit;
```

PROC GPLOT
Settings defined with the SYMBOL statement are automatically used by PROC GPLOT.

Line plot

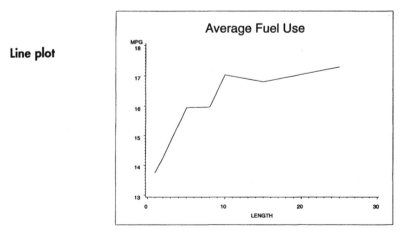

Adding data points to a line plot

The SYMBOL statement VALUE= option controls how points are represented on your plot. VALUE= names the character displayed at each data point. In addition to the standard printable characters, you can use special plotting symbols. In the example below, the DIAMOND symbol is used.

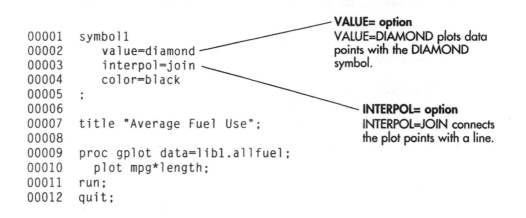

```
00001   symbol1
00002       value=diamond
00003       interpol=join
00004       color=black
00005   ;
00006
00007   title "Average Fuel Use";
00008
00009   proc gplot data=lib1.allfuel;
00010     plot mpg*length;
00011   run;
00012   quit;
```

VALUE= option
VALUE=DIAMOND plots data points with the DIAMOND symbol.

INTERPOL= option
INTERPOL=JOIN connects the plot points with a line.

Line plot with data points
When a plotting symbol is named in the VALUE= option and INTERPOL=JOIN, points are displayed *and* joined with a straight line.

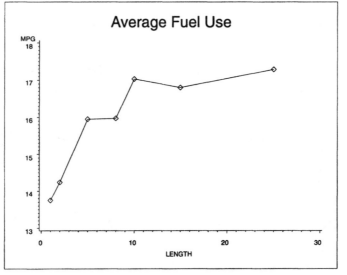

Plotting symbols
Characters shown in quotes must also be in quotes in the VALUE= option. For example: VALUE="+". For other symbols use the unquoted name, as with DIAMOND in the example. More symbols are available. See the reference in "More Information."

✳	":" (colon)
⊕	"+" (plus sign)
⊙	"-" (hyphen)
⬚	"_" (underscore)
○	circle
●	dot
♯	hash
△	triangle
◇	diamond
✳	star
□	square

How to fix the zigzag line problem

Plot points are connected in the order they appear in the input SAS data set. If the horizontal axis variable is not in sorted order, points will not be connected correctly. If your plot appears as a zigzag, you need to sort the input data set. The example uses the SAS data set LIB1.ALLFUEL1, shown below. Note that the horizontal axis variable, LENGTH, is not in sort order.

LENGTH is not sorted
LENGTH is the x axis variable for the plot.

```
                     LIB1.ALLFUEL1

         OBS      LENGTH       TOTAL        MPG

          1         10        0.64835     17.0327
          2          2        0.15603     14.2366
          3          1        0.08035     13.7487
          4          5        0.34026     15.9502
          5         25        1.59152     17.2900
          6          8        0.54998     15.9710
          7         15        0.99652     16.8029
```

```
00001    symbol1
00002        value=diamond
00003        height=2
00004        interpol=join              Join data points with a line
00005        color=black
00006    ;
00007
00008    title "Average Fuel Use";
00009
00010    proc gplot data=lib1.allfuel1;
00011      plot mpg*length;
00012    run;
00013    quit;
```

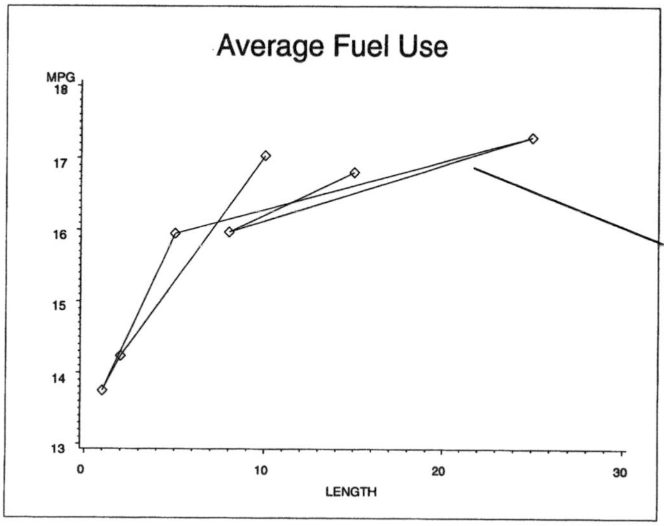

Zigzag plot line
Points are plotted and connected in the order of the x axis variable LENGTH.

To fix the zigzag problem, sort the plotting data set by the *x* axis variable,

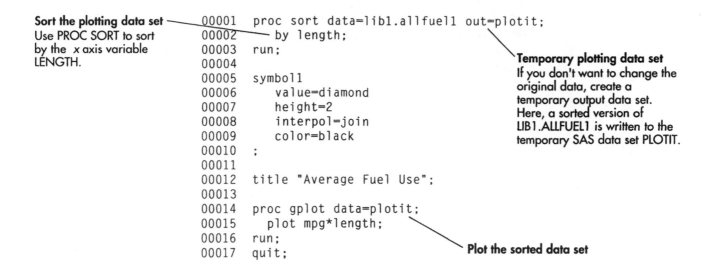

Sort the plotting data set
Use PROC SORT to sort by the *x* axis variable LENGTH.

```
00001   proc sort data=lib1.allfuel1 out=plotit;
00002      by length;
00003   run;
00004
00005   symbol1
00006      value=diamond
00007      height=2
00008      interpol=join
00009      color=black
00010   ;
00011
00012   title "Average Fuel Use";
00013
00014   proc gplot data=plotit;
00015      plot mpg*length;
00016   run;
00017   quit;
```

Temporary plotting data set
If you don't want to change the original data, create a temporary output data set. Here, a sorted version of LIB1.ALLFUEL1 is written to the temporary SAS data set PLOTIT.

Plot the sorted data set

Plot drawn from the sorted data

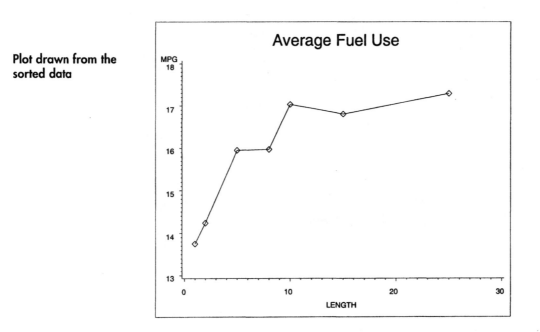

Changing the plot line type

Use the SYMBOL statement LINE= option to change the line type used to connect points. The default is line type 1, a solid line. There are several line types available. Types 1 through 25 are shown below; more are available. You must use both the INTERPOL= and the LINE= options to control line type.

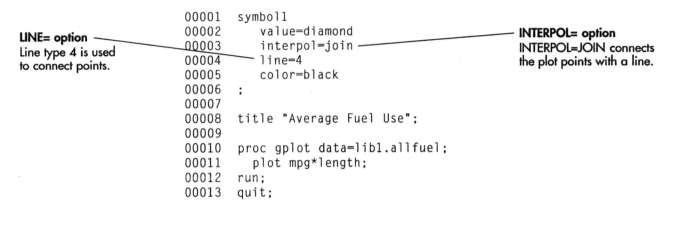

LINE= option
Line type 4 is used to connect points.

```
00001   symbol1
00002     value=diamond
00003     interpol=join
00004     line=4
00005     color=black
00006   ;
00007
00008   title "Average Fuel Use";
00009
00010   proc gplot data=lib1.allfuel;
00011     plot mpg*length;
00012   run;
00013   quit;
```

INTERPOL= option
INTERPOL=JOIN connects the plot points with a line.

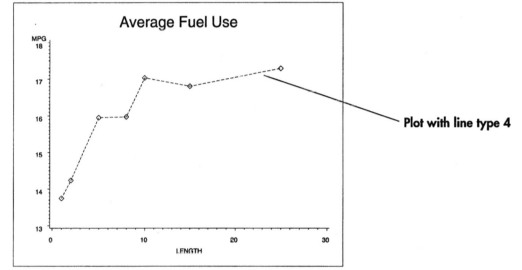

Plot with line type 4

Line types 1 through 25

Changing the plot line thickness

Use the SYMBOL statement WIDTH= option to control line thickness. The value specified is a number. Results for a given width specification will vary depending on your output device. Experimentation may be necessary to get the look you want.

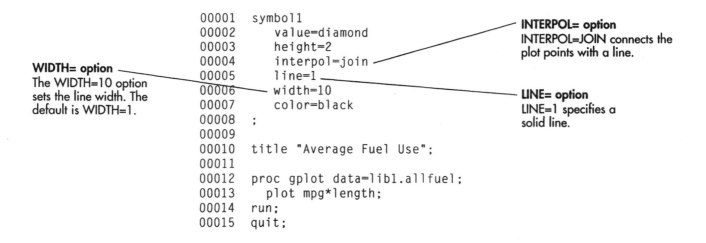

WIDTH= option
The WIDTH=10 option sets the line width. The default is WIDTH=1.

INTERPOL= option
INTERPOL=JOIN connects the plot points with a line.

LINE= option
LINE=1 specifies a solid line.

```
00001    symbol1
00002       value=diamond
00003       height=2
00004       interpol=join
00005       line=1
00006       width=10
00007       color=black
00008    ;
00009
00010    title "Average Fuel Use";
00011
00012    proc gplot data=lib1.allfuel;
00013       plot mpg*length;
00014    run;
00015    quit;
```

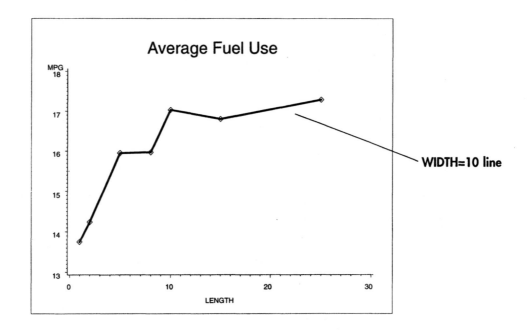

WIDTH=10 line

More Information

PROC GPLOT, general reference
> Chapter 31, "The GPLOT Procedure", *SAS/GRAPH Software: Reference, Volume 2, Version 6, First Edition*, pp. 1073-1130

SYMBOL statement, general reference
> Chapter 16, "The SYMBOL Statement", *SAS/GRAPH Software: Reference, Volume 1*, pp. 399-440

INTERPOL= option in the SYMBOL statement, syntax, interpolation options
> "SYMBOL Statement Options" in Chapter 16, "The SYMBOL Statement", *SAS/GRAPH Software: Reference, Volume 1*, pp. 413-418

LINE= option in the SYMBOL statement, syntax
> "SYMBOL Statement Options" in Chapter 16, "The SYMBOL Statement", *SAS/GRAPH Software: Reference, Volume 1*, p. 419

VALUE= option in the SYMBOL statement, syntax
> "SYMBOL Statement Options" in Chapter 16, "The SYMBOL Statement", *SAS/GRAPH Software: Reference, Volume 1*, pp. 420-422

WIDTH= option in the SYMBOL statement, syntax
> "SYMBOL Statement Options" in Chapter 16, "The SYMBOL Statement", *SAS/GRAPH Software: Reference, Volume 1*, pp. 422

line types, list
> "Selecting Line Types" in Chapter 16, "The SYMBOL Statement", *SAS/GRAPH Software: Reference, Volume 1*, p. 429

using the SYMBOL statement, discussion
> "Introduction to the SYMBOL Statement" in Chapter 19, "Introduction to Plots", *SAS/GRAPH Software: Usage*, pp. 233-235

using INTERPOL=JOIN, example
> "Plot of Two Variables" in Chapter 31, "The GPLOT Procedure", *SAS/GRAPH Software: Reference, Volume 2*, pp. 1112-1114

> "Joining the Data Points" in Chapter 19, "Introduction to Plots", *SAS/GRAPH Software: Usage, Version 6, First Edition*, pp. 239-240

special plotting symbols, list of examples and names
> "SYMBOL Statement Options" in Chapter 16, "The SYMBOL Statement", *SAS/GRAPH Software: Reference, Volume 1*, p. 421

20 Smoothing Plot Lines

> **In This Chapter**
>
> - **Using line smoothing options**
> - **How to plot a regression line**
> - **Adding confidence limits to regression plots**

Using line smoothing options

The SYMBOL statement INTERPOL= option controls how data points are connected. INTERPOL=JOIN connects points using a straight line with a vertex or "kink" at each data point. There are several INTERPOL= settings that smooth the plot vertices. In the example below, INTERPOL=SPLINE is used. The smoothing method you use may depend on requirements for statistical validity or may be a matter of esthetics.

```
00001   symbol1
00002      value=diamond
00003      height=2
00004      interpol=spline
00005      color=black
00006   ;
00007
00008   title "Average Fuel Use";
00009
00010   proc gplot data=lib1.allfuel;
00011     plot mpg*length;
00012   run;
00013   quit;
```

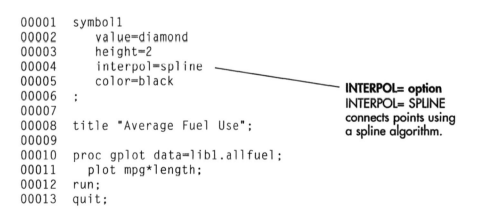

INTERPOL= option
INTERPOL= SPLINE connects points using a spline algorithm.

Closer Look

Before using statistical interpolations, be sure the method you choose will be valid for the conclusions you draw from the plot. With the statistical interpolations, there are several parameters you can adjust to make sure your plot accurately represents the data. See "More Information" for special interpolation references.

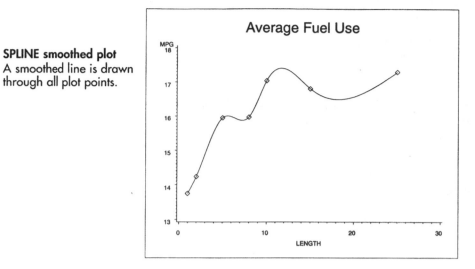

SPLINE smoothed plot
A smoothed line is drawn through all plot points.

How to plot a regression line

The INTERPOL= option can be used to request special data representations including regression plots. There are several regression options to cover specific statistical requirements. The simplest regression request is INTERPOL=R. This generates a linear regression line.

```
00001   symbol
00002      value=diamond
00003      height=2
00004      interpol=r
00005      color=black
00006   ;
00007
00008   title "Average Fuel Use";
00009
00010   proc gplot data=lib1.allfuel;
00011     plot mpg*length;
00012   run;
00013   quit;
```

INTERPOL= option
INTERPOL=R generates a regression line through the plot points.

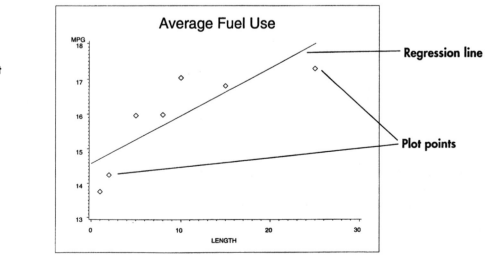

INTERPOL=R plot

Regression line

Plot points

Adding confidence limits to regression plots

You can display regression line confidence limits. The example generates a cubic regression with 90% confidence limits for the predicted mean values. The regression and confidence limit requests are part of the INTERPOL= option. The CO= option names the confidence limit line color. The confidence limit line type is determined by adding one to the plot line type. The default plot line type is 1, so the default confidence limit line type is 2.

CO= option
CO=GRAYAA
generates gray
confidence limit lines.

INTERPOL= option
INTERPOL=RCCLM90 generates
a cubic regression with 90%
confidence limits.

```
00001    symbol1
00002       value=triangle
00003       interpol=rcclm90
00004       co=grayaa
00005       color=black
00006    ;
00007
00008    title h=2 "Average Fuel Use";
00009    title2 h=1.5 "90% Confidence Limit";
00010    title3 h=1.5 "For Mean Predicted Values";
00011
00012    proc gplot data=lib1.allfuel;
00013       plot mpg*length;
00014    run;
00015    quit;
```

RC requests a cubic regression

$$\text{interpol}=\text{rcclm90}$$

**CLM90 requests 90% for
mean predicted value
confidence limits**

Average Fuel Use
90% Confidence Limit
For Mean Predicted Values

Cubic regression line

Confidence limit line

More Information

SYMBOL statement, general reference

Chapter 16, "The SYMBOL Statement", *SAS/GRAPH Software: Reference, Volume 1, Version 6, First Edition*, pp. 399-440

PROC GPLOT, general reference

Chapter 31, "The GPLOT Procedure", *SAS/GRAPH Software: Reference, Volume 2,* pp. 1073-1130

INTERPOL= option, SYMBOL statement, reference, syntax, available interpolation methods

"SYMBOL Statement Options" in Chapter 16, "The SYMBOL Statement", *SAS/GRAPH Software: Reference, Volume 1*, pp. 410-418

MODE= option, effect on special interpolation methods

"SYMBOL Statement Options" in Chapter 16, "The SYMBOL Statement", *SAS/GRAPH Software: Reference, Volume 1*, p. 419

VALUE= option

"SYMBOL Statement Options" in Chapter 16, "The SYMBOL Statement", *SAS/GRAPH Software: Reference, Volume 1*, pp. 420-422

regression interpolation options

"SYMBOL Statement Options" in Chapter 16, "The SYMBOL Statement", *SAS/GRAPH Software: Reference, Volume 1*, pp. 415-416

regression lines and confidence limits, example

"Using Regression Analysis Interpolation and Color Options" in Chapter 16, "The SYMBOL Statement", *SAS/GRAPH Software: Reference, Volume 1*, pp. 430-431

"Fitting a Regression Line" in Chapter 22, "Producing Scatter Plots", *SAS/GRAPH Software: Usage, Version 6, First Edition*, pp. 304-307

line smoothing methods, example

"Using Spline Interpolation" in Chapter 22, "Producing Scatter Plots", *SAS/GRAPH Software: Usage*, pp. 307-309

confidence limit requests

"SYMBOL Statement Options" in Chapter 16, "The SYMBOL Statement", *SAS/GRAPH Software: Reference, Volume 1*, pp. 415-416

21 Adding a Second Axis

In This Chapter

- Adding a second axis with the PLOT2 statement
- How to identify each plot
- Why isn't the SYMBOL2 statement being used?

Adding a second axis with the PLOT2 statement

You can show the relationship between an *x* axis variable and two different *y* axis variables with the PLOT2 statement. The PLOT2 statement generates a second set of points and a second vertical axis on the right-hand side of the graph.

SYMBOL statements control the display of points generated by the PLOT2 statement. If only a SYMBOL1 statement with a COLOR= option is used, it will apply to the points generated by the PLOT statement, and the PLOT2 points will be displayed with the default symbol settings.

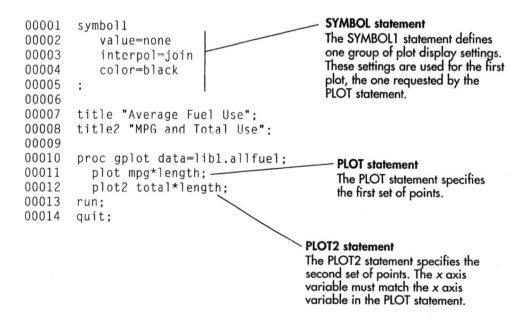

```
00001   symbol1
00002      value=none
00003      interpol=join
00004      color=black
00005   ;
00006
00007   title "Average Fuel Use";
00008   title2 "MPG and Total Use";
00009
00010   proc gplot data=lib1.allfuel;
00011     plot mpg*length;
00012     plot2 total*length;
00013   run;
00014   quit;
```

SYMBOL statement
The SYMBOL1 statement defines one group of plot display settings. These settings are used for the first plot, the one requested by the PLOT statement.

PLOT statement
The PLOT statement specifies the first set of points.

PLOT2 statement
The PLOT2 statement specifies the second set of points. The *x* axis variable must match the *x* axis variable in the PLOT statement.

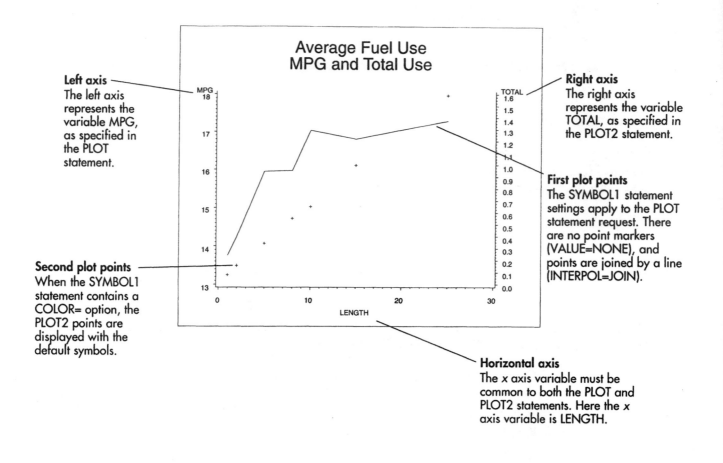

Left axis
The left axis represents the variable MPG, as specified in the PLOT statement.

Right axis
The right axis represents the variable TOTAL, as specified in the PLOT2 statement.

First plot points
The SYMBOL1 statement settings apply to the PLOT statement request. There are no point markers (VALUE=NONE), and points are joined by a line (INTERPOL=JOIN).

Second plot points
When the SYMBOL1 statement contains a COLOR= option, the PLOT2 points are displayed with the default symbols.

Horizontal axis
The x axis variable must be common to both the PLOT and PLOT2 statements. Here the x axis variable is LENGTH.

How to identify each plot

The PLOT2 statement adds a second axis and set of points, but a legend distinguishing the two plots is not automatically generated. Use two SYMBOL statements to apply distinctive plotting symbols and lines to each plot; then use the LEGEND and OVERLAY options on both the PLOT and PLOT2 statements to generate a legend identifying the plots.

You can also use LEGEND statements to create customized legends. To apply customized legends, use the LEGEND= option in the PLOT statement instead of the LEGEND option. See Chapter 40 for more on custom legends.

First SYMBOL statement
SYMBOL1 is applied to the left-hand axis plot.

Second SYMBOL statement
When the SYMBOL1 statement has a COLOR= option, the SYMBOL2 settings are applied to the plot generated by the PLOT2 statement.

PLOT statement
The LEGEND and OVERLAY options generate a legend identifying the first plot line.

```
00001  symbol1
00002     interpol=join
00003     value=dot
00004     height=2
00005     line=1
00006     color=black
00007  ;
00008
00009  symbol2
00010     interpol=join
00011     value=circle
00012     height=2
00013     line=3
00014     color=black
00015  ;
00016
00017  title "Fuel Use";
00018  title2 "MPG and Total Use";
00019
00010  proc gplot data=lib1.allfuel;
00021     plot mpg*length / legend overlay;
00022     plot2 total*length / legend overlay;
00023  run;
00024  quit;
```

First plot symbol
The solid dot and line type 1 distinguish the first plot.

Second plot symbol
The circle (hollow dot) and line type 3 distinguish the second plot.

PLOT2 statement
The LEGEND and OVERLAY options generate a legend identifying the second plot line.

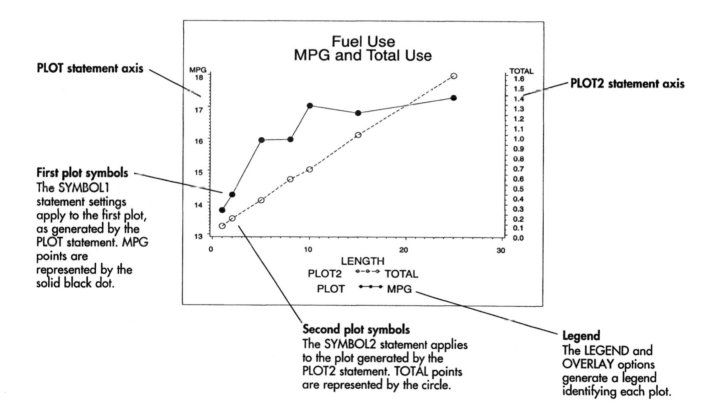

PLOT statement axis

PLOT2 statement axis

First plot symbols
The SYMBOL1 statement settings apply to the first plot, as generated by the PLOT statement. MPG points are represented by the solid black dot.

Second plot symbols
The SYMBOL2 statement applies to the plot generated by the PLOT2 statement. TOTAL points are represented by the circle.

Legend
The LEGEND and OVERLAY options generate a legend identifying each plot.

Why isn't the SYMBOL2 statement being used?

If a SYMBOL1 statement is used *without* a COLOR= option, the SYMBOL1 settings are combined with the next available color to generate the symbol settings applied to the second plot. To avoid unexpected results, always use the COLOR= option in SYMBOL statements.

Color list

This COLORS= graphics option specifies that two colors are available. If you do not specify a color list, the default list is used. Normally, the default color list contains at least two colors.

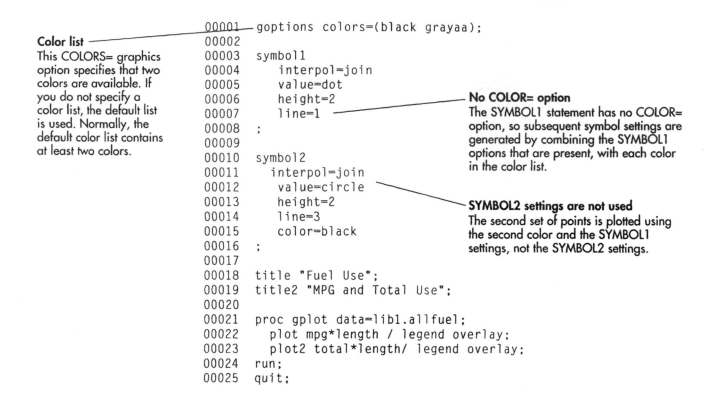

```
00001   goptions colors=(black grayaa);
00002
00003   symbol1
00004       interpol=join
00005       value=dot
00006       height=2
00007       line=1
00008   ;
00009
00010   symbol2
00011       interpol=join
00012       value=circle
00013       height=2
00014       line=3
00015       color=black
00016   ;
00017
00018   title "Fuel Use";
00019   title2 "MPG and Total Use";
00020
00021   proc gplot data=lib1.allfuel;
00022     plot mpg*length / legend overlay;
00023     plot2 total*length/ legend overlay;
00024   run;
00025   quit;
```

No COLOR= option

The SYMBOL1 statement has no COLOR= option, so subsequent symbol settings are generated by combining the SYMBOL1 options that are present, with each color in the color list.

SYMBOL2 settings are not used

The second set of points is plotted using the second color and the SYMBOL1 settings, not the SYMBOL2 settings.

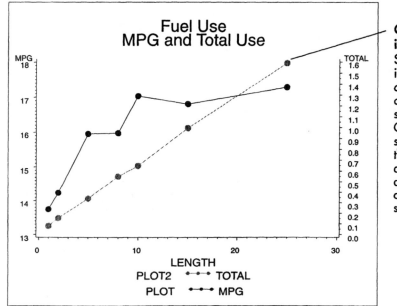

CIRCLE plot character is not used.

SYMBOL1 settings, including the plotting character DOT, are combined with the second color, GRAYAA. These settings are applied to the second plot. To avoid this problem, always use a COLOR= option in the SYMBOL statement.

More Information

PROC GPLOT, general reference

Chapter 31, "The GPLOT Procedure", *SAS/GRAPH Software: Reference, Volume 2, Version 6, First Edition*, pp. 1073-1130

SYMBOL statement, general reference

Chapter 16, "The SYMBOL Statement", *SAS/GRAPH Software: Reference, Volume 1*, pp. 399-440

rules for applying SYMBOL settings

"Symbol Sequences", in Chapter 16, "The SYMBOL Statement", *SAS/GRAPH Software: Reference, Volume 1*, pp. 405-408

PLOT2 statement, syntax, example

"PLOT2 Statement" in Chapter 31, "The GPLOT Procedure", *SAS/GRAPH Software: Reference, Volume 2*, pp. 1120-1129

using a second plot axis, discussion and examples

"Displaying a Second Scale of Values on a Right Vertical Axis" in Chapter 21, "Producing Plots with Legends", *SAS/GRAPH Software: Usage, Version 6, First Edition*, pp. 290-296

INTERPOL= option in the SYMBOL statement, syntax, interpolation options

"SYMBOL Statement Options" in Chapter 16, "The SYMBOL Statement", *SAS/GRAPH Software: Reference, Volume 1*, pp. 413-418

LINE= option in the SYMBOL statement, syntax

"SYMBOL Statement Options" in Chapter 16, "The SYMBOL Statement", *SAS/GRAPH Software: Reference, Volume 1*, p. 419

VALUE= option in the SYMBOL statement, syntax

"SYMBOL Statement Options" in Chapter 16, "The SYMBOL Statement", *SAS/GRAPH Software: Reference, Volume 1*, pp. 420-422

line types, list

"Selecting Line Types" in Chapter 16, "The SYMBOL Statement", *SAS/GRAPH Software: Reference, Volume 1*, p. 429

use of LEGEND and LEGEND= options with the OVERLAY option

"The GPLOT Procedure", in Chapter 4, "SAS/GRAPH Procedures", *SAS Technical Report P-215, SAS/GRAPH Software: Changes and Enhancements, Release 6.07*, p. 53

22 Plotting Multiple Sets of Points

In This Chapter

- Using a third variable to generate multiple plots in a single set of axes
- Controlling the number of plots when using a third variable
- Using multiple plot requests and overlays

Using a third variable to generate multiple plots in a single set of axes

You can generate multiple plots with a third-variable plot request specified in the PLOT statement. The third variable is also called the z variable or classification variable.

```
PLOT y*x=z;
```

For each value of the z variable a separate set of points is plotted relating the x and y variables.

The SAS data set LIB1.TYPEFUEL is used in the following example. A partial listing of LIB1.TYPEFUEL is shown below. When TYPE is used as the third variable, a plot is generated for each unique value of TYPE. The variable TYPE has four unique values: SUBCOMPACT, COMPACT, MIDSIZE, and LARGE; so four plots are generated on a single set of axes.

**SAS data set
LIB1.TYPEFUEL**
(partial listing)

		LIB1.TYPEFUEL		
OBS	TYPE	LENGTH	TOTAL	MPG
1	SUBCOMPACT	1	0.04846	20.6352
2	SUBCOMPACT	2	0.12261	16.3122
		.		
		.		
9	COMPACT	2	0.13546	14.7641
10	COMPACT	5	0.26073	19.1771
		.		
		.		
15	MIDSIZE	1	0.07625	13.1145
16	MIDSIZE	2	0.16520	12.1067
		.		
		.		
22	LARGE	1	0.10822	9.2401
23	LARGE	2	0.26925	7.4282

```
00001    symbol1
00002        interpol=join
00003        value=diamond
00004        height=1
00005        line=1
00006        color=black
00007    ;
00008
00009    symbol2
00010        interpol=join
00011        value=circle
00012        height=1
00013        line=3
00014        color=black
00015    ;
00016
00017    symbol3
00018        interpol=join
00019        value=dot
00020        height=1
00021        line=5
00022        color=black
00023    ;
00024
00025    symbol4
00026        interpol=join
00027        value=star
00028        height=1
00029        line=8
00030        color=black
00031    ;
00032
00033    title "Fuel Use and Car Type";
00034
00035    proc gplot data=lib1.typefuel;
00036      plot mpg*length=type;
00037    run;
00038    quit;
```

SYMBOL statements
Four SYMBOL statements (lines 1-31) define settings to distinguish the four sets of points. If you do not use the COLOR= option, symbol settings are cycled through all colors in the color list before using the settings in the next SYMBOL statement. To avoid unexpected results, always use the COLOR= option.

Third-variable plot request
The PLOT statement with a third variable generates a plot for each unique value of the third variable TYPE.

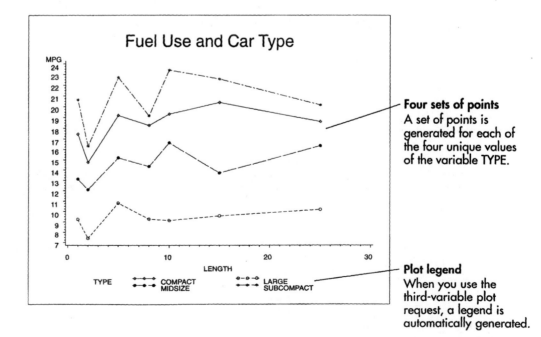

Four sets of points
A set of points is generated for each of the four unique values of the variable TYPE.

Plot legend
When you use the third-variable plot request, a legend is automatically generated.

Controlling the number of plots when using a third variable

A set of points is plotted for each unique value of a third variable. If there are many unique values of this variable your graph may be overcrowded with plot lines. You can control the number of plots generated with a WHERE statement. The WHERE statement limits the data read by PROC GPLOT.

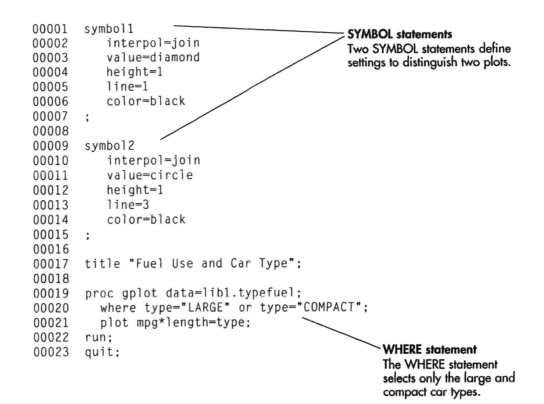

```
00001    symbol1
00002       interpol=join
00003       value=diamond
00004       height=1
00005       line=1
00006       color=black
00007    ;
00008
00009    symbol2
00010       interpol=join
00011       value=circle
00012       height=1
00013       line=3
00014       color=black
00015    ;
00016
00017    title "Fuel Use and Car Type";
00018
00019    proc gplot data=lib1.typefuel;
00020       where type="LARGE" or type="COMPACT";
00021       plot mpg*length=type;
00022    run;
00023    quit;
```

SYMBOL statements
Two SYMBOL statements define settings to distinguish two plots.

WHERE statement
The WHERE statement selects only the large and compact car types.

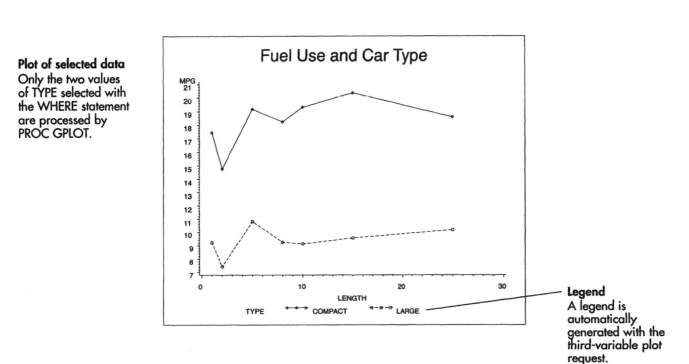

Plot of selected data
Only the two values of TYPE selected with the WHERE statement are processed by PROC GPLOT.

Legend
A legend is automatically generated with the third-variable plot request.

Using multiple plot requests and overlays

If your data are not organized properly for use with a third-variable plot request, you can generate multiple plots in a single set of axes by using multiple plot requests and the OVERLAY option.

The following example plots the SAS data set LIB1.FUEL2, as shown below. A third-variable plot request cannot be used to plot the variables SUBCOM and LARGE against LENGTH, so each variable is plotted against LENGTH with a separate plot request and the resulting plots are overlayed on the same set of axes. The LEGEND option displays a legend identifying each overlay plot.

Input data set
The LIB1.FUEL2 data set holds information on miles-per-gallon for various trip lengths for subcompact and large cars. Each observation holds data for both types of cars.

```
                    LIB1.FUEL2

   OBS      SUBCOM       LARGE      LENGTH

    1      20.6352      9.2401         1
    2      16.3122      7.4282         2
    3      22.6963     10.8119         5
    4      19.1297      9.2644         8
    5      23.3921      9.1327        10
    6      22.5562      9.5771        15
    7      20.1433     10.1883        25
```

The LEGEND option generates a default legend identifying each overlay plot. You can apply a customized legend by using the LEGEND= option instead of LEGEND. The LEGEND= option names a legend defined with a LEGEND statement. In this example, "Car Types" is used to label the legend instead of the default "PLOT."

```
00019    legend1 label=("Car Types");        ── Define LEGEND1 settings
00020
00021    proc gplot data=lib1.fuel2;
00022       plot subcom*length
00023            large*length /
00024          overlay
00025          vaxis=axis1
00026          legend=legend1       ── Assign LEGEND1 to the overlay
00027       ;                          plot with the LEGEND= option
```

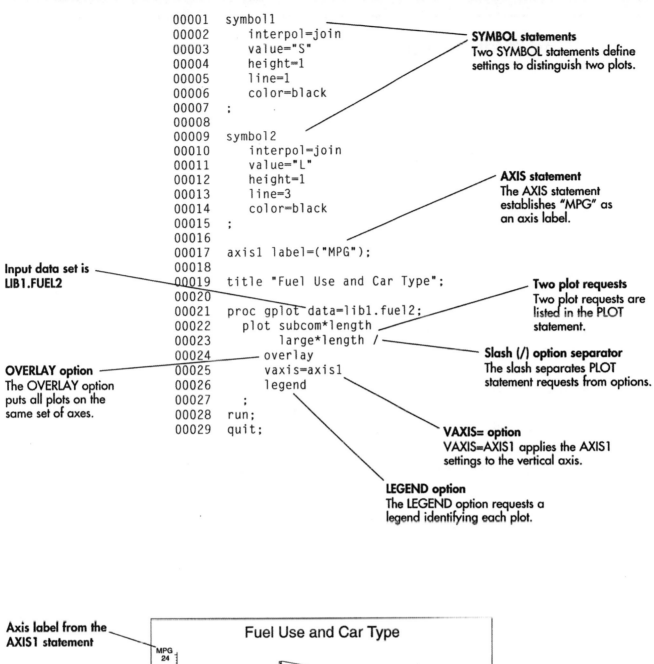

```
00001    symbol1
00002       interpol=join
00003       value="S"
00004       height=1
00005       line=1
00006       color=black
00007    ;
00008
00009    symbol2
00010       interpol=join
00011       value="L"
00012       height=1
00013       line=3
00014       color=black
00015    ;
00016
00017    axis1 label=("MPG");
00018
00019    title "Fuel Use and Car Type";
00020
00021    proc gplot data=lib1.fuel2;
00022       plot subcom*length
00023            large*length /
00024            overlay
00025            vaxis=axis1
00026            legend
00027       ;
00028    run;
00029    quit;
```

SYMBOL statements
Two SYMBOL statements define settings to distinguish two plots.

AXIS statement
The AXIS statement establishes "MPG" as an axis label.

Input data set is LIB1.FUEL2

Two plot requests
Two plot requests are listed in the PLOT statement.

Slash (/) option separator
The slash separates PLOT statement requests from options.

OVERLAY option
The OVERLAY option puts all plots on the same set of axes.

VAXIS= option
VAXIS=AXIS1 applies the AXIS1 settings to the vertical axis.

LEGEND option
The LEGEND option requests a legend identifying each plot.

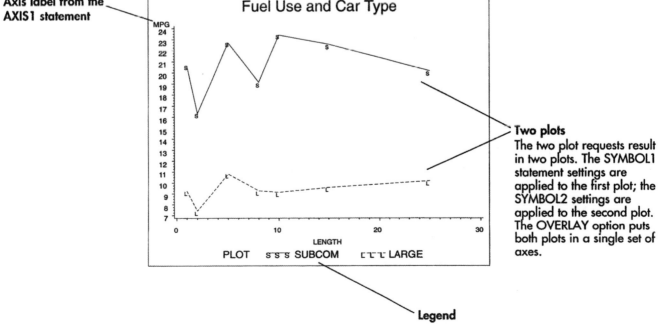

Axis label from the AXIS1 statement

Two plots
The two plot requests result in two plots. The SYMBOL1 statement settings are applied to the first plot; the SYMBOL2 settings are applied to the second plot. The OVERLAY option puts both plots in a single set of axes.

Legend

GPLOT procedure, general reference

Chapter 31, "The GPLOT Procedure", *SAS/GRAPH Software: Reference, Volume 2, Version 6, First Edition*, pp. 1073-1130

PLOT statement, general reference

"PLOT Statement" in Chapter 31, "The GPLOT Procedure", *SAS/GRAPH Software: Reference, Volume 2*, pp. 1100-1120

OVERLAY option, reference

"Options" in Chapter 31, "The GPLOT Procedure", *SAS/GRAPH Software: Reference, Volume 2*, p. 1107

LEGEND= option

"Options" in Chapter 31, "The GPLOT Procedure", *SAS/GRAPH Software: Reference, Volume 2*, p. 1106

LEGEND statement, general reference

Chapter 13, "The LEGEND Statement", *SAS/GRAPH Software: Reference, Volume 1*, pp. 303-345

third-variable plots, example

"Plots of Three Variables with a Legend" in Chapter 31, "The GPLOT Procedure", *SAS/GRAPH Software: Reference, Volume 2*, pp. 1118-1120

"Producing a Plot with a Legend" in Chapter 21, "Producing Plots with Legends", *SAS/GRAPH Software: Usage, Version 6, First Edition*, pp. 285-287

LABEL= option, AXIS statement

"AXIS Statement Options" in Chapter 9, "The AXIS Statement", *SAS/GRAPH Software: Reference, Volume 1*, pp. 221-222

SYMBOL statement, general reference

Chapter 16, "The SYMBOL Statement", *SAS/GRAPH Software: Reference, Volume 1*, pp. 399-440

Overlay plots, discussion

"Displaying Multiple Plots on One Set of Axes" in Chapter 20, "Producing Multiple Plots", *SAS/GRAPH Software: Usage*, pp. 261-262

using the AXIS statement and VAXIS= option, example

"Modifying the Vertical Axis" in Chapter 20, "Producing Multiple Plots", *SAS/GRAPH Software: Usage*, pp. 265-266

using the FOOTNOTE statement to create a legend, example

"Adding an Explanatory Footnote" in Chapter 20, "Producing Multiple Plots", *SAS/GRAPH Software: Usage*, pp. 268-270

using the SYMBOL statement to distinguish plot lines, example

"Defining Symbol Characteristics for Each Plot" in Chapter 21, "Producing Plots with Legends", *SAS/GRAPH Software: Usage*, pp. 287-288

SAS data set structure for third-variable plots, example

"Structuring Data to Produce a Classification Variable" in Chapter 21, "Producing Plots with Legends", *SAS/GRAPH Software: Usage*, pp. 296-299

WHERE= data set option, reference

"WHERE=" in Chapter 15, "SAS Data Set Options", *SAS Language: Reference, Version 6, First Edition*, pp. 731-732

Filling an Area under a Line

23

In This Chapter

- **Filling under a line**
- **Filling under multiple lines**

Filling under a line

The area under a plot can be filled using the PLOT statement AREAS= option. However, the AREAS= option is ignored unless the points in your plot are connected with a line. Use a SYMBOL statement with the INTERPOL= option to connect points. The PATTERN statement controls the color and pattern of the area fill.

In the following example, a WHERE statement is used to select only the observations where the value of TYPE =LARGE. Since TYPE is the third variable in the third-variable plot request and there is only one value of TYPE, only one line is plotted.

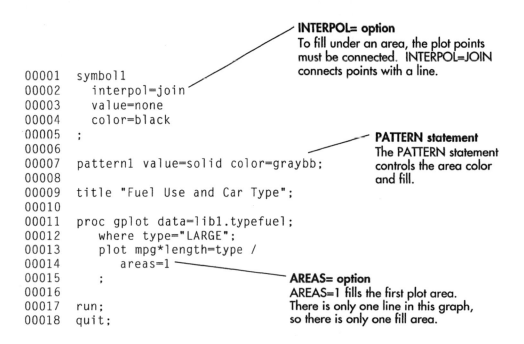

```
00001   symbol1
00002     interpol=join
00003     value=none
00004     color=black
00005   ;
00006
00007   pattern1 value=solid color=graybb;
00008
00009   title "Fuel Use and Car Type";
00010
00011   proc gplot data=lib1.typefuel;
00012      where type="LARGE";
00013      plot mpg*length=type /
00014         areas=1
00015      ;
00016
00017   run;
00018   quit;
```

INTERPOL= option
To fill under an area, the plot points must be connected. INTERPOL=JOIN connects points with a line.

PATTERN statement
The PATTERN statement controls the area color and fill.

AREAS= option
AREAS=1 fills the first plot area. There is only one line in this graph, so there is only one fill area.

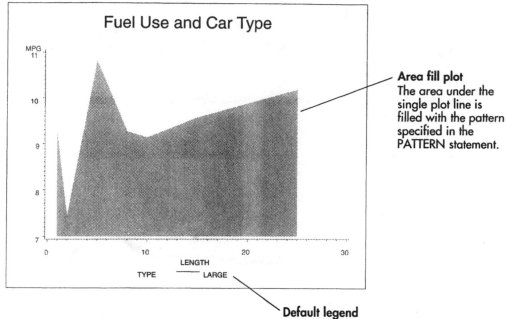

Fuel Use and Car Type

Area fill plot
The area under the single plot line is filled with the pattern specified in the PATTERN statement.

Default legend
No LEGEND statement is used, so the default legend is displayed. When your plot contains just one area, legends may not be useful. To turn off legends, use the PLOT statement NOLEGEND option.

Filling under multiple lines

You can apply distinctive fills between two or more lines. The space between the lines is filled in the order in which the lines are drawn. To prevent high areas from obscuring low areas, you must ensure that the line with the lowest vertical axis values is drawn first, followed by areas in ascending order of vertical axis values. Use a PATTERN statement for each area to control the appearance of the fill.

In this example, the WHERE statement is used to select two values of the variable TYPE, from the data set LIB1.TYPEFUEL. Because TYPE is used in the third-variable plot request, there are two plot lines.

Areas are filled in the order that lines are drawn on the plot. To prevent lower areas from being covered by higher areas, you need to ensure that the first line plotted is the lowest, that is, the one with the lowest vertical axis values. When using a third-variable plot request:

```
PLOT  y*x=z;
```

you may need to alter the values of the z variable, so its sort order corresponds to the relative values of the vertical axis variable y. See Chapter 24 for an example of this process.

SYMBOL statements
The SYMBOL statements use INTERPOL=JOIN to connect the plot points.

LEGEND statement
The LEGEND statement specifies how the area pattern is displayed in the legend. Here the width of the legend bar will be three times its height. (See Chapter 40 for more on the LEGEND statement.)

```
00001   symbol1 interpol=join value=none color=black;
00002   symbol2 interpol=join value=none color=black;;
00003
00004   pattern1 value=solid color=graycc;
00005   pattern2 value=solid color=gray88;
00006
00007   legend1 shape=bar(3,1);
00008
00009   title "Fuel Use and Car Type";
00010
00011   proc gplot data=lib1.typefuel
00012     where type="LARGE" or type="SUBCOMPACT";
00013     plot mpg*length=type /
00014       areas=2
00015       legend=legend1
00016     ;
00017
00018   run;
00019   quit;
```

PATTERN statements
The PATTERN statements specify the color and fill pattern for two areas.

AREAS= option
AREAS=2 fills two plot areas.

LEGEND= option
LEGEND=LEGEND1 applies the LEGEND1 settings to the plot.

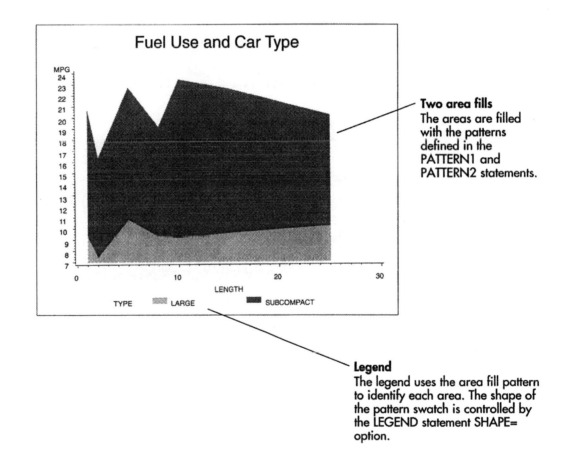

Two area fills
The areas are filled with the patterns defined in the PATTERN1 and PATTERN2 statements.

Legend
The legend uses the area fill pattern to identify each area. The shape of the pattern swatch is controlled by the LEGEND statement SHAPE= option.

 Closer Look
SYMBOL statements control the display of plot lines. The example above uses SYMBOL statements with the COLOR option even though plot lines are not shown in area plots. If you do not use the COLOR= option, symbol settin are cycled through all available colors before the next SYMBOL statement settings are used. This can result unexpected results. You may want to allow SAS/GRAPH to cycle through symbol settings so you don't have inclu a separate SYMBOL statement for each color. If you do not want SAS/GRAPH to cycle through symbol settin always include a COLOR= option with the SYMBOL statement.

More Information

GPLOT procedure, general reference

Chapter 31, "The GPLOT Procedure", *SAS/GRAPH Software: Reference, Volume 2, Version 6, First Edition,* pp. 1073-1130

PLOT statement, general reference

"PLOT Statement" in Chapter 31, "The GPLOT Procedure", *SAS/GRAPH Software: Reference, Volume 2,* pp. 1100-1120

AREAS= option

"Options" in Chapter 31, "The GPLOT Procedure", *SAS/GRAPH Software: Reference, Volume 2,* p. 1103

LEGEND= option

"Options" in Chapter 31, "The GPLOT Procedure", *SAS/GRAPH Software: Reference, Volume 2,* p. 1106

LEGEND statement, general reference

Chapter 13, "The LEGEND Statement", *SAS/GRAPH Software: Reference, Volume 1,* pp. 303-345

SHAPE= option in the LEGEND statement

"LEGEND Statement Options" in Chapter 13, "The LEGEND Statement", *SAS/GRAPH Software: Reference, Volume 1,* pp. 312-313

PATTERN statement, general reference

Chapter 15, "The PATTERN Statement", *SAS/GRAPH Software: Reference, Volume 1,* pp. 365-398

SYMBOL statement, general reference

Chapter 16, "The SYMBOL Statement", *SAS/GRAPH Software: Reference, Volume 1,* pp. 399-440

INTERPOL= option in the SYMBOL statement

"SYMBOL Statement Options" in Chapter 16, "The SYMBOL Statement", *SAS/GRAPH Software: Reference, Volume 1,* pp. 410-418

filling areas under a line, example

"Filling Areas below the Plot Lines" in Chapter 20, "Producing Multiple Plots", *SAS/GRAPH Software: Usage, Version 6, First Edition,* pp. 270-273

Example 1, "Filling Areas in a Two-Dimensional Plot", *SAS/GRAPH Software: Examples, Version 6, First Edition,* pp. 1-4

filling areas under overlaid lines, example

"Using the AREAS= Option with Overlaid Plots" in Chapter 31, "The GPLOT Procedure", *SAS/GRAPH Software: Reference, Volume 2,* pp. 1116-1117

Creating a Cumulative Area Plot

In This Chapter

- **What is a cumulative area plot?**
- **Data for the cumulative plot**
- **Creating the plot**

What is a cumulative area plot?

A cumulative area plot shows a total and the components of that total. The magnitude of the components is shown not by a distance from the horizontal axis, but by the distance from the component below it.

Cumulative area plot

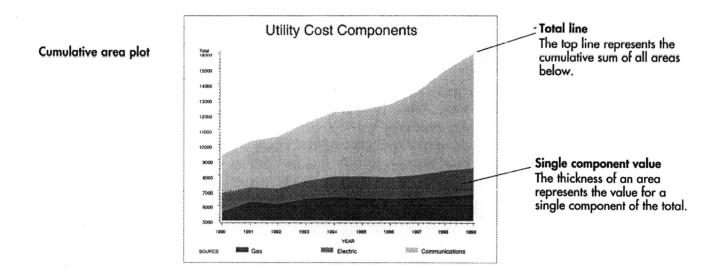

Total line
The top line represents the cumulative sum of all areas below.

Single component value
The thickness of an area represents the value for a single component of the total.

Data for the cumulative plot

The SAS data set LIB1.UTILYEAR, shown below, holds data for three utility cost categories over 10 years. These data are used as the basis for the example plot.

LIB1.UTILYEAR does not contain variables holding the total utility cost for each year or cumulative costs for any combination of categories. In order to create a cumulative plot, an intermediate data set is generated that contains these cumulative totals. This intermediate data set is plotted instead of LIB1.UTILYEAR.

Plot data
LIB1.UTILYEAR holds the data shown in the cumulative area plot. Before the data can be plotted, they must be restructured to represent cumulative sums instead of values for individual utility categories.

```
                    LIB1.UTILYEAR

        OBS    YEAR     GAS     ELEC    TELE

         1     1990     5600    1250    2450
         2     1991     6250     950    3000
         3     1992     6100    1025    3400
         4     1993     6450    1175    3800
         5     1994     6575    1350    4200
         6     1995     6500    1425    4350
         7     1996     6450    1425    4775
         8     1997     6525    1500    5500
         9     1998     6600    1700    6550
        10     1999     6750    1725    7500
```

Creating the plot

A DATA step and a PROC GPLOT step are used to create the cumulative area plot. The DATA step reads the data set LIB1.UTILYEAR, calculates cumulative totals, and writes these totals to the temporary SAS data set PLOTIT. Cumulative totals are held in the variable COST. These totals are identified by the variable SOURCE.

SOURCE is used in a third-variable plot request, so there is one line for each of its three values. The values assigned to SOURCE are important because they determine the order in which these lines are drawn. The lines are drawn in ascending order of the three values. The line for "1_Gas" is drawn first, the line for "2_Elec" second, and the line for "3_Tele" third. The lines representing the lowest y axis values must be drawn first to avoid "hiding" low areas behind high areas. The key point is that low y values must correspond to low third-variable values. This relationship between the relative values of the vertical axis variable and the sort sequence of the third variable is enforced by using 1, 2, and 3 to prefix the values of SOURCE as the value of COST increases by accumulating expenses for each utility category. A LEGEND statement is used to display "Gas", "Electric", and "Communications" instead of "1_Gas", "2_Elec", and "3_Tele."

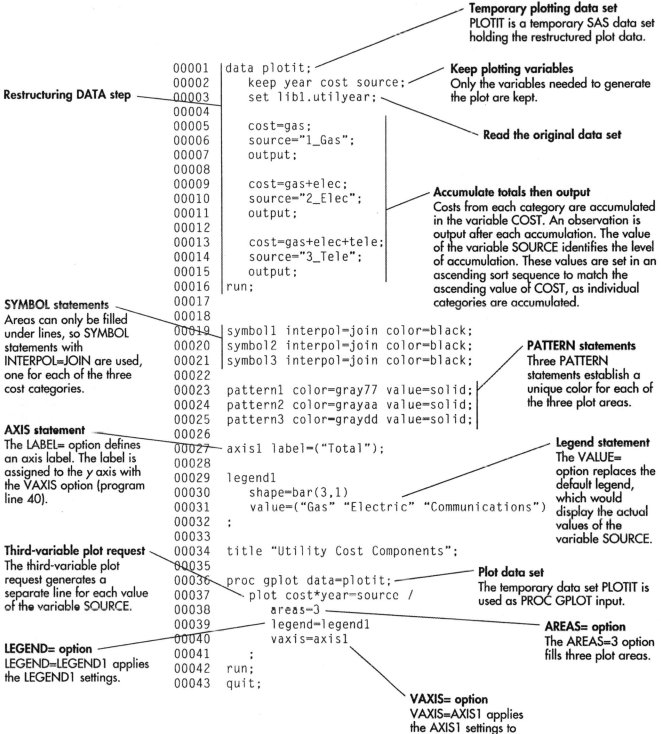

Temporary plotting data set
PLOTIT is a temporary SAS data set holding the restructured plot data.

Restructuring DATA step

Keep plotting variables
Only the variables needed to generate the plot are kept.

Read the original data set

Accumulate totals then output
Costs from each category are accumulated in the variable COST. An observation is output after each accumulation. The value of the variable SOURCE identifies the level of accumulation. These values are set in an ascending sort sequence to match the ascending value of COST, as individual categories are accumulated.

SYMBOL statements
Areas can only be filled under lines, so SYMBOL statements with INTERPOL=JOIN are used, one for each of the three cost categories.

PATTERN statements
Three PATTERN statements establish a unique color for each of the three plot areas.

AXIS statement
The LABEL= option defines an axis label. The label is assigned to the y axis with the VAXIS option (program line 40).

Legend statement
The VALUE= option replaces the default legend, which would display the actual values of the variable SOURCE.

Third-variable plot request
The third-variable plot request generates a separate line for each value of the variable SOURCE.

Plot data set
The temporary data set PLOTIT is used as PROC GPLOT input.

AREAS= option
The AREAS=3 option fills three plot areas.

LEGEND= option
LEGEND=LEGEND1 applies the LEGEND1 settings.

VAXIS= option
VAXIS=AXIS1 applies the AXIS1 settings to the vertical axis.

```
00001  data plotit;
00002     keep year cost source;
00003     set lib1.utilyear;
00004
00005     cost=gas;
00006     source="1_Gas";
00007     output;
00008
00009     cost=gas+elec;
00010     source="2_Elec";
00011     output;
00012
00013     cost=gas+elec+tele;
00014     source="3_Tele";
00015     output;
00016  run;
00017
00018
00019  symbol1 interpol=join color=black;
00020  symbol2 interpol=join color=black;
00021  symbol3 interpol=join color=black;
00022
00023  pattern1 color=gray77 value=solid;
00024  pattern2 color=grayaa value=solid;
00025  pattern3 color=graydd value=solid;
00026
00027  axis1 label=("Total");
00028
00029  legend1
00030     shape=bar(3,1)
00031     value=("Gas" "Electric" "Communications")
00032  ;
00033
00034  title "Utility Cost Components";
00035
00036  proc gplot data=plotit;
00037     plot cost*year=source /
00038        areas=3
00039        legend=legend1
00040        vaxis=axis1
00041     ;
00042  run;
00043  quit;
```

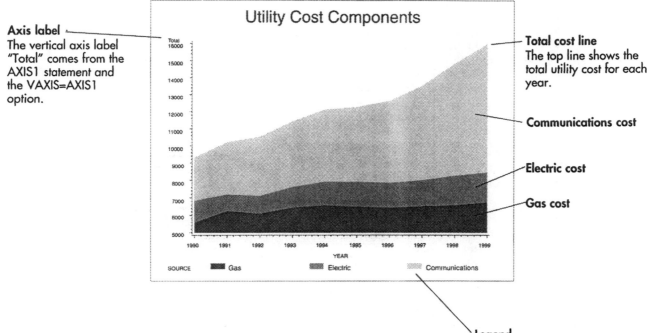

Axis label
The vertical axis label "Total" comes from the AXIS1 statement and the VAXIS=AXIS1 option.

Total cost line
The top line shows the total utility cost for each year.

Communications cost

Electric cost

Gas cost

Legend
The legend is generated automatically when you use the third-variable plot request. Legend text and pattern swatches are set in the LEGEND statement.

PLOTIT data set
PLOTIT is the temporary data set generated from LIB1.UTILYEAR.

```
          PLOTIT DATA SET

OBS   YEAR    COST    SOURCE

 1    1990    5600    1_Gas
 2    1990    6850    2_Ele
 3    1990    9300    3_Tel
 4    1991    6250    1_Gas
 5    1991    7200    2_Ele
 6    1991   10200    3_Tel
 7    1992    6100    1_Gas
 8    1992    7125    2_Ele
 9    1992   10525    3_Tel
10    1993    6450    1_Gas
11    1993    7625    2_Ele
12    1993   11425    3_Tel
13    1994    6575    1_Gas
14    1994    7925    2_Ele
15    1994   12125    3_Tel
```

```
          PLOTIT DATA SET

OBS   YEAR    COST    SOURCE

16    1995    6500    1_Gas
17    1995    7925    2_Ele
18    1995   12275    3_Tel
19    1996    6450    1_Gas
20    1996    7875    2_Ele
21    1996   12650    3_Tel
22    1997    6525    1_Gas
23    1997    8025    2_Ele
24    1997   13525    3_Tel
25    1998    6600    1_Gas
26    1998    8300    2_Ele
27    1998   14850    3_Tel
28    1999    6750    1_Gas
29    1999    8475    2_Ele
30    1999   15975    3_Tel
```

More Information

DATA step, general reference

Chapter 2, "The DATA Step", *SAS Language: Reference, Version 6, First Edition*, pp. 13-42

OUTPUT statement, reference

"OUTPUT" in Chapter 9, "SAS Language Statements", *SAS Language: Reference*, pp. 447-448

GPLOT procedure, general reference

Chapter 31, "The GPLOT Procedure", *SAS/GRAPH Software: Reference, Volume 2, Version 6, First Edition*, pp. 1073-1130

PLOT statement, general reference

"PLOT Statement" in Chapter 31, "The GPLOT Procedure", *SAS/GRAPH Software: Reference, Volume 2*, pp. 1100-1120

AREAS= option

"Options" in Chapter 31, "The GPLOT Procedure", *SAS/GRAPH Software: Reference, Volume 2*, p. 1103

LEGEND= option

"Options" in Chapter 31, "The GPLOT Procedure", *SAS/GRAPH Software: Reference, Volume 2*, p. 1106

LEGEND statement, general reference

Chapter 13, "The LEGEND Statement", *SAS/GRAPH Software: Reference, Volume 1*, pp. 303-345

SHAPE= option in the LEGEND statement

"LEGEND Statement Options" in Chapter 13, "The LEGEND Statement", *SAS/GRAPH Software: Reference, Volume 1*, pp. 312-313

PATTERN statement, general reference

Chapter 15, "The PATTERN Statement", *SAS/GRAPH Software: Reference, Volume 1*, pp. 365-398

SYMBOL statement, general reference

Chapter 16, "The SYMBOL Statement", *SAS/GRAPH Software: Reference, Volume 1*, pp. 399-440

INTERPOL= option in the SYMBOL statement

"SYMBOL Statement Options" in Chapter 16, "The LEGEND Statement", *SAS/GRAPH Software: Reference, Volume 1*, pp. 410-418

filling areas under a line, example

"Filling Areas below the Plot Lines" in Chapter 20, "Producing Multiple Plots", *SAS/GRAPH Software: Usage, Version 6, First Edition*, pp. 270-273

Example 1, "Filling Areas in a Two-Dimensional Plot", *SAS/GRAPH Software: Examples, Version 6, First Edition*, pp. 1-4

Using Plot Appearance Options

In This Chapter

- Drawing reference lines
- Filling in the plot frame
- Setting the axes origin to zero

Drawing reference lines

Use the AUTOHREF and AUTOVREF options to draw reference lines at each major tick mark. The AUTOHREF option draws vertical reference lines on the horizontal axis. The AUTOVREF option draws horizontal reference lines on the vertical axis. You can use one or both options.

Use the LVREF= and LHREF= options to control the appearance of the reference lines. These options set the line type. There are several line types available, including dashed and solid lines. See Chapter 19 for a table of line types.

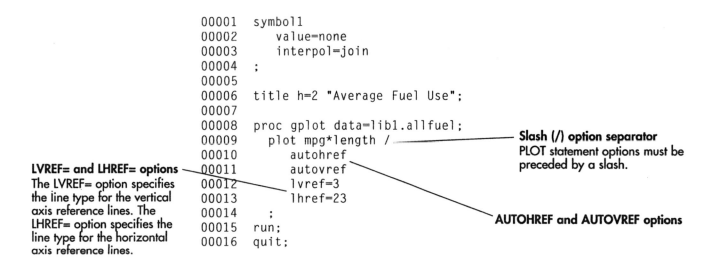

```
00001   symbol1
00002      value=none
00003      interpol=join
00004   ;
00005
00006   title h=2 "Average Fuel Use";
00007
00008   proc gplot data=lib1.allfuel;
00009     plot mpg*length /
00010         autohref
00011         autovref
00012         lvref=3
00013         lhref=23
00014     ;
00015   run;
00016   quit;
```

Slash (/) option separator
PLOT statement options must be preceded by a slash.

LVREF= and LHREF= options
The LVREF= option specifies the line type for the vertical axis reference lines. The LHREF= option specifies the line type for the horizontal axis reference lines.

AUTOHREF and AUTOVREF options

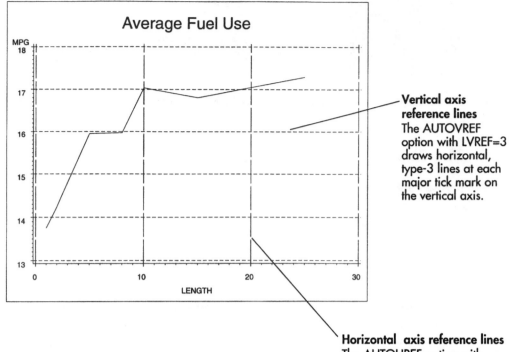

Vertical axis reference lines
The AUTOVREF option with LVREF=3 draws horizontal, type-3 lines at each major tick mark on the vertical axis.

Horizontal axis reference lines
The AUTOHREF option with LHREF=23 draws vertical, type-23 lines at each major tick mark on the horizontal axis.

Filling in the plot frame

Use the CFRAME= option to fill the plot frame with a color. The color must be valid for your graphics output device. In the following example, the grayscale color **GRAYEE** is used.

```
00001   symbol1
00002      value=none
00003      interpol=join
00004   ;
00005
00006   title h=2 "Average Fuel Use";
00007
00008   proc gplot data=lib1.allfuel;
00009     plot mpg*length /
00010       cframe=grayee                    CFRAME= option
00011     ;
00012   run;
00013   quit;
```

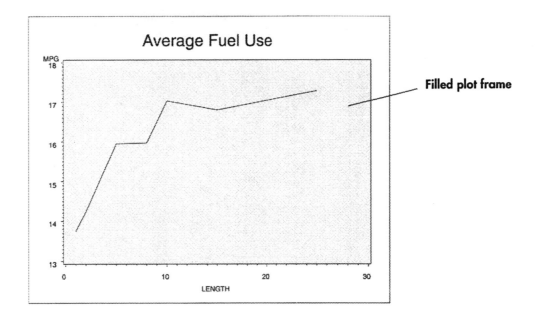

Filled plot frame

Setting the axes origin to zero

The VZERO and HZERO options force axes tick marks to begin at zero. If you do not use these options, PROC GPLOT will use axes starting points based on the actual data values. VZERO sets the vertical axis starting point to zero. HZERO sets the horizontal axis starting point to zero. You can use one or both options. These options are ignored if the data contain negative values.

```
00001   symbol1
00002      value=none
00003      interpol=join
00004   ;
00005
00006   title h=2 "Average Fuel Use";
00007
00008   proc gplot data=lib1.allfuel;
00009     plot mpg*length /
00010        vzero                      VZERO option
00011          ;
00012   run;
00013   quit;
```

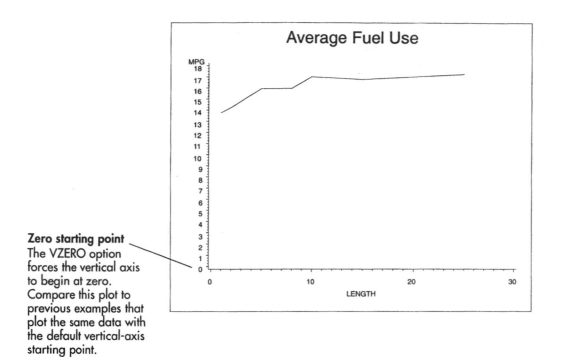

Zero starting point
The VZERO option forces the vertical axis to begin at zero. Compare this plot to previous examples that plot the same data with the default vertical-axis starting point.

Other appearance options
The table lists other options you can use to control the appearance of your plot. These options are fully documented under the reference for the PLOT statement, in "More Information."

Option	Action
CAXIS=color	sets the axis line and tick mark color
CHREF=color	sets the color of reference lines drawn on the horizontal axis
CTEXT=color	sets the color of all text on axes, including tick mark and axes labels
CVREF=color	sets the color of reference lines drawn on the vertical axis
FRAME	draws a frame around the plot area
GRID	draws a grid of horizontal and vertical reference lines at all major tick marks
HMINOR=n	sets the number of minor tick marks drawn between each major tick mark on the horizontal axis
HREF=value list	draws vertical reference lines on the horizontal axis at each point in the value list
NOAXES	removes plot axes
VMINOR=n	sets the number of minor tick marks drawn between each major tick mark on the vertical axis
VREF=value list	draws horizontal reference lines on the vertical axis at each point in the value list
VREVERSE	reverses the values on the vertical axis so the highest values are at the bottom

More Information

GPLOT procedure, general reference

Chapter 31, "The GPLOT Procedure", *SAS/GRAPH Software: Reference, Volume 2, Version 6, First Edition*, pp. 1073-1130

PLOT statement, general reference

"PLOT Statement" in Chapter 31, "The GPLOT Procedure", *SAS/GRAPH Software: Reference, Volume 2*, pp. 1100-1120

AUTOHREF and AUTOVREF options, reference

"Options" in Chapter 31, "The GPLOT Procedure", *SAS/GRAPH Software: Reference, Volume 2*, p. 1104

CFRAME= option, reference

"Options" in Chapter 31, "The GPLOT Procedure", *SAS/GRAPH Software: Reference, Volume 2*, p. 1104

HZERO option, reference

"Options" in Chapter 31, "The GPLOT Procedure", *SAS/GRAPH Software: Reference, Volume 2*, p. 1106

LHREF= and LVREF= options, reference

"Options" in Chapter 31, "The GPLOT Procedure", *SAS/GRAPH Software: Reference, Volume 2*, pp. 1106-1107

line types, table

"Selecting Line Types" in Chapter 16, "The SYMBOL Statement", *SAS/GRAPH Software: Reference, Volume 1*, p. 429

VZERO option, reference

"Options" in Chapter 31, "The GPLOT Procedure", *SAS/GRAPH Software: Reference, Volume 2*, p. 1108

Part 4
Working with Maps

Chapter 26 - Understanding Map Data Sets

Chapter 27 - Creating a Map

Chapter 28 - Using Value Ranges in Maps

Chapter 29 - Handling Empty Areas

Chapter 30 - Selecting Map Colors and Fills

Understanding Map Data Sets

In This Chapter

• What are map data sets?
• How are map data used?
• Projecting map data sets

What are map data sets?

Map data sets are standard SAS data sets with each observation representing a point. A group of these points defines a shape. A map outline is the result of connecting the points with a line. Each shape in a map data set is identified by an ID variable such as a FIPS (Federal Information Processing Standards) code for a United States map or a country id number for a continental map of Asia. The map ID variables are matched with ID variables in your response data set to relate response data to map areas.

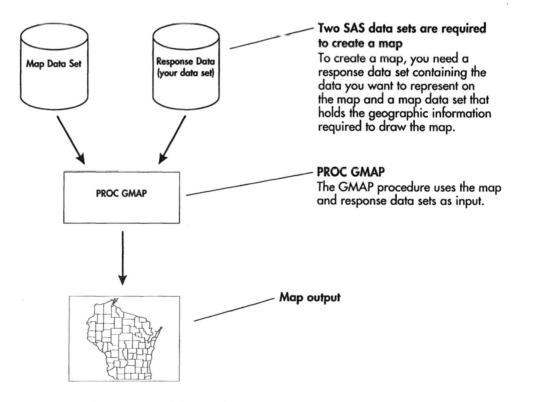

Two SAS data sets are required to create a map
To create a map, you need a response data set containing the data you want to represent on the map and a map data set that holds the geographic information required to draw the map.

PROC GMAP
The GMAP procedure uses the map and response data sets as input.

Map output

The first few observations from two Institute-supplied maps are shown below. The map data set MAPS.US represents the United States, with outlines for each state. It has about 1,500 observations. The map data set MAPS.COUNTIES is a United States map with outlines for all the states and counties. MAPS.COUNTIES has about 370,000 observations.

MAPS.US map data set
(partial listing)

```
                    Map Data For MAPS.US

  OBS        X           Y        SEGMENT      STATE
   1      0.16175    -0.10044        1            1
   2      0.12306    -0.10415        1            1
   3      0.12296    -0.10678        1            1
   4      0.12666    -0.11010        1            1
   5      0.12629    -0.11467        1            1
   6      0.11828    -0.11797        1            1
   7      0.12129    -0.11622        1            1
   8      0.11728    -0.10824        1            1
                                 .
                                 .
                                 .
```

MAPS.COUNTIES map data set
(partial listing)

```
                    Map Data For MAPS.COUNTIES

  OBS      X          Y       COUNTY   DENSITY   SEGMENT    STATE
   1    1.51450    0.57006      1        6         1          1
   2    1.51343    0.57004      1        3         1          1
   3    1.51343    0.57081      1        3         1          1
   4    1.51240    0.57081      1        6         1          1
   5    1.51192    0.57082      1        6         1          1
   6    1.50820    0.57084      1        0         1          1
   7    1.50817    0.56884      1        6         1          1
   8    1.50817    0.56879      1        6         1          1
                            .
                            .
                            .
```

The X and Y variables in these data sets hold the x and y coordinates of a point on the map. The values for the variable STATE are FIPS codes that uniquely identify each of the 50 states. In the data set MAPS.COUNTIES, the variable COUNTY is a number that uniquely identifies each county within the state.

How are map data used?

One or more variables in a map data set are ID variables. ID variables match geographic areas to observations in the response data. In the map data set MAPS.COUNTIES, STATE and COUNTY are the ID variables. To map data onto the MAPS.COUNTIES map or a map derived from it, you need variables in your response data set called STATE and COUNTY. The values of these variables must match corresponding values in the data set MAPS.COUNTIES. See Chapter 6 for more on data sets used for mapping.

Number of lakes in each county
These are the response data represented on the map.

x and y coordinates of the county outline points

LAKES	STATE	COUNTY
51	55	1
17	55	3
68	55	5
6	55	7
15	55	9
46	55	11

STATE	COUNTY	X	Y
55	1	-0.00068	-0.009373
55	1	-0.00643	-0.009381
55	1	0.001452	-0.009379
55	1	0.001692	-0.010134
55	3	0.780451	0.291261
55	3	0.801183	0.310009

Response data set

Map data set

The ID variables STATE and COUNTY match data values from the response data set to points in the map data set.

Projecting map data sets

Some SAS Institute-supplied maps are unprojected. This means that the *x* and *y* coordinates have not been prepared to represent the map on a flat surface, such as a piece of paper or display screen. If your map looks like a distorted mirror image, the map data set is unprojected. Use the GPROJECT procedure to create a usable map.

Unprojected map
Unprojected maps display as a distorted mirror image.

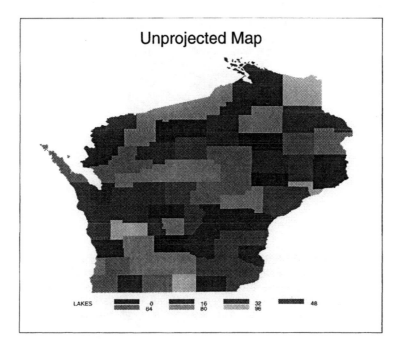

In the example below, the map data set MAPS.COUNTIES is subsetted with a WHERE statement. Only state 55 (Wisconsin) data are read and projected. The resulting map data set WICOUNTY generates an undistorted map.

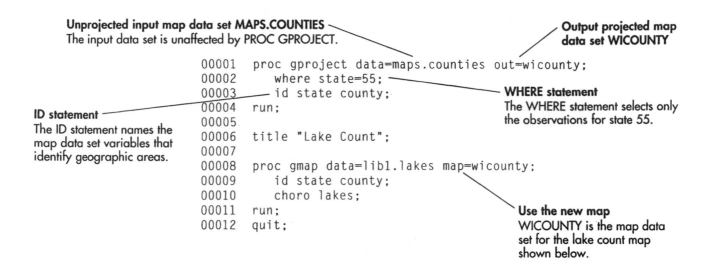

Unprojected input map data set MAPS.COUNTIES
The input data set is unaffected by PROC GPROJECT.

Output projected map data set WICOUNTY

```
00001    proc gproject data=maps.counties out=wicounty;
00002       where state=55;
00003       id state county;
00004    run;
00005
00006    title "Lake Count";
00007
00008    proc gmap data=lib1.lakes map=wicounty;
00009       id state county;
00010       choro lakes;
00011    run;
00012    quit;
```

ID statement
The ID statement names the map data set variables that identify geographic areas.

WHERE statement
The WHERE statement selects only the observations for state 55.

Use the new map
WICOUNTY is the map data set for the lake count map shown below.

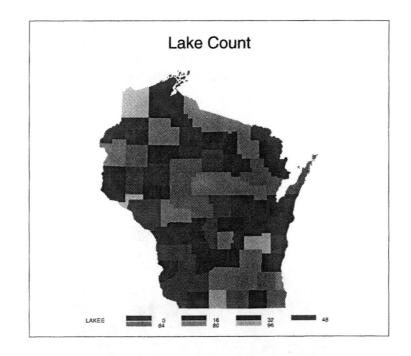

Projected map
The projected map displays correctly on a flat surface.

In the examples above, MAPS is the libref for the standard SAS map library. MAPS is the conventional libref for this library, but at your site it could have a different name. To find the map library, use the display manager LIB command to list available libraries. If you are running on an MVS mainframe system in batch mode, check your job output listing for a MAPS DDNAME. It's possible that the map library is not automatically available to your SAS session or job. In this case, you should contact your SAS software representative about the location of the map library.

More Information

SAS map data sets, discussion and reference

"SAS/GRAPH Map Data Sets" in Chapter 29, "The GMAP Procedure", *SAS/GRAPH Software: Reference, Volume 2, Version 6, First Edition*, pp. 1057-1061

"The Map Data Set" in Chapter 27, "Introduction to Maps", *SAS/GRAPH Software: Usage, Version 6, First Edition*, pp. 358-360

"Data Considerations" in Chapter 29, "The GMAP Procedure", *SAS/GRAPH Software: Reference, Volume 2*, pp. 1007-1012

SAS Technical Report P-196 SAS/GRAPH Software: Map Data Sets, Release 6.06

FIPS codes, discussion and table showing code and state name

"Using FIPS Codes and Province Codes", in Chapter 29, "The GMAP Procedure", *SAS/GRAPH Software: Reference, Volume 2*, pp. 1058-1059

using the WHERE statement to subset maps, discussion and example

"Using Map Data Sets", in Chapter 29, "The GMAP Procedure", *SAS/GRAPH Software: Reference, Volume 2*, pp. 1060-1061

GPROJECT procedure, reference

Chapter 33, "The GPROJECT Procedure", *SAS/GRAPH Software: Reference, Volume 2*, pp. 1147-1168

creating maps, discussion and examples

Chapter 27, "Introduction to Maps", *SAS/GRAPH Software: Usage, Version 6, First Edition*, pp. 355-382

Creating a Map

In This Chapter

- **What types of maps are available?**
- **Mapping numeric data**
- **How to specify midpoints**
- **Specifying the number of midpoints**
- **Mapping with character variables**
- **How to create an empty map**

What types of maps are available?

The GMAP procedure can produce several types of maps. The most commonly used is the choropleth map. Choropleth (or choro) maps represent data with patterns and colors on a two-dimensional surface. In this and in the following mapping chapters, only choropleth maps are used in the examples.

In addition to choropleth maps, the following map types are available:

block map   data are represented with a three-dimensional block in each geographic area

prism map   data are represented by the height of the geographic area

surface map   data are represented by a spike centered on each geographic area

Mapping numeric data

In the following example, the data set LIB1.LAKES is represented on a county map of the state of Wisconsin. Geographic areas are identified by state FIPS (Federal Information Processing Standards) code and county number. The FIPS code for Wisconsin is 55. See Chapter 26 for more on how to create a county map for a single state.

Data set LIB1.LAKES
Shown here are the first six observations from the data set LIB1.LAKES used in the following examples. The variables STATE and COUNTY identify the geographic unit associated with each lake count.

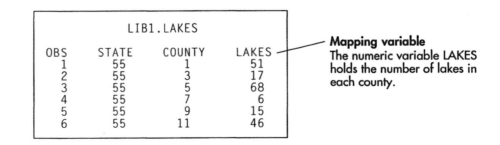

OBS	STATE	COUNTY	LAKES
1	55	1	51
2	55	3	17
3	55	5	68
4	55	7	6
5	55	9	15
6	55	11	46

LIB1.LAKES

Mapping variable
The numeric variable LAKES holds the number of lakes in each county.

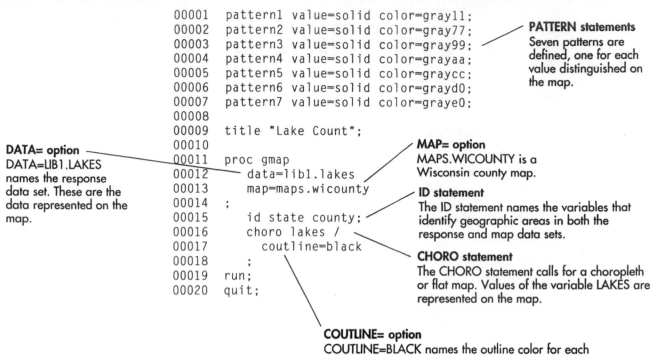

```
00001    pattern1 value=solid color=gray11;
00002    pattern2 value=solid color=gray77;
00003    pattern3 value=solid color=gray99;
00004    pattern4 value=solid color=grayaa;
00005    pattern5 value=solid color=graycc;
00006    pattern6 value=solid color=grayd0;
00007    pattern7 value=solid color=graye0;
00008
00009    title "Lake Count";
00010
00011    proc gmap
00012        data=lib1.lakes
00013        map=maps.wicounty
00014    ;
00015        id state county;
00016        choro lakes /
00017           coutline=black
00018        ;
00019    run;
00020    quit;
```

PATTERN statements
Seven patterns are defined, one for each value distinguished on the map.

DATA= option
DATA=LIB1.LAKES names the response data set. These are the data represented on the map.

MAP= option
MAPS.WICOUNTY is a Wisconsin county map.

ID statement
The ID statement names the variables that identify geographic areas in both the response and map data sets.

CHORO statement
The CHORO statement calls for a choropleth or flat map. Values of the variable LAKES are represented on the map.

COUTLINE= option
COUTLINE=BLACK names the outline color for each geographic area. When COUTLINE= is not used, there is no outlining. Any CHORO statement options must be preceded by a slash (/).

Lake count map
PROC GMAP calculates a number of midpoints around which to group the values of the variable LAKES. For the data set LIB1.LAKES, the default number of midpoints is seven. You usually do not know in advance what the default number of midpoints will be.

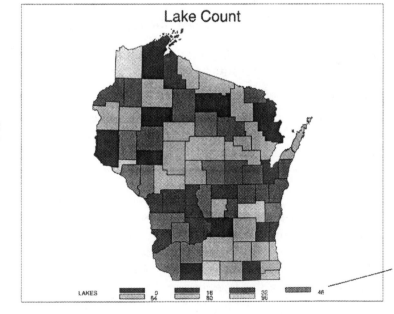

Legend
A legend is automatically generated to identify each midpoint on the map.

How to specify midpoints

In the previous example, PROC GMAP uses an internal method to calculate the number of midpoints or data levels to show on the map. Each midpoint represents a median. All observations where the value of the variable LAKES is between the midpoint and halfway to the next midpoint are represented by the single midpoint value. You can choose your own midpoints with the MIDPOINTS= option. Normally, midpoints should be evenly spaced.

```
00001    pattern1 value=solid color=gray77;
00002    pattern2 value=solid color=graybb;
00003    pattern3 value=solid color=grayee;
00004
00005    title "Lake Count"
00006
00007    proc gmap
00008       data=lib1.lakes
00009       map=maps.wicounty
00010    ;
00011       id state county;
00012       choro lakes /
00013          coutline = black
00014          midpoints = 30 60 90;
00015    run;
00016    quit;
```

PATTERN statements
Three patterns are defined, one for each midpoint.

MIDPOINTS= option
The MIDPOINTS= option lists exactly the midpoints you want on the map.

Map with three midpoints
This map is generated using only the three midpoints specified in the MIDPOINTS= option.

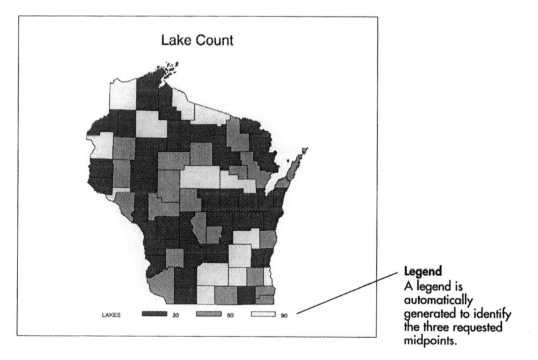

Legend
A legend is automatically generated to identify the three requested midpoints.

Specifying the number of midpoints

In the previous example, the exact midpoint values are specified. You also have the choice of specifying only the number of midpoints you want, by using the LEVELS= option. When you use LEVELS=, PROC GMAP calculates the requested number of evenly spaced midpoint values.

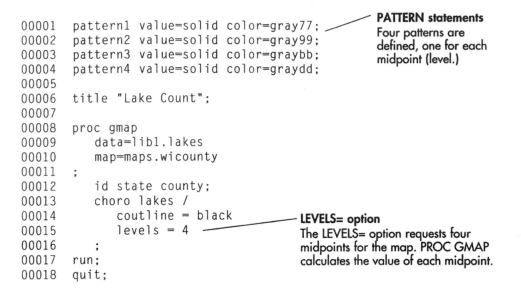

```
00001    pattern1 value=solid color=gray77;
00002    pattern2 value=solid color=gray99;
00003    pattern3 value=solid color=graybb;
00004    pattern4 value=solid color=graydd;
00005
00006    title "Lake Count";
00007
00008    proc gmap
00009       data=lib1.lakes
00010       map=maps.wicounty
00011    ;
00012       id state county;
00013       choro lakes /
00014          coutline = black
00015          levels = 4
00016       ;
00017    run;
00018    quit;
```

PATTERN statements
Four patterns are defined, one for each midpoint (level.)

LEVELS= option
The LEVELS= option requests four midpoints for the map. PROC GMAP calculates the value of each midpoint.

LEVELS= map
The response data are grouped around four evenly spaced midpoints.

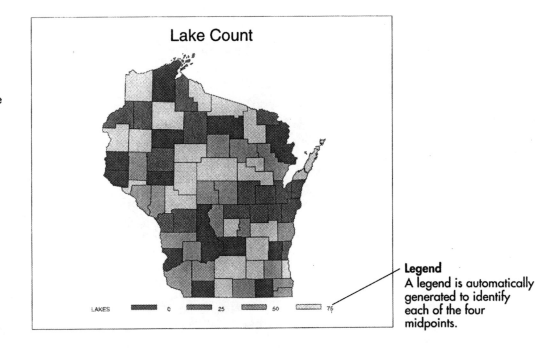

Lake Count

Legend
A legend is automatically generated to identify each of the four midpoints.

You can override midpointing of numeric data with the DISCRETE option in the CHORO statement. For example:

```
choro lakes / discrete;
```

This option forces PROC GMAP to map each unique numeric value. There is no grouping of data around midpoints. Character variables are always mapped as discrete values.

Mapping with character variables

You can map character variables with PROC GMAP. In the data set LIB1.SALESREP shown below, NAME is a character variable identifying the sales representative for various states. With character variables, PROC GMAP does not calculate midpoint groups; therefore, each value of NAME is mapped.

Data set LIB1.SALESREP

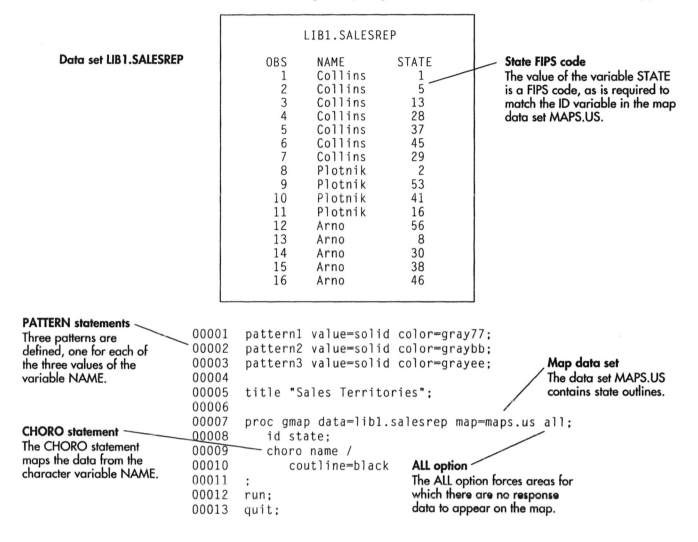

```
                LIB1.SALESREP

      OBS     NAME        STATE
       1      Collins        1
       2      Collins        5
       3      Collins       13
       4      Collins       28
       5      Collins       37
       6      Collins       45
       7      Collins       29
       8      Plotnik        2
       9      Plotnik       53
      10      Plotnik       41
      11      Plotnik       16
      12      Arno          56
      13      Arno           8
      14      Arno          30
      15      Arno          38
      16      Arno          46
```

State FIPS code
The value of the variable STATE is a FIPS code, as is required to match the ID variable in the map data set MAPS.US.

PATTERN statements
Three patterns are defined, one for each of the three values of the variable NAME.

CHORO statement
The CHORO statement maps the data from the character variable NAME.

```
00001   pattern1 value=solid color=gray77;
00002   pattern2 value=solid color=graybb;
00003   pattern3 value=solid color=grayee;
00004
00005   title "Sales Territories";
00006
00007   proc gmap data=lib1.salesrep map=maps.us all;
00008      id state;
00009      choro name /
00010           coutline=black
00011   ;
00012   run;
00013   quit;
```

Map data set
The data set MAPS.US contains state outlines.

ALL option
The ALL option forces areas for which there are no response data to appear on the map.

Sales rep map
The sales territory of each sales rep is shown. When the ALL option is used, the entire map is displayed, even empty areas.

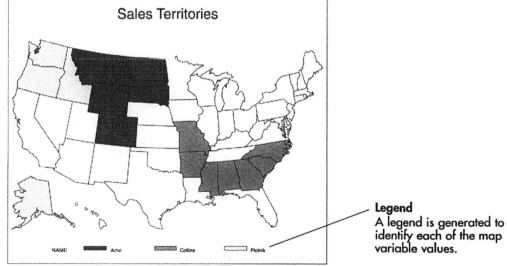

Sales Territories

Legend
A legend is generated to identify each of the map variable values.

How to create an empty map

You can create an empty map with PROC GMAP. One method is demonstrated below, where the map data set is also used as the response data set. The LEVELS=1 option requests only one data level, so only a single pattern is required. A PATTERN statement defines a single pattern with an empty fill. The ID statement names the ID variables from the map data set. The OBS=1 data set option reduces processing time. You need only one, but at least one, observation for PROC GMAP to function. The ALL option forces the display of all map areas even if there are no response data.

Empty pattern
The PATTERN1 statement defines the single empty pattern required for the map.

Response data set
Use the map data set as the response data set. This ensures that the ID variables will be compatible. The OBS=1 data set option reduces processing time.

LEVELS=1 option
Specifying LEVELS=1 means only one pattern is required to fill the map. That pattern is defined as empty in the PATTERN1 statement.

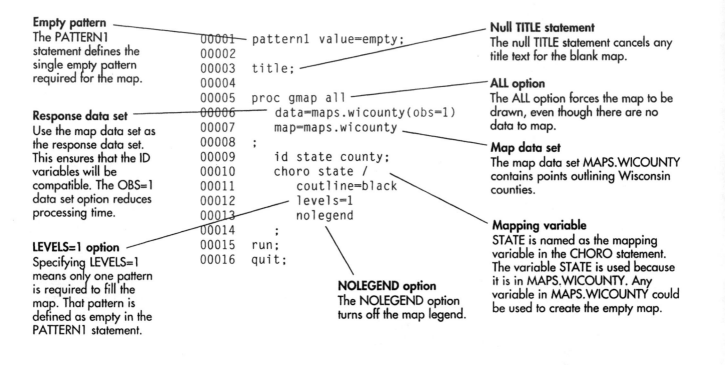

```
00001   pattern1 value=empty;
00002
00003   title;
00004
00005   proc gmap all
00006       data=maps.wicounty(obs=1)
00007       map=maps.wicounty
00008   ;
00009       id state county;
00010       choro state /
00011           coutline=black
00012           levels=1
00013           nolegend
00014       ;
00015   run;
00016   quit;
```

Null TITLE statement
The null TITLE statement cancels any title text for the blank map.

ALL option
The ALL option forces the map to be drawn, even though there are no data to map.

Map data set
The map data set MAPS.WICOUNTY contains points outlining Wisconsin counties.

Mapping variable
STATE is named as the mapping variable in the CHORO statement. The variable STATE is used because it is in MAPS.WICOUNTY. Any variable in MAPS.WICOUNTY could be used to create the empty map.

NOLEGEND option
The NOLEGEND option turns off the map legend.

Blank map
Titles and legends are turned off and all areas are filled with the empty pattern.

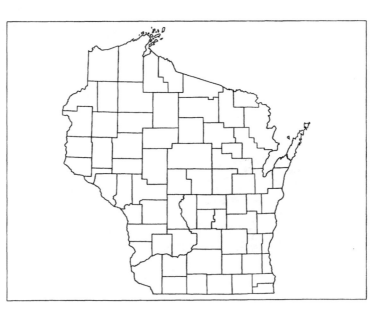

More Information

GMAP procedure, general reference

Chapter 29, "The GMAP Procedure", *SAS/GRAPH Software: Reference, Volume 2, Version 6, First Edition*, pp. 1001-1062

ALL option, reference

"Options" in Chapter 29, "The GMAP Procedure", *SAS/GRAPH Software: Reference, Volume 2*, p. 1016

ALL option, example

"Using the ALL Option" in Chapter 28, "Producing Choropleth Maps", *SAS/GRAPH Software: Usage, Version 6, First Edition*, pp. 389-390

ID statement, reference

"ID Statement" in Chapter 29, "The GMAP Procedure", *SAS/GRAPH Software: Reference, Volume 2*, p. 1017

COUTLINE= option, reference

"CHORO Statement" in Chapter 29, "The GMAP Procedure", *SAS/GRAPH Software: Reference, Volume 2*, p. 1032

LEVELS= option, reference

"CHORO Statement" in Chapter 29, "The GMAP Procedure", *SAS/GRAPH Software: Reference, Volume 2*, p. 1033

MIDPOINTS= option, reference

"CHORO Statement" in Chapter 29, "The GMAP Procedure", *SAS/GRAPH Software: Reference, Volume 2*, p. 1033

LEVEL= and MIDPOINTS= options, discussion

"Controlling Response Levels" in Chapter 27, "Introduction to Maps", *SAS/GRAPH Software: Usage*, pp. 368-369

NOLEGEND option, reference

"CHORO Statement" in Chapter 29, "The GMAP Procedure", *SAS/GRAPH Software: Reference, Volume 2*, p. 1034

CHORO (choropleth) map, example

"Simple Choropleth Map" in Chapter 29, "The GMAP Procedure", *SAS/GRAPH Software: Reference, Volume 2*, pp. 1036-1037

"Producing the Map" in Chapter 27, "Introduction to Maps", *SAS/GRAPH Software: Usage*, pp. 366-367

mapping process, discussion and examples

Chapter 27, "Introduction to Maps", *SAS/GRAPH Software: Usage, Version 6, First Edition*, pp. 355-382

Chapter 28, "Producing Choropleth Maps", *SAS/GRAPH Software: Usage*, pp. 383-394

block, prism, and surface maps, examples

"Overview" in Chapter 29, "The GMAP Procedure", *SAS/GRAPH Software: Reference, Volume 2*, pp. 1002-1004

block map, reference

"BLOCK Statement" in Chapter 29, "The GMAP Procedure", *SAS/GRAPH Software: Reference, Volume 2*, pp. 1017-1030

prism map, reference

"PRISM Statement" in Chapter 29, "The GMAP Procedure", *SAS/GRAPH Software: Reference, Volume 2*, pp. 1039-1049

surface map, reference

"SURFACE Statement" in Chapter 29, "The GMAP Procedure", *SAS/GRAPH Software: Reference, Volume 2*, pp. 1050-1056

FIPS codes, table of codes and state names

"Using FIPS Codes and Province Codes" in Chapter 29, "The GMAP Procedure", *SAS/GRAPH Software: Reference, Volume 2*, pp. 1058-1059

placing state names on a US map, placing text on maps, example

Example 11 "Labeling States on a United States Map", *SAS/GRAPH Software: Examples, Version 6, First Edition*, pp. 71-78

Note: *SAS/GRAPH Software Examples* contains several interesting mapping examples.

Using Value Ranges in Maps

In This Chapter

- **Creating your own value ranges for maps**

Creating your own value ranges for maps

You can create your own data groups for use with PROC GMAP. First, use the FORMAT procedure to create a custom format of the desired data ranges and labels, then use the FORMAT statement in the GMAP procedure to apply your custom format to the mapping variable. (See Chapter 27 for more on the response and map data sets used in this example.)

PROC FORMAT step

```
00001    proc format;
00002        value lakecat
00003            0 -< 15      = "less than 15"
00004           15 -< 40      = "less than 40"
00005           40 -  high    = "40 or more"
00006        ;
00007    run;
00008
00009    pattern1 value=solid color=gray77;
00010    pattern2 value=solid color=graybb;
00011    pattern3 value=solid color=grayee;
00012
00013    title "Lake Count";
00014
00015    proc gmap
00016        data=lib1.lakes
00017        map=maps.wicounty
00018    ;
00019        format lakes lakecat.;
00020        id state county;
00021        choro lakes /
00022            discrete
00023            coutline = black
00024        ;
00025    run;
00026    quit;
```

Custom format name
Name the custom format in the VALUE statement. Here the format is called LAKECAT.

Ranges and labels
List the value ranges and the text used to label them.

PATTERN statements
Three patterns are defined, one for each value range.

FORMAT statement
The FORMAT statement applies the custom format to the mapping variable LAKES. The format name must end with a period.

DISCRETE option
The DISCRETE option forces the mapping of each unique formatted value instead of internally calculated midpoints.

Custom format map

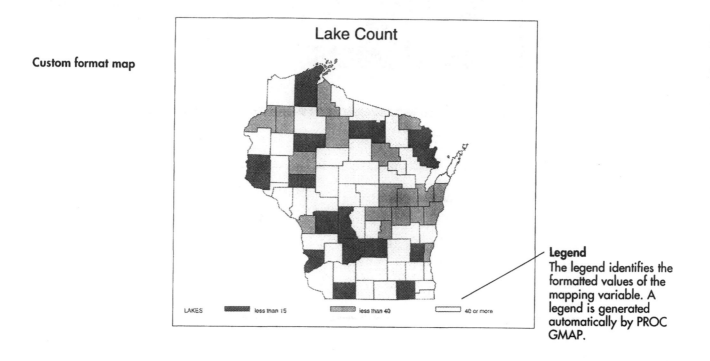

Lake Count

Legend
The legend identifies the formatted values of the mapping variable. A legend is generated automatically by PROC GMAP.

📖 More Information

FORMAT procedure, reference

Chapter 18, "The FORMAT Procedure", *SAS Procedures Guide, Version 6, Third Edition*, pp. 275-312

specifying format ranges

"Details", in Chapter 18, "The FORMAT Procedure", *SAS Procedures Guide*, p. 294-295

creating a numeric format, example

"Categorizing Variable Values with Customized Formats", in Chapter 8, "Classifying Variables into Categories", *SAS Language and Procedures: Usage 2, Version 6, First Edition*, pp. 151-153

retrieving formats from SAS libraries

Chapter 26, "The FORMAT Procedure", *SAS Technical Report P-222, Changes and Enhancements to Base SAS Software, Release 6.07*, p. 208

DISCRETE option, reference

"Options" in Chapter 29, "The GMAP Procedure", *SAS/GRAPH Software: Reference, Volume 2, Version 6, First Edition*, p. 1033

formatting mapping variables, example

"Choropleth Map with Formatted Numeric Values" in Chapter 29, "The GMAP Procedure", *SAS/GRAPH Software: Reference, Volume 2*, pp. 1037-1039

"Selecting Response Levels with User-Written Formats" in Chapter 27, "Introduction to Maps", *SAS/GRAPH Software: Usage, Version 6, First Edition*, pp. 369-371

 **Handling Empty Areas**

In This Chapter

- **Default handling of empty areas**
- **Displaying empty areas**

Default handling of empty areas

Map data sets normally contain outlines for several areas: all the countries in a continent or all the provinces or states in a country. There may be geographic areas in the map data set for which there are no response data. By default, PROC GMAP does not draw these empty areas. When empty areas are scattered throughout the map, the familiar map shape may be disrupted. This problem is illustrated in the following example.

```
00001    pattern1 value=solid color=gray77;
00002    pattern2 value=solid color=graybb;
00003    pattern3 value=solid color=grayee;
00004
00005    title "US Jobsites";
00006
00007    proc gmap data=lib1.jobsites  map=maps.us;
00008       id state;
00009       choro sites /
00010          levels = 3
00011          coutline = black
00012       ;
00013    run;
```

Response data set
The response data set LIB1.JOBSITES does not have an observation for all states.

Map data set
The data set MAPS.US is a United States map with state boundaries.

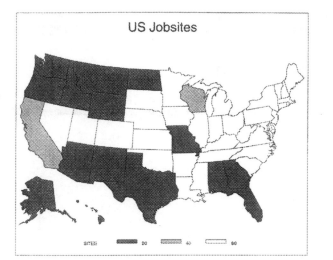

Map with empty areas
States for which there are no response data are not displayed on the map.

Displaying empty areas

Use the ALL option in the PROC GMAP statement to ensure that all geographic areas in the map are displayed, even if there are no corresponding response data.

```
00001    pattern1 value=solid color=gray77;
00002    pattern2 value=solid color=graybb;
00003    pattern3 value=solid color=grayee;
00004
00005    title "US Jobsites";
00006
00007    proc gmap data=lib1.jobsites  map=maps.us all;
00008       id state;
00009       choro sites /
00010          levels = 3
00011          coutline = black
00012       ;
00013    run;
```

ALL option

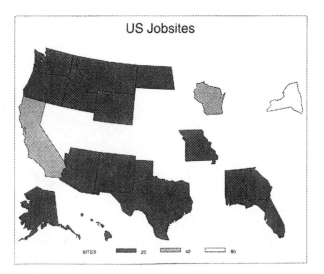

Empty areas displayed
When the ALL option is used, the full map is displayed.

📖 More Information

ALL option, reference

"Options" in Chapter 29, "The GMAP Procedure", *SAS/GRAPH Software: Reference, Volume 2, Version 6, First Edition*, p. 1016

using the ALL option, example

"Displaying Map Areas without Response Values" in Chapter 28, "Producing Choropleth Maps", *SAS/GRAPH Software: Usage, Version 6, First Edition*, pp. 388-391

Selecting Map Colors and Fills

In This Chapter

- **Controlling fill patterns**
- **Changing color and assigning an empty pattern**
- **How user-defined and default patterns are selected**

Controlling fill patterns

Use PATTERN statements to control the area fills in your map. PATTERN statements define settings for a combination of fill pattern and fill color. PROC GMAP automatically applies any existing pattern settings to a map. The order in which settings are defined determines how they will be applied. The settings in the PATTERN1 (or PATTERN) statement are applied to the first area, PATTERN2 is applied to the second area, PATTERN3 is applied to the third area, etc. Include the COLOR= option with each PATTERN statement to ensure that fills are used only once and not cycled through all available colors.

PATTERN statements are global, which means they are in effect from the point they appear in your program and remain in effect until explicitly changed or your SAS session ends. Place PATTERN statements before the PROC GMAP step you want them to apply to. An example PATTERN statement is shown below.

VALUE= option
The VALUE= option sets the fill pattern. In addition to the "M" and "X" values described below, you can specify VALUE=SOLID for a solid fill or VALUE=EMPTY for no fill.

PATTERN1
The "1" names this as the first pattern to use. PATTERN and PATTERN1 are equivalent.

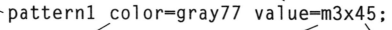

```
pattern1 color=gray77 value=m3x45;
```

COLOR= option
The COLOR= option names the color to use for this pattern. You can name any color valid for your output device. If the color you select is not valid, PROC GMAP selects a substitute. Here, a grayscale color is selected.

M3
The "M" indicates that this is a map pattern. The "3" selects a line density from the range 1 to 5.

X45
"X" indicates crosshatching. "45" means the crosshatching will be at a 45° angle. Besides "X" you can use "N" to fill with parallel lines instead of a crosshatch.

Normally, you want to define a pattern for each map area. In the following example, three levels are distinguished on the map and three patterns are defined to fill the areas.

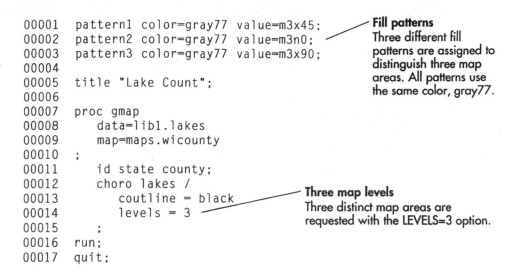

```
00001    pattern1 color=gray77 value=m3x45;
00002    pattern2 color=gray77 value=m3n0;
00003    pattern3 color=gray77 value=m3x90;
00004
00005    title "Lake Count";
00006
00007    proc gmap
00008       data=lib1.lakes
00009       map=maps.wicounty
00010    ;
00011       id state county;
00012       choro lakes /
00013          coutline = black
00014          levels = 3
00015       ;
00016    run;
00017    quit;
```

Fill patterns
Three different fill patterns are assigned to distinguish three map areas. All patterns use the same color, gray77.

Three map levels
Three distinct map areas are requested with the LEVELS=3 option.

Map with three hatch fills
The three fill patterns are assigned in ascending order of the LAKES midpoint values.

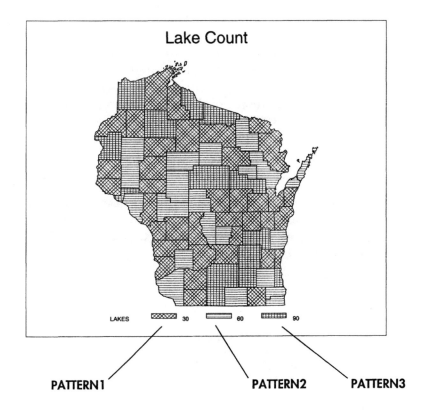

PATTERN1   PATTERN2   PATTERN3

Changing color and assigning an empty pattern

You can assign any valid combination of color and fill values to a pattern. You can also use the value EMPTY to assign no fill to an area.

```
00001    pattern1 color=gray99 value=solid;
00002    pattern2 color=graycc value=solid;
00003    pattern3 color=black  value=empty;
00004
00005    title "Lake Count";
00006
00007    proc gmap
00008       data=lib1.lakes
00009       map=maps.wicounty
00010    ;
00011       id state county;
00012       choro lakes /
00013          coutline = black
00014          levels = 3
00015       ;
00016    run;
00017    quit;
```

Changing fill color
The first two patterns use a solid fill with two different grayscale colors.

Defining an empty fill
VALUE=EMPTY means no fill. Even though a fill color is not used, the COLOR= option ensures that additional pattern sequences are not generated by cycling through the available colors.

Three mapping levels
The LEVELS=3 option requests that three areas be distinguished on the map. The three patterns defined above are applied to these areas.

Map with two colors and an empty area

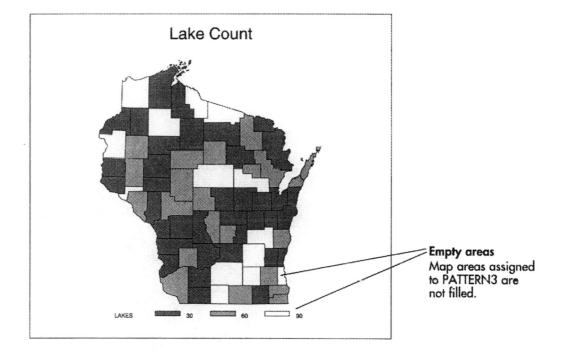

Empty areas
Map areas assigned to PATTERN3 are not filled.

You can use the PATTERN statement to define pattern sequences. This saves you from having to enter a separate PATTERN statement for each fill. If you need only a small number of patterns, your program will be easier to understand and to change if you use a separate PATTERN statement for each fill. If you need a large or unknown number of unique patterns you can use pattern sequences to avoid writing many PATTERN statements. The COLORS= and CPATTERN= graphics options can be used to control the colors used in pattern sequences. See the references in "More Information" regarding pattern sequences and the PATTERN statement.

How user-defined and default patterns are selected

PROC GMAP always attempts to distinguish map areas with unique patterns. If you do not assign patterns, defaults are used. If you do not assign enough patterns to distinguish all map areas, PROC GMAP first uses the patterns you do assign, then selects defaults to fill the remaining areas. In the following example, three patterns are defined, but four are required to fill the map. The fourth pattern is a default selected by PROC GMAP.

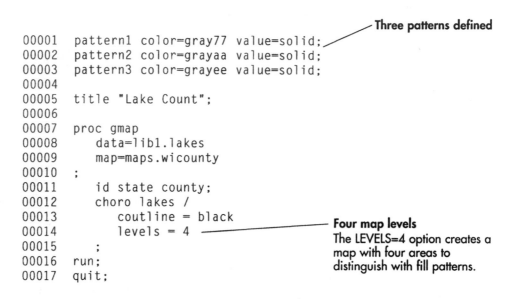

```
00001    pattern1 color=gray77 value=solid;
00002    pattern2 color=grayaa value=solid;
00003    pattern3 color=grayee value=solid;
00004
00005    title "Lake Count";
00006
00007    proc gmap
00008       data=lib1.lakes
00009       map=maps.wicounty
00010    ;
00011       id state county;
00012       choro lakes /
00013          coutline = black
00014          levels = 4
00015       ;
00016    run;
00017    quit;
```

Three patterns defined

Four map levels
The LEVELS=4 option creates a map with four areas to distinguish with fill patterns.

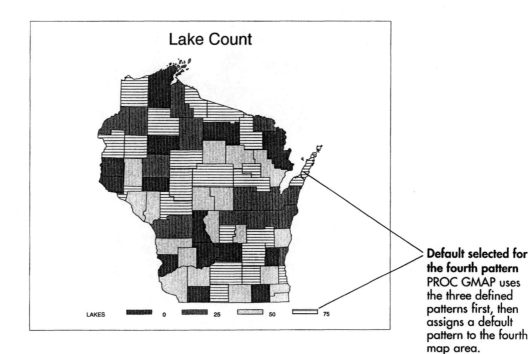

Lake Count

LAKES   0   25   50   75

Default selected for the fourth pattern
PROC GMAP uses the three defined patterns first, then assigns a default pattern to the fourth map area.

More Information

PATTERN statement, general reference

Chapter 15, "The PATTERN Statement", *SAS/GRAPH Software: Reference, Volume 1, Version 6, First Edition*, pp. 365-398

default patterns

"Default Pattern Sequences" in Chapter 15, "The PATTERN Statement", *SAS/GRAPH Software: Reference, Volume 1*, p. 371

pattern sequences generated with the PATTERN statement

"Pattern Sequences Generated by PATTERN Statements" in Chapter 15, "The PATTERN Statement", *SAS/GRAPH Software: Reference, Volume 1*, pp. 371-373

COLOR= option, description and reference

"PATTERN Statement Options" in Chapter 15, "The PATTERN Statement", *SAS/GRAPH Software: Reference, Volume 1*, p. 374

VALUE= option, description and reference

"PATTERN Statement Options" in Chapter 15, "The PATTERN Statement", *SAS/GRAPH Software: Reference, Volume 1*, p. 376-379

using map chart patterns, examples

"Selecting Patterns for Map Areas" in Chapter 27, "Introduction to Maps", *SAS/GRAPH Software: Usage, Version 6, First Edition*, pp. 371-374

"Map and Block Patterns with the GMAP Procedure" in Chapter 15, "The PATTERN Statement", *SAS/GRAPH Software: Reference, Volume 1*, pp. 395-397

using colors, general reference

Chapter 7, "SAS/GRAPH Colors", *SAS/GRAPH Software: Reference, Volume 1*, pp. 177-197

grayscale colors

"Gray-scale Color Codes" in Chapter 7, "SAS/GRAPH Colors", *SAS/GRAPH Software: Reference, Volume 1*, p. 183

LEVELS= option, reference

"Options" in Chapter 29, "The GMAP Procedure", *SAS/GRAPH Software: Reference, Volume 2*, p. 1033

Part 5
Working with Pie Charts

Chapter 31 - Creating a Pie Chart

Chapter 32 - Labeling Pie Slices

Chapter 33 - Creating Multiple Pie Charts per Page

Chapter 34 - Controlling Pie Chart Appearance

Chapter 35 - Selecting Pie Chart Colors and Fills

Creating a Pie Chart

In This Chapter

- **Using PROC GCHART to create pie charts**
- **Charting a numeric variable**
- **Controlling the number of slices with numeric variables**
- **Selecting your own midpoints**
- **Showing all slices with a numeric variable**
- **Making slices represent sums**

Using PROC GCHART to create pie charts

Use the GCHART procedure with the PIE statement to generate a pie chart. An example is shown below. By default, the width of each slice represents frequency (count). In the example, there is a slice for each value of the charting variable ROOM, and the width of each slice represents the count of meetings in each room.

```
00001   title "Meetings Per Room";
00002
00003   proc gchart data=lib1.meetings;
00004      pie room;
00005   run;
00006   quit;
```

PROC GCHART step

Input SAS data set

PIE statement
The PIE statement generates a pie chart with a slice for each value of the variable ROOM.

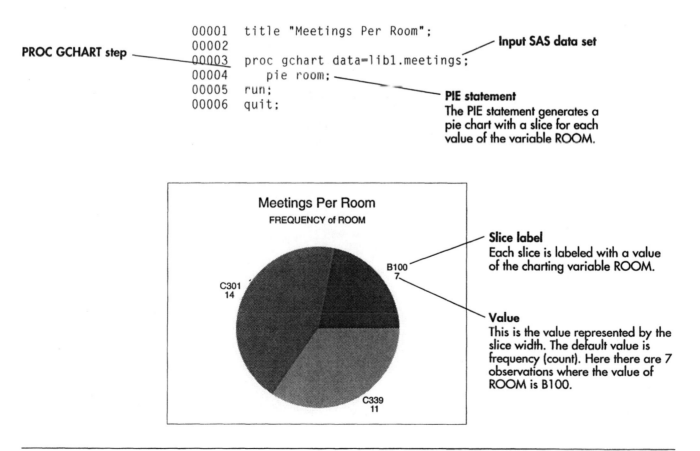

Slice label
Each slice is labeled with a value of the charting variable ROOM.

Value
This is the value represented by the slice width. The default value is frequency (count). Here there are 7 observations where the value of ROOM is B100.

Charting a numeric variable

PROC GCHART uses an internal method to calculate a number of midpoints when charting a numeric variable. A midpoint is a median representing all observations that fall between the midpoint value and halfway to the next midpoint. Midpoints are used because there may be many values between any two numeric values.

In the example below, the numeric variable HOURS is charted. You can see the values of HOURS in the data set LIB1.MEETINGS shown in "Data Used in Examples" at the end of this book. PROC GCHART calculates six midpoints to represent the values of HOURS.

```
00001   title "Length of Meetings";
00002
00003   proc gchart data=lib1.meetings;
00004      pie hours;
00005   run;
00006   quit;
```

Numeric charting variable HOURS

Numeric variable pie chart
One slice is generated for each midpoint.

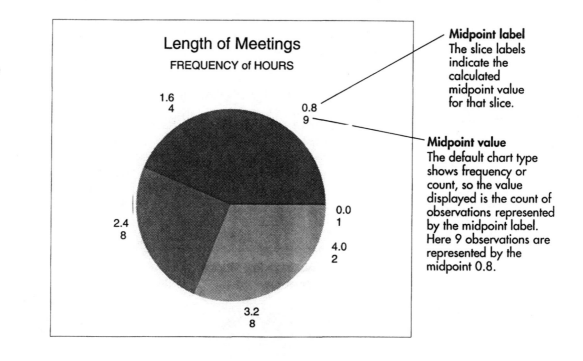

Midpoint label
The slice labels indicate the calculated midpoint value for that slice.

Midpoint value
The default chart type shows frequency or count, so the value displayed is the count of observations represented by the midpoint label. Here 9 observations are represented by the midpoint 0.8.

Controlling the number of slices with numeric variables

Use the LEVELS= option to request a number of evenly spaced midpoints. There is one slice for each midpoint or level. When you use PIE statement options, such as LEVELS=, you must precede the options list with a slash (/).

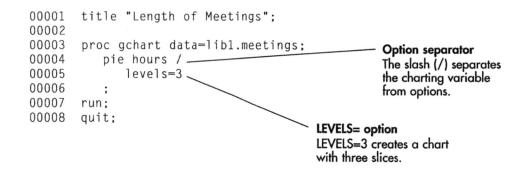

```
00001    title "Length of Meetings";
00002
00003    proc gchart data=lib1.meetings;
00004       pie hours /
00005          levels=3
00006       ;
00007    run;
00008    quit;
```

Option separator
The slash (/) separates the charting variable from options.

LEVELS= option
LEVELS=3 creates a chart with three slices.

LEVELS= chart

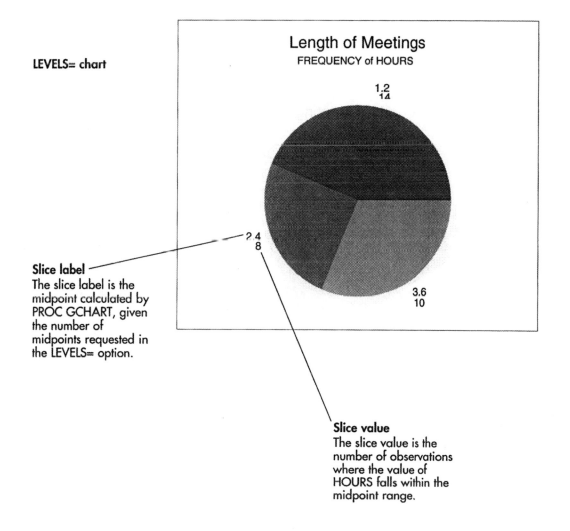

Slice label
The slice label is the midpoint calculated by PROC GCHART, given the number of midpoints requested in the LEVELS= option.

Slice value
The slice value is the number of observations where the value of HOURS falls within the midpoint range.

Selecting your own midpoints

As described in the previous section, PROC GCHART calculates a set of midpoints when charting numeric values. Use the MIDPOINTS= option to specify the exact midpoints used in a pie chart. You can specify a list of midpoints, as shown in the example below, or you can use a start value, end value, and increment value. The MIDPOINTS= option can also be used with character variables to limit or reorder pie chart slices. See references in "More Information."

```
00001   title "Length of Meetings";
00002
00003   proc gchart data=lib1.meetings;
00004      pie hours /
00005         midpoints= 1.0 1.5 3.0
00006      ;
00007   run;
00008   quit;
```

MIDPOINTS= option
List the midpoints you want represented on the chart. Use one or more blanks to separate values.

MIDPOINTS= chart

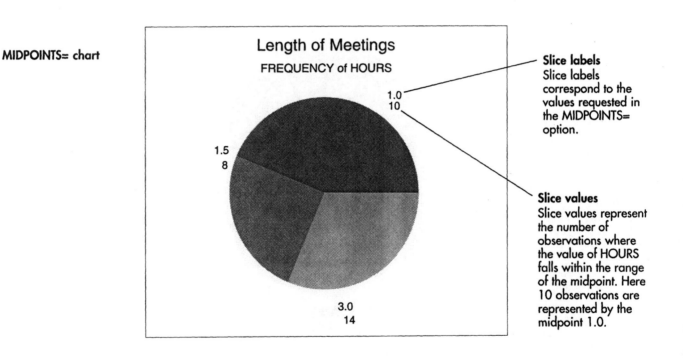

Slice labels
Slice labels correspond to the values requested in the MIDPOINTS= option.

Slice values
Slice values represent the number of observations where the value of HOURS falls within the range of the midpoint. Here 10 observations are represented by the midpoint 1.0.

Showing all slices with a numeric variable

If you want to show the actual values of a numeric variable instead of mid-points, use the DISCRETE option. When DISCRETE is used, the value represented on the chart is the count of observations for each unique value of the charting variable. Values are not grouped around midpoints. Character variables are always charted as discrete values.

```
00001    title "Length of Meetings";
00002
00003    proc gchart data=lib1.meetings;
00004       pie hours /
00005          discrete
00006       ;
00007    run;
00008    quit;
```

DISCRETE option
The DISCRETE option disables midpointing for numeric variables. Each unique value of the numeric variable HOURS is treated separately.

DISCRETE chart
Each unique value of the charting variable HOURS is represented by a slice.

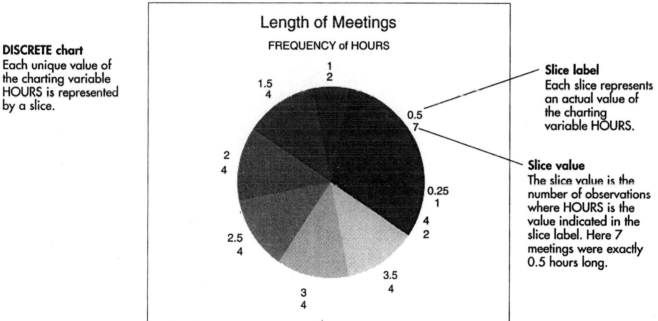

Slice label
Each slice represents an actual value of the charting variable HOURS.

Slice value
The slice value is the number of observations where HOURS is the value indicated in the slice label. Here 7 meetings were exactly 0.5 hours long.

Making slices represent sums

You can make the width of each slice represent a sum instead of a count. Use the SUMVAR= option to name a numeric variable to be summed for each value of the charting variable.

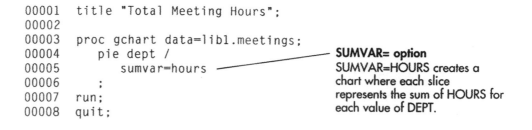

```
00001   title "Total Meeting Hours";
00002
00003   proc gchart data=lib1.meetings;
00004      pie dept /
00005          sumvar=hours
00006      ;
00007   run;
00008   quit;
```

SUMVAR= option
SUMVAR=HOURS creates a chart where each slice represents the sum of HOURS for each value of DEPT.

SUMVAR= chart

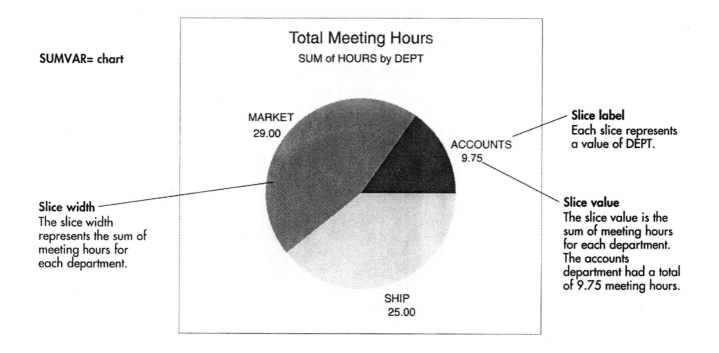

Total Meeting Hours
SUM of HOURS by DEPT

MARKET 29.00

ACCOUNTS 9.75

SHIP 25.00

Slice label
Each slice represents a value of DEPT.

Slice width
The slice width represents the sum of meeting hours for each department.

Slice value
The slice value is the sum of meeting hours for each department. The accounts department had a total of 9.75 meeting hours.

As with bar charts, you can use the TYPE= option with the PIE statement. This means you could specify that the pie chart represent percentages or means. Percentages are not very useful with pie charts because the relative width of each slice shows percentage or proportion anyway. You can display the percentage value with the PERCENT= option. See Chapter 32 for an example. Use the SUMVAR= option with TYPE= MEAN to show means. See Chapter 10 for an example of using these options with bar charts.

More Information

PIE statement, general reference

"PIE statement", in Chapter 23, "The GCHART Procedure", *SAS/GRAPH Software: Reference, Volume 2, Version 6, First Edition*, pp. 809-827

DISCRETE option, reference

"Options", in Chapter 23, "The GCHART Procedure", *SAS/GRAPH Software: Reference, Volume 2*, p. 813

LEVELS= option, reference

"Options", in Chapter 23, "The GCHART Procedure", *SAS/GRAPH Software: Reference, Volume 2*, p. 814

MIDPOINTS= option, reference with start-end-increment syntax

"Options", in Chapter 23, "The GCHART Procedure", *SAS/GRAPH Software: Reference, Volume 2*, pp. 814-815

SUMVAR= option, reference

"Options", in Chapter 23, "The GCHART Procedure", *SAS/GRAPH Software: Reference, Volume 2*, p. 816

TYPE= option, reference

"Options", in Chapter 23, "The GCHART Procedure", *SAS/GRAPH Software: Reference, Volume 2*, pp. 816-817

MIDPOINTS= option, examples with character and numeric variables

"Manipulating Midpoints", in Chapter 10, "Introduction to Pie Charts", *SAS/GRAPH Software: Usage, Version 6, First Edition*, pp. 118-124

Labeling Pie Slices

In This Chapter

- Specifying a value to display and its location
- Displaying only percentage values
- Using arrow leaders and the INSIDE location value

Specifying a value to display and its location

There are three values you can display with each slice in a pie chart:

- SLICE - the value of the midpoint of the charting variable
- VALUE - the count, sum, mean, or percentage associated with the slice
- PERCENT - the percentage of the total accounted for by the slice

The SLICE=, VALUE=, and PERCENT= options, respectively, control the display of these values.

To control the placement values displayed on a pie chart, you can assign the following values to the SLICE=, VALUE=, and PERCENT= options:

- OUTSIDE - outside the slice
- INSIDE - inside the slice
- ARROW - outside the slice with an arrow leading to the slice
- NONE - don't display the value

By default, SLICE and VALUE are displayed on the pie. OUTSIDE is the default placement for these values. You can request other combinations of values and location. In the following example, the PERCENT value is added to the pie chart and located outside the slice.

```
00001   title "Meetings Per Room";
00002
00003   proc gchart data=lib1.meetings;
00004      pie room /
00005         percent=outside
00006      ;
00007   run;
00008   quit;
```

Slash (/) option separator
When PIE statement options are used, they must follow a slash (/) to distinguish them from the charting variable.

PERCENT= option
PERCENT=OUTSIDE requests that the percentage value be displayed outside each pie slice.

Percentage values displayed outside each slice

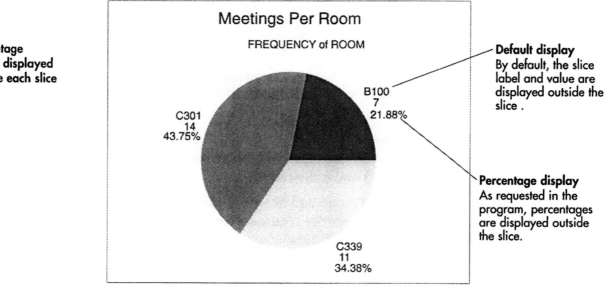

Meetings Per Room

FREQUENCY of ROOM

C301
14
43.75%

B100
7
21.88%

C339
11
34.38%

Default display
By default, the slice label and value are displayed outside the slice .

Percentage display
As requested in the program, percentages are displayed outside the slice.

Displaying only percentage values

The slice midpoint label and value are displayed by default. To display only the percentage value, you need to suppress the label and value and request the percentage display.

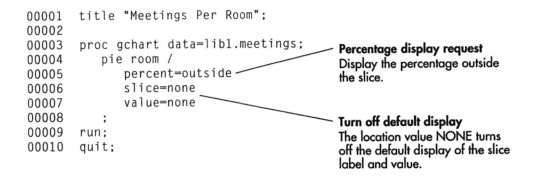

```
00001    title "Meetings Per Room";
00002
00003    proc gchart data=lib1.meetings;
00004       pie room /
00005          percent=outside
00006          slice=none
00007          value=none
00008       ;
00009    run;
00010    quit;
```

Percentage display request
Display the percentage outside the slice.

Turn off default display
The location value NONE turns off the default display of the slice label and value.

Percentages-only chart

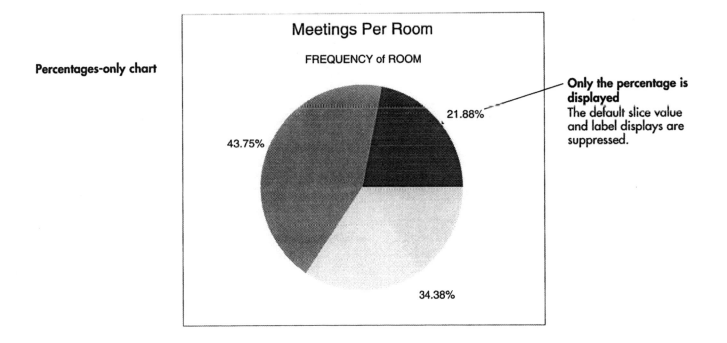

Only the percentage is displayed
The default slice value and label displays are suppressed.

Using arrow leaders and the INSIDE location value

Arrow leaders are often useful when slices are narrow. The arrow leads the eye from the number to the pie slice. The INSIDE location displays a value inside the slice.

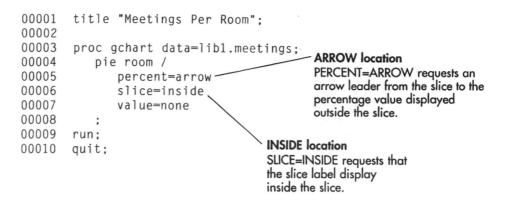

```
00001    title "Meetings Per Room";
00002
00003    proc gchart data=lib1.meetings;
00004       pie room /
00005          percent=arrow
00006          slice=inside
00007          value=none
00008       ;
00009    run;
00010    quit;
```

ARROW location
PERCENT=ARROW requests an arrow leader from the slice to the percentage value displayed outside the slice.

INSIDE location
SLICE=INSIDE requests that the slice label display inside the slice.

ARROW and INSIDE chart

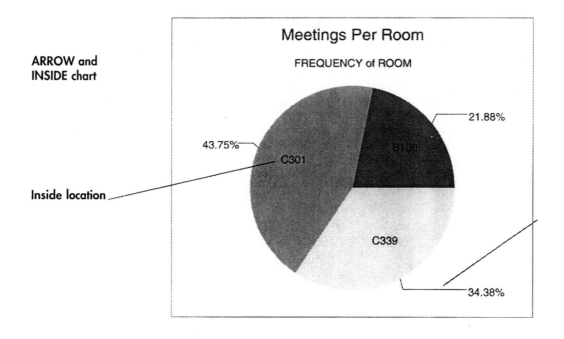

Inside location

When you request an inside display location, the label text may be obscured by the surrounding slice fill. There is currently no straightforward method to "knockout" a text box from the surrounding fill to display the label.

Any combination of location option values is valid, but when you use ARROW and OUTSIDE together, the arrow leader may interfere with other text. Check your chart to make sure that text and arrow placement and the appearance of inside text are acceptable.

📖 More Information

PERCENT= option, reference

"Options", in Chapter 23, "The GCHART Procedure", *SAS/GRAPH Software: Reference, Volume 2, Version 6, First Edition*, p. 816

SLICE= option, reference

"Options", in Chapter 23, "The GCHART Procedure", *SAS/GRAPH Software: Reference, Volume 2*, p. 816

VALUE= option, reference

"Options", in Chapter 23, "The GCHART Procedure", *SAS/GRAPH Software: Reference, Volume 2*, p. 817

label display options, description

"Slice Labeling Options", in Chapter 23, "The GCHART Procedure", *SAS/GRAPH Software: Reference, Volume 2*, pp. 819-821

label display options, examples

"Controlling the Content and Position of Midpoint Labels", in Chapter 11, "Enhancing the Appearance of Pie Charts", *SAS/GRAPH Software: Usage, Version 6, First Edition*, pp. 143-146

33 Creating Multiple Pie Charts per Page

In This Chapter

- Creating multiple charts with the GROUP= option
- Controlling page layout

Creating multiple charts with the GROUP= option

When you use the GROUP= option in the PIE statement, a separate chart is generated for each unique value of the grouping variable. In the example below, three pie charts are generated because the grouping variable DEPT has three unique values: ACCOUNTS, MARKET, and SHIP.

By default, the multiple charts generated with the GROUP= option are displayed on separate pages. To display all charts on a single page use the ACROSS= or DOWN= option (or both). In the example, ACROSS=3 is specified. This places three charts in a single row across the page.

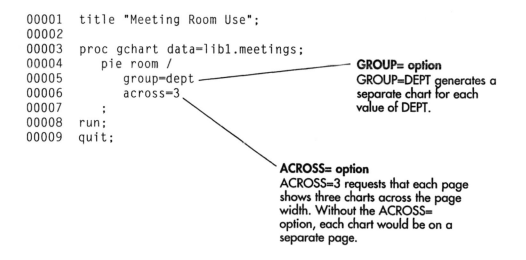

```
00001   title "Meeting Room Use";
00002
00003   proc gchart data=lib1.meetings;
00004      pie room /
00005         group=dept
00006         across=3
00007      ;
00008   run;
00009   quit;
```

GROUP= option
GROUP=DEPT generates a separate chart for each value of DEPT.

ACROSS= option
ACROSS=3 requests that each page shows three charts across the page width. Without the ACROSS= option, each chart would be on a separate page.

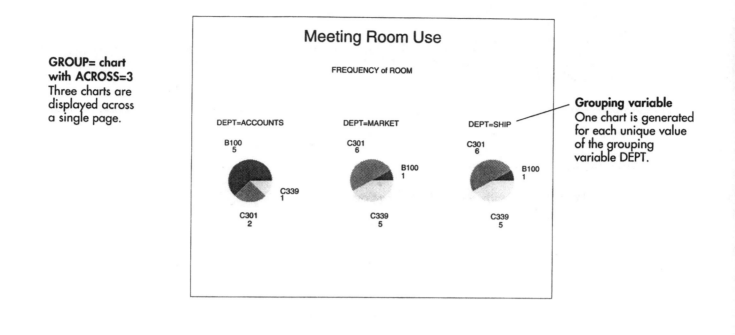

GROUP= chart with ACROSS=3
Three charts are displayed across a single page.

Grouping variable
One chart is generated for each unique value of the grouping variable DEPT.

Controlling page layout

You can combine the ACROSS= and DOWN= options to specify a page layout grid. In the following example, a 2 x 2 grid is specified by using ACROSS=2 and DOWN=2. Up to four charts can be placed on a page. In the example, there are only three charts to display. Charts are displayed across the page first, then down.

```
00001   title "Meeting Room Use";
00002
00003   proc gchart data=lib1.meetings;
00004      pie room /
00005         group=dept
00006         across=2
00007         down=2
00008      ;
00009   run;
00010   quit;
```

ACROSS= and DOWN= options
Combine the ACROSS= and DOWN= options to define a grid in which to display multiple charts.

You can place multiple graphs of any type in a page grid with PROC GREPLAY templates. Templates offer considerable flexibility but require some initial setup. Several ready-made templates are supplied by SAS Institute in the catalog SASHELP.TEMPLT.

2 x 2 page grid
ACROSS=2 and
DOWN=2 define a
2 x 2 grid with four
graph positions. There
are only three charts,
so the fourth position is
empty.

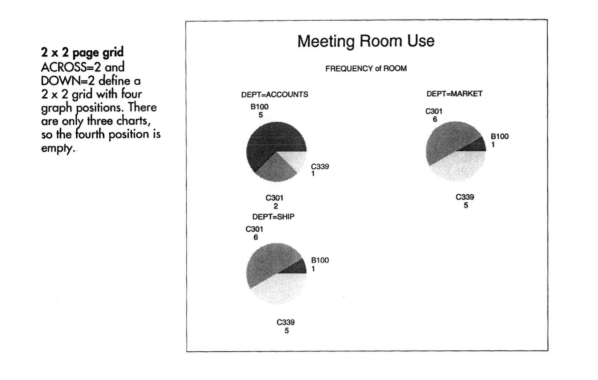

More Information

ACROSS= option, reference

"Options", in Chapter 23, "The GCHART Procedure", *SAS/GRAPH Software: Reference, Volume 2, Version 6, First Edition*, p. 811

DOWN= option, reference

"Options", in Chapter 23, "The GCHART Procedure", *SAS/GRAPH Software: Reference, Volume 2*, p. 813

GROUP= option, reference

"Options", in Chapter 23, "The GCHART Procedure", *SAS/GRAPH Software: Reference, Volume 2*, p. 814

grouping with multiple charts per page, examples

"Pie Chart Using Groups", in Chapter 23, "The GCHART Procedure", *SAS/GRAPH Software: Reference, Volume 2*, pp. 823-824

"Arranging the Pie Charts in the Output", in Chapter 11, "Enhancing the Appearance of Pie Charts", SAS/GRAPH Software: Usage, Version 6, First Edition, pp. 149-150

using SAS/GRAPH templates, examples

Chapter 55, "Displaying More than One Graph in Graphics Output", SAS/GRAPH Software: Usage, pp. 771-790

Controlling Pie Chart Appearance

34

In This Chapter

- Adding exploded slices
- Outlining slices
- Making a slice invisible
- Matching text and slice color
- Turning off the chart type heading
- Changing the location of the first slice
- Controlling slice order

Adding exploded slices

Use the EXPLODE= option to create a chart with one or more slices pulled out from the pie. Identify the slices to pull out, by midpoint value. The midpoints specified must match values in the data exactly, including upper- and lowercase for character variables.

```
00001   title "Meeting Room Use";
00002
00003   proc gchart data=lib1.meetings;
00004      pie room /
00005         explode="B100"
00006      ;
00007   run;
00008   quit;
```

EXPLODE= option
The EXPLODE= option names a slice to pull out from the rest of the chart. Here the charting variable is ROOM and the slice to explode is for room B100.

Since PROC GCHART calculates a set of default midpoints when charting a numeric variable, you probably won't know in advance what the midpoints are. In this case, create a chart without the EXPLODE= option and note the midpoint values. Then add an EXPLODE= option naming one of the generated midpoints. Alternatively, you can use the MIDPOINTS= option to specify midpoints. Any of these values can then be listed in the EXPLODE= option.

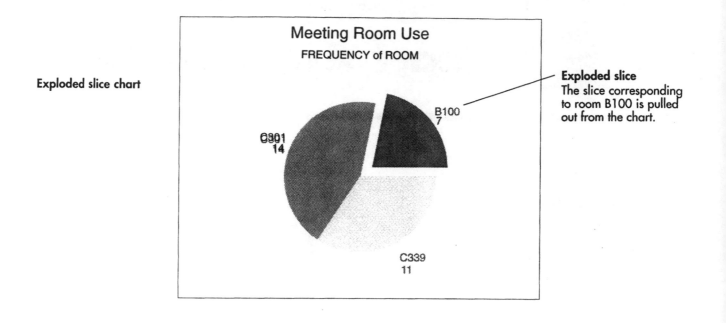

Exploded slice chart

Exploded slice
The slice corresponding to room B100 is pulled out from the chart.

Outlining slices

You can add an outline around each slice in the chart. This helps make the slices stand out. Use the COUTLINE= option and name the desired outline color.

```
00001   title "Meeting Room Use";
00002
00003   proc gchart data=lib1.meetings;
00004     pie room /
00005        coutline=black
00006     ;
00007   run;
00008   quit;
```

COUTLINE= option.

Outlined chart
Each slice is outlined in black.

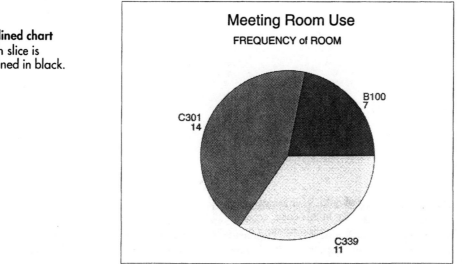

Making a slice invisible

You can remove a slice from the pie with the INVISIBLE= option. Name the midpoints of the slices you want to make invisible. You must specify the exact midpoint value of the invisible slices. Even though the slice is not displayed, the data corresponding to the invisible slice are still taken into account to generate the chart.

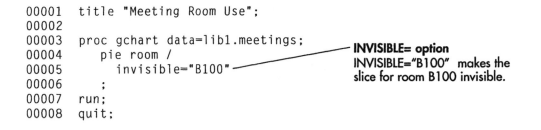

```
00001   title "Meeting Room Use";
00002
00003   proc gchart data=lib1.meetings;
00004      pie room /
00005         invisible="B100"
00006      ;
00007   run;
00008   quit;
```

INVISIBLE= option
INVISIBLE="B100" makes the slice for room B100 invisible.

INVISIBLE= chart

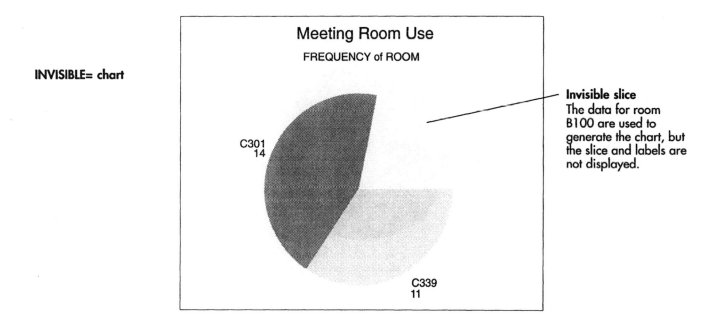

Invisible slice
The data for room B100 are used to generate the chart, but the slice and labels are not displayed.

Matching text and slice color

Use the MATCHCOLOR option to match the color of the slice label text with the color of the slice fill. Note that light colors that work well as fills may be hard to read when applied to text.

```
00001   title "Meeting Room Use";
00002
00003   proc gchart data=lib1.meetings;
00004      pie room /
00005         matchcolor ───────────────── MATCHCOLOR option
00006      ;
00007   run;
00008   quit;
```

MATCHCOLOR chart

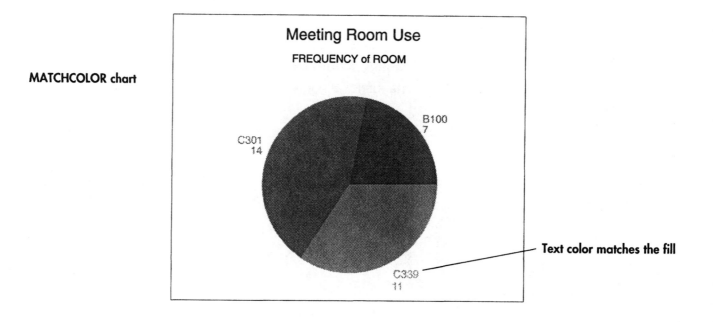

Turning off the chart type heading

By default, a subtitle heading is displayed that describes the chart. For the chart in the previous example, "FREQUENCY of ROOM" is the heading. You can turn this heading off with the NOHEADING option.

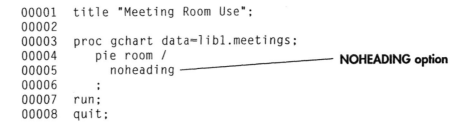

```
00001    title "Meeting Room Use";
00002
00003    proc gchart data=lib1.meetings;
00004      pie room /
00005        noheading ─────────────── NOHEADING option
00006        ;
00007    run;
00008    quit;
```

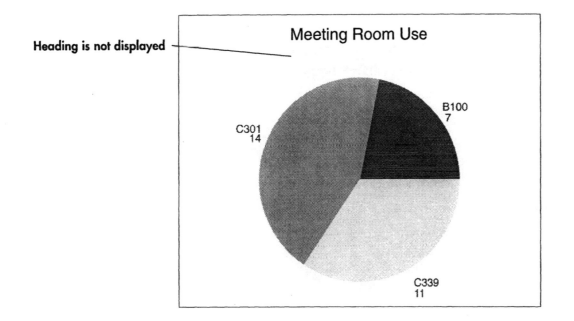

Heading is not displayed ────

Meeting Room Use

C301
14

B100
7

C339
11

Closer Look

In addition to the NOHEADING option, you can use the NOGROUPHEADING option to remove the headings displayed when the GROUP= option is used.

Changing the location of the first slice

By default, the first slice in the chart begins at the 3 o'clock position. You can change the starting position with the ANGLE= option. The angle specified is measured counterclockwise from the 3 o'clock position. To place the first slice at the top of the chart use ANGLE=90.

```
00001   title "Meeting Room Use";
00002
00003   proc gchart data=lib1.meetings;          ANGLE= option
00004      pie room /
00005         angle=90
00006      ;
00007   run;
00008   quit;
```

New starting position "B100" is the first slice charted. The ANGLE=90 option starts the chart at the 12 o'clock position instead of the default 3 o'clock position.

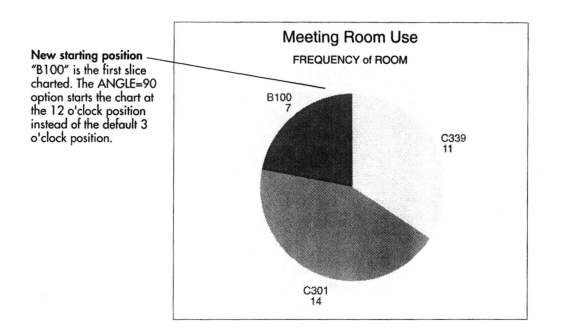

Controlling slice order

By default, slices are arranged counterclockwise in midpoint order, that is, in alphabetic or numeric order of the values of the charting variable. You can rearrange the slices with the MIDPOINTS= option. Name the midpoints you want, in the order that you want them.

```
00001    title "Meeting Room Use";
00002
00003    proc gchart data=lib1.meetings;
00004       pie room /
00005           midpoints = "C301" "B100" "C339"
00006       ;
00007    run;
00008    quit;
```

MIDPOINTS= option
You must list all the midpoints you want in the chart.

Ordered slices
The slice sequence is determined by the order of values in the MIDPOINT= option. By default, the first slice begins at the 3 o'clock position.

Meeting Room Use
FREQUENCY of ROOM

More Information

ANGLE= option, reference

"Options", in Chapter 23, "The GCHART Procedure", *SAS/GRAPH Software: Reference, Volume 2, Version 6, First Edition*, p. 812

COUTLINE= option, reference

"Options", in Chapter 23, "The GCHART Procedure", *SAS/GRAPH Software: Reference, Volume 2*, p. 812

EXPLODE= option, reference

"Options", in Chapter 23, "The GCHART Procedure", *SAS/GRAPH Software: Reference, Volume 2*, p. 813

INVISIBLE= option, reference

"Options", in Chapter 23, "The GCHART Procedure", *SAS/GRAPH Software: Reference, Volume 2*, p. 814

MATCHCOLOR option, reference

"Options", in Chapter 23, "The GCHART Procedure", *SAS/GRAPH Software: Reference, Volume 2*, p. 814

MIDPOINTS= option, reference

"Options", in Chapter 23, "The GCHART Procedure", *SAS/GRAPH Software: Reference, Volume 2*, pp. 814-815

NOHEADING option, reference

"Options", in Chapter 23, "The GCHART Procedure", *SAS/GRAPH Software: Reference, Volume 2*, p. 816

midpoints, description

"The Chart Variable and Midpoint Values", in Chapter 23, "The GCHART Procedure", *SAS/GRAPH Software: Reference, Volume 2*, pp. 817-818

reordering slices (midpoints), example

"Reordering Midpoints", in Chapter 10, "Introduction to Pie Charts", *SAS/GRAPH Software: Usage, Version 6, First Edition*, pp. 118-119

outlining slices, example

"Choosing an Outline Color for Slices", in Chapter 11, "Enhancing the Appearance of Pie Charts", *SAS/GRAPH Software: Usage*, pp. 136-137

exploding slices, example

"Exploding a Pie Slice", in Chapter 11, "Enhancing the Appearance of Pie Charts", *SAS/GRAPH Software: Usage*, pp. 137-138

making a slice invisible, example

"Making a Pie Slice Invisible", in Chapter 11, "Enhancing the Appearance of Pie Charts", *SAS/GRAPH Software: Usage*, pp. 138-140

changing the starting angle of the first slice, example

"Changing the Starting Angle of the Pie", in Chapter 11, "Enhancing the Appearance of Pie Charts", *SAS/GRAPH Software: Usage*, pp. 146-148

Selecting Pie Chart Colors and Fills

Controlling fill patterns

In This Chapter

- **Controlling fill patterns**
- **Varying the fill pattern**
- **Varying fill color**
- **Controlling color and fill**

Controlling fill patterns

Each pie chart slice is filled with a color and pattern. The fill can be solid, empty, angled lines, or a crosshatch. The colors available are dependent on the output device selected.

By default, PROC GCHART attempts to distinguish each slice by choosing a unique color-fill combination. You can override the default colors and fills with PATTERN statements. If you do not define enough patterns to fill all slices, PROC GCHART selects default patterns to fill the remaining slices.

PATTERN statements are global, which means they are in effect from the point they appear in your program and remain in effect until explicitly changed or your SAS session ends. Place PATTERN statements before the PROC GCHART step you want them to apply to. An example PATTERN statement is shown below.

VALUE= option
The VALUE= option sets the fill pattern. In addition to "P" and "X" described below, you can specify VALUE=SOLID for a solid fill or VALUE=EMPTY for no fill.

PATTERN1
The "1" names this as the first pattern to use. PATTERN and PATTERN1 are equivalent.

```
pattern1 color=gray77 value=p3x45;
```

COLOR= option
The COLOR= option names the color to use for this pattern. Color can be anything valid for your output device. If the color you select is not valid, PROC GCHART selects a substitute.

P3
The "P" indicates that this is a pie chart pattern. The "3" indicates hatching density in the range from 1 to 5.

X45
"X" indicates crosshatching. "45" means the hatching will be at a 45° angle. Besides "X", you can use "N" to hatch with parallel lines.

Varying the fill pattern

In the following example, three unique patterns are defined by varying the VALUE= setting. The color setting in each pattern is gray77.

```
00001    pattern1 color=gray77 value=p3x45;
00002    pattern2 color=gray77 value=p3n0;
00003    pattern3 color=gray77 value=p3x90;
00004
00005    title "Meeting Room Use";
00006
00007    proc gchart data=lib1.meetings;
00008       pie room;
00009    run;
00010    quit;
```

PATTERN statements
Three different fill patterns are assigned to distinguish three slices. All fill colors are gray77.

ROOM values
In this example, the variable ROOM has three unique values, so there will be three slices in the chart. One pattern is defined for each slice.

First slice pattern
The PATTERN1 statement settings are applied to the first slice. By default, the first slice begins at the 3 o'clock position. The fill pattern is p3x45.

Second slice pattern
The second slice is filled with pattern p3n0.

Third slice pattern
The fill pattern is p3x90.

Varying fill color

This example shows the effect of varying a solid color. The colors available are dependent on your output device. Here grayscale colors are used. See "More Information" for references on grayscale colors.

```
00001    pattern1 color=gray77 value=solid;
00002    pattern2 color=graybb value=solid;
00003    pattern3 color=black value=solid;
00004
00005    title "Meeting Room Use";
00006
00007    proc gchart data=lib1.meetings;
00008       pie room;
00009    run;
00010    quit;
```

Fill colors
Three different colors are assigned to distinguish three slices. All fills are solid.

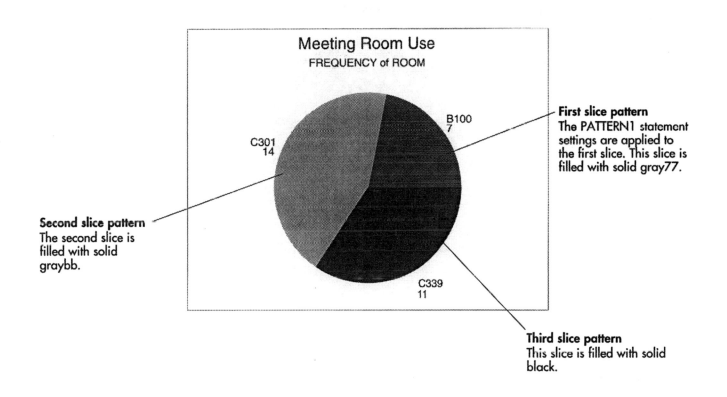

First slice pattern
The PATTERN1 statement settings are applied to the first slice. This slice is filled with solid gray77.

Second slice pattern
The second slice is filled with solid graybb.

Third slice pattern
This slice is filled with solid black.

Controlling color and fill

Color and fill can be used in any combination that is valid for your output device.

```
00001    pattern1 color=gray77 value=solid;
00002    pattern2 color=graybb value=solid;
00003    pattern3 color=black value=p3x135;
00004
00005    title "Meeting Room Use";
00006
00007    proc gchart data=lib1.meetings;
00008       pie room;
00009    run;
00010    quit;
```

PATTERN statements
Fill patterns and colors can be used together to create many unique fills.

Chart with three fill patterns
The three patterns defined in the program are applied to the three slices. Each slice has a unique color-fill combination.

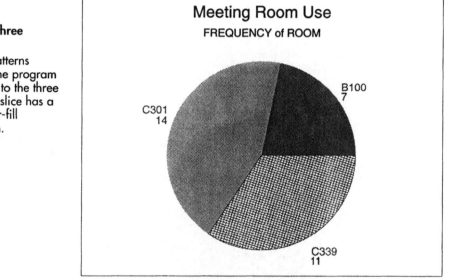

Meeting Room Use
FREQUENCY of ROOM

B100
7

C301
14

C339
11

You can use the PATTERN statement to define pattern sequences. This saves you from having to enter a separate PATTERN statement for each fill. If you need only a small number of patterns and know the output device where the graphs will be reproduced, your program will be easier to understand and to change if you use a separate PATTERN statement for each fill. If you need a large or unknown number of unique patterns you can use pattern sequences to avoid writing many PATTERN statements. The COLORS= and CPATTERN= graphics options can be used to control the colors in pattern sequences. See the references in "More Information" regarding pattern sequences and the PATTERN statement.

More Information

PATTERN statement, general reference

Chapter 15, "The PATTERN Statement", *SAS/GRAPH Software: Reference, Volume 1, Version 6, First Edition*, pp. 365-398

default patterns

"Default Pattern Sequences" in Chapter 15, "The PATTERN Statement", *SAS/GRAPH Software: Reference, Volume 1*, p. 371

pattern sequences generated with the PATTERN statement

"Pattern Sequences Generated by PATTERN Statements" in Chapter 15, "The PATTERN Statement", *SAS/GRAPH Software: Reference, Volume 1*, pp. 371-373

COLOR= option, description and reference

"PATTERN Statement Options" in Chapter 15, "The PATTERN Statement", *SAS/GRAPH Software: Reference, Volume 1*, p. 374

VALUE= option, description and reference

"PATTERN Statement Options" in Chapter 15, "The PATTERN Statement", *SAS/GRAPH Software: Reference, Volume 1*, pp. 376-381

using pie chart patterns, description and examples

"PATTERN Statement Options" in Chapter 15, "The PATTERN Statement", *SAS/GRAPH Software: Reference, Volume 1*, pp. 374-381

"Selecting Fill Patterns and Colors" in Chapter 11, "Enhancing the Appearance of Pie Charts", *SAS/GRAPH Software: Usage, Version 6, First Edition*, pp. 132-136

"Pie and Star Patterns with the GCHART Procedure" in Chapter 15, "The PATTERN Statement", *SAS/GRAPH Software: Reference, Volume 1*, pp. 394-395

overriding pattern color in the PIE statement, CFILL= option

"Options" in Chapter 23, "The GCHART Procedure", *SAS/GRAPH Software: Reference, Volume 2*, p. 812

overriding pattern fill in the PIE statement, FILL= option

"Options" in Chapter 23, "The GCHART Procedure", *SAS/GRAPH Software: Reference, Volume 2*, p. 813

pie patterns, description

"Selecting Patterns for the Pies" in Chapter 23, "The GCHART Procedure", *SAS/GRAPH Software: Reference, Volume 2*, p. 819

using colors, general reference

Chapter 7, "SAS/GRAPH Colors", *SAS/GRAPH Software: Reference, Volume 1*, pp. 177-197

grayscale colors

"Gray-scale Color Codes" in Chapter 7, "SAS/GRAPH Colors", *SAS/GRAPH Software: Reference, Volume 1*, p. 183

Part 6
Fine-Tuning
Your Graph

Chapter 36 - Controlling Titles and Footnotes

Chapter 37 - Adding Dollar Signs and Decimal Places

Chapter 38 - Displaying Dates with Plots and Charts

Chapter 39 - Controlling Axes on Plots and Charts

Chapter 40 - Controlling Legends

Chapter 41 - Creating Mulitple Graphs from a Single
           Data Set

Chapter 42 - Saving and Reviewing Graphs

36

Controlling Titles and Footnotes

In This Chapter

- Controlling title font, color, and size
- Adding titles and footnotes
- Changing text orientation
- Changing text within a line

Controlling title font, color, and size

Text displayed with TITLE, FOOTNOTE, NOTE, AXIS, and LEGEND statements is controlled with FONT=, COLOR=, HEIGHT=, and other options.

Many fonts are provided with SAS/GRAPH software. For some output devices, you can also use device-specific hardware fonts. The setting for the FONT= option must be a valid font name from the list of available fonts.

The HEIGHT= option controls text size. The default height units are character cells. The exact dimensions of a character cell can vary. You can also use the inch (IN), centimeter (CM), and percent (PCT) units. The PCT unit specifies a percentage of the graphics output area.

Settings for the COLOR= option must be valid color names for the current output device.

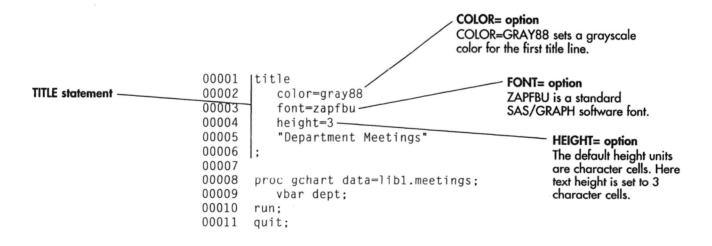

COLOR= option
COLOR=GRAY88 sets a grayscale color for the first title line.

TITLE statement

```
00001  title
00002     color=gray88
00003     font=zapfbu
00004     height=3
00005     "Department Meetings"
00006  ;
00007
00008  proc gchart data=lib1.meetings;
00009     vbar dept;
00010  run;
00011  quit;
```

FONT= option
ZAPFBU is a standard SAS/GRAPH software font.

HEIGHT= option
The default height units are character cells. Here text height is set to 3 character cells.

Title text
The font, color, and size attributes of the title are set with TITLE statement options.

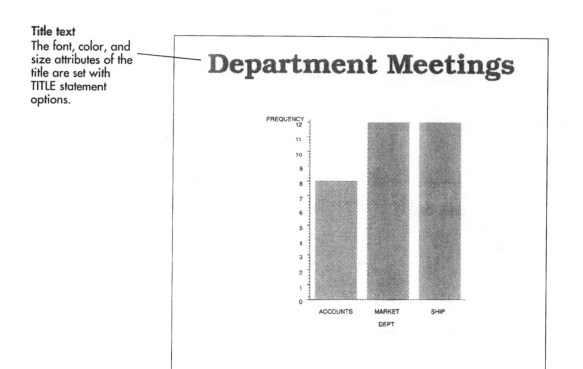

Common text options
These options can be used with TITLE, FOOTNOTE, AXIS, LEGEND, and NOTE statements. Several other options are also available.

Option	Units and Setting Description	Examples
HEIGHT=	CELLS - character cells, default PCT - percentage of display area CM - centimeters IN - inches	HEIGHT=3 CELLS HEIGHT=8.5 PCT HEIGHT=2.5 CM HEIGHT=0.75 IN
FONT=	standard font name hardware font name (hardware fonts are device specific)	FONT=ZAPFBU FONT=HWPS1008
COLOR=	color name (The color must be supported by the current output device.)	COLOR=RED COLOR=GRAY88 COLOR=BLACK
ANGLE=	degrees (the entire text line is rotated by the specified angle counterclockwise from the baseline of the text string)	ANGLE=90 ANGLE=−90
ROTATE=	degrees (each character is rotated by the specified angle counterclockwise from the baseline of the text string)	ROTATE=90 ROTATE=−90

Adding titles and footnotes

To generate multiple title lines, use multiple TITLE statements. Up to ten TITLE statements are allowed: TITLE1 (or TITLE) through TITLE10.

Use FOOTNOTE statements to define footnotes. Footnote text is centered at the bottom of the graphics display area. All options available for titles are available for footnotes. As with the TITLE statement, up to ten FOOTNOTE statements are allowed.

In the following example, the BOX= option is used to draw a box around the footnote. BOX= is one of several options available in text placement statements such as TITLE and FOOTNOTE.

TITLE statement
This statement defines the first title line.

```
00001   title
00002       color=black
00003       font=zapfbu
00004       height=6 pct
00005       "Department Meetings"
00006   ;
00007
00008   title2
00009       color=gray88
00010       height= 3 pct
00011       "Meeting Count"
00012   ;
00013
00014   footnote
00015       color=black
00016       box=2
00017       height=2 pct
00018       "For Latest Fiscal Year"
00019   ;
00020
00021   proc gchart data=lib1.meetings;
00022       vbar dept;
00023   run;
00024   quit;
```

Percentage height unit
PCT specifies text size as a percentage of the graphics display area. A percentage setting is device and scale independent.

TITLE2 statement
The TITLE2 statement defines the second title line.

BOX= option
The BOX= option draws a box around the footnote text. BOX=2 sets the box line thickness to 2. The range for line thickness is 1 to 4.

The HEIGHT= option is used in several statements that specify text. The HEIGHT= units can be CELLS (character cells), CM (centimeters), IN (inches), or PCT (percent). Only PCT is independent of scale and of the hardware device that displays your graph. If you do not use PCT, the size or aspect ratio of text may change when you display your graph on a different device.

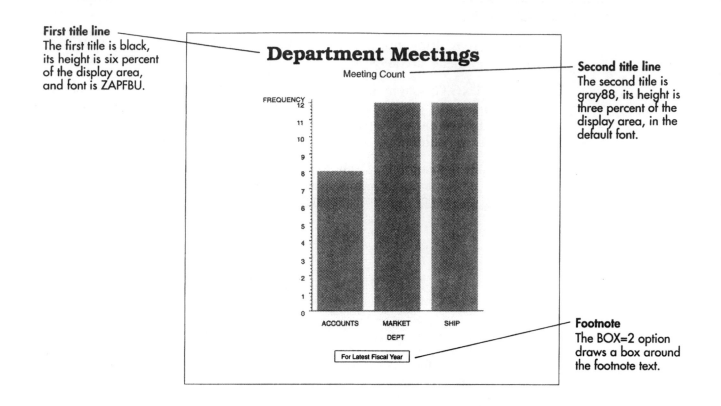

First title line
The first title is black, its height is six percent of the display area, and font is ZAPFBU.

Second title line
The second title is gray88, its height is three percent of the display area, in the default font.

Footnote
The BOX=2 option draws a box around the footnote text.

Changing text orientation

The ANGLE= and ROTATE= options can be used to change text line and letter orientation. ANGLE= changes the angle of the entire text line relative to horizontal. ROTATE= changes the angle of individual letters. When ANGLE=90, title text is placed on the left edge of the graphics output area and footnote text is placed on the right edge. When ANGLE=–90, titles are placed on the right edge and footnotes on the left edge. For other angles, text is rotated counterclockwise from its normal position on the page. Negative angles rotate text in the clockwise direction.

```
00001   title
00002      color=gray88
00003      font=zapfbu
00004      height=3
00005      "Department Meetings"
00006   ;
00007
00008   footnote
00009      angle=-90
00010      "For Internal Use Only"
00011   ;
00012
00013
00014   proc gchart data=lib1.meetings;
00015      vbar dept;
00016   run;
00017   quit;
```

ANGLE= option
The ANGLE=-90 option rotates the entire text line in a clockwise direction relative to the horizontal.

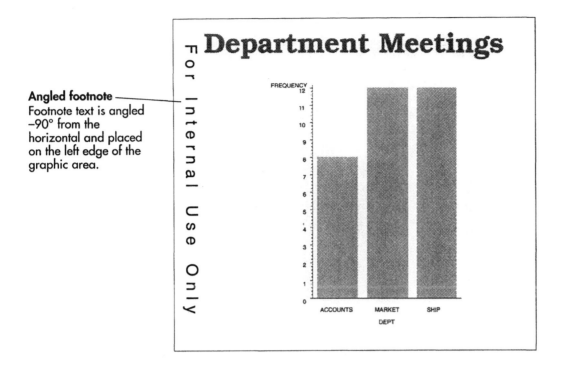

Angled footnote
Footnote text is angled −90° from the horizontal and placed on the left edge of the graphic area.

You can use the ANGLE= and ROTATE= options together to reorient letters in angled text.

```
00001   title
00002       color=gray88
00003       font=zapfbu
00004       height=3
00005       "Department Meetings"
00006   ;
00007
00008   footnote
00009       angle=-90
00010       rotate=90
00011       "For Internal Use Only"
00012   ;
00013
00014   proc gchart data=lib1.meetings;
00015       vbar dept;
00016   run;
00017   quit;
```

ANGLE= option
ANGLE=−90 option rotates the entire footnote line.

ROTATE= option
ROTATE=90 rotates individual letters in the angled line back to the standard orientation.

 The LANGLE= option is similar to the ANGLE= option except that at LANGLE=90 and LANGLE=−90 text is centered on the page rather than the left or right edge.

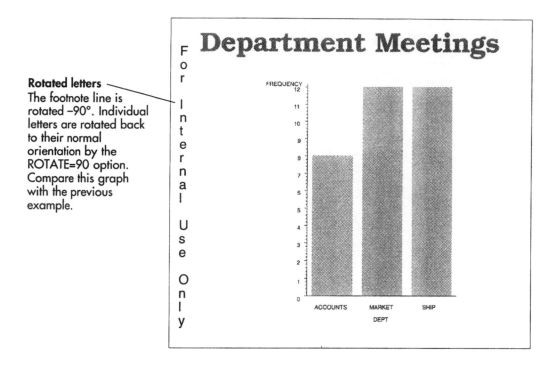

Rotated letters
The footnote line is rotated –90°. Individual letters are rotated back to their normal orientation by the ROTATE=90 option. Compare this graph with the previous example.

Changing text within a line

Multiple sets of text control options can be used within a single line. Place the options before the text you want them to apply to.

```
00001   title height=2 color=gray88 "Chart of "
00002         height=4 color=black  "All"
00003         height=2 color=gray88 " Meetings"
00004   ;
00005
00006   proc gchart data=lib1.meetings;
00007      vbar dept;
00008   run;
00009   quit;
```

Multiple text control options in a single line

In addition to the TITLE and FOOTNOTE statements discussed in this chapter, you can also use the NOTE statement. By default, NOTE statement text is left-justified at the top of the graphics output area, but you can use the MOVE= option to place it anywhere. The MOVE= option can also be used in TITLE and FOOTNOTE statements. No space is reserved for NOTE statement text as it is for TITLE and FOOTNOTE statement text. This means notes can overwrite other graphics elements. NOTE statements are not global. They must be used within the SAS/GRAPH procedure you want them to apply to.

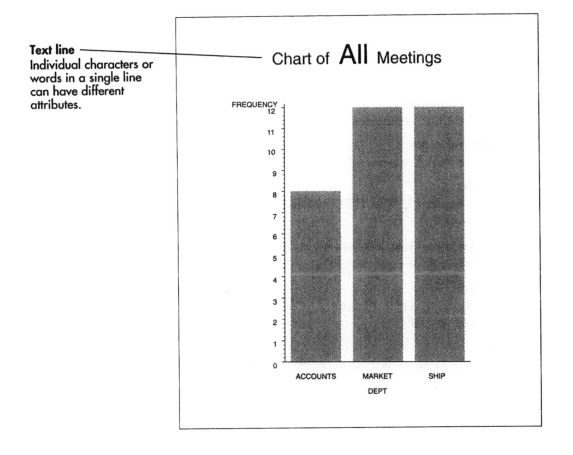

Text line
Individual characters or words in a single line can have different attributes.

More Information

SAS/GRAPH fonts, general reference
Chapter 6, "SAS/GRAPH Fonts", *SAS/GRAPH Software: Reference, Volume 1, Version 6, First Edition*, pp. 155-175

hardware fonts, discussion and reference
"Hardware Fonts" in Chapter 6, "SAS/GRAPH Fonts", *SAS/GRAPH Software: Reference, Volume 1*, pp. 161-164

standard SAS/GRAPH fonts, reference and examples
"SAS/GRAPH Software Fonts" in Chapter 6, "SAS/GRAPH Fonts", *SAS/GRAPH Software: Reference, Volume 1*, pp. 166-174

SAS Technical Report P-170, Type Styles and Fonts for Use with SAS/GRAPH Software

SAS/GRAPH colors, general reference
Chapter 7, "SAS/GRAPH Colors", *SAS/GRAPH Software: Reference, Volume 1*, pp. 177-197

using color with specific devices
"Device Capabilities" in Chapter 7, "SAS/GRAPH Colors", *SAS/GRAPH Software: Reference, Volume 1*, pp. 194-197

FOOTNOTE statement, general reference

Chapter 11, "The FOOTNOTE Statement", *SAS/GRAPH Software: Reference, Volume 1*, pp. 271-289

FOOTNOTE statement, examples

"Examples" in Chapter 11, "The FOOTNOTE Statement", *SAS/GRAPH Software: Reference, Volume 1*, pp. 285-289

NOTE statement, general reference

Chapter 14, "The NOTE Statement", *SAS/GRAPH Software: Reference, Volume 1*, pp. 347-364

TITLE statement, general reference

Chapter 17, "The TITLE Statement", *SAS/GRAPH Software: Reference, Volume 1*, pp. 441-463

TITLE statement, examples

"Examples" in Chapter 17, "The TITLE Statement", *SAS/GRAPH Software: Reference, Volume 1*, pp. 456-462

Chapter 40, "Displaying Text in Footnotes, Notes, and Titles", *SAS/GRAPH Software: Usage, Version 6, First Edition*, pp. 543-561

ANGLE= option, reference

"TITLE Statement Options" in Chapter 17, "The TITLE Statement", *SAS/GRAPH Software: Reference, Volume 1*, p. 446

BOX= option, reference

"TITLE Statement Options" in Chapter 17, "The TITLE Statement", *SAS/GRAPH Software: Reference, Volume 1*, pp. 447-448

COLOR= option, reference

"TITLE Statement Options" in Chapter 17, "The TITLE Statement", *SAS/GRAPH Software: Reference, Volume 1*, p. 448

HEIGHT= option, reference

"TITLE Statement Options" in Chapter 17, "The TITLE Statement", *SAS/GRAPH Software: Reference, Volume 1*, pp. 449-450

LANGLE= option, reference

"TITLE Statement Options" in Chapter 17, "The TITLE Statement", *SAS/GRAPH Software: Reference, Volume 1*, p. 451

ROTATE= option, reference

"TITLE Statement Options" in Chapter 17, "The TITLE Statement", *SAS/GRAPH Software: Reference, Volume 1*, pp. 452-453

37 Adding Dollar Signs and Decimal Places

In This Chapter

- **Controlling decimal places**
- **Using formats**
- **Displaying dollar signs**

Controlling decimal places

You can control the display of decimal places with a SAS format. Use the FORMAT statement to assign a format to a variable. In the following example, the 5.2 format displays values of the variable TOTAL in five total spaces with two decimal places.

```
00001   symbol1
00002      value=none
00003      interpol=join
00004   ;
00005
00006   title "Average Fuel Use";
00007
00008   proc gplot data=lib1.allfuel;
00009      format total 5.2;  ———————— FORMAT statement
00010      plot total*length;
00011   run;
00012   quit;
```

There are many SAS formats available. The standard numeric format and the DOLLAR format shown in this chapter are among the most commonly used. Also available are the COMMA and PERCENT formats that display values with commas or percent signs. See "More Information" for a list of available formats. In addition to the standard SAS formats, you can create your own formats with PROC FORMAT. See Chapters 16 and 28 for examples.

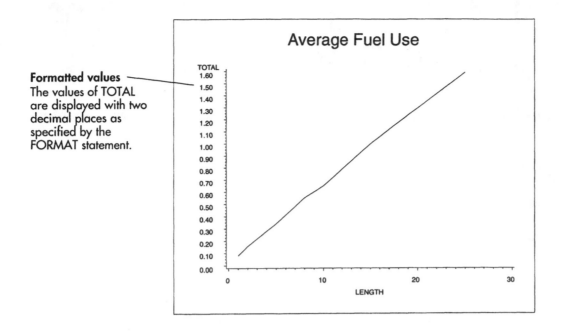

Formatted values
The values of TOTAL are displayed with two decimal places as specified by the FORMAT statement.

Using formats

Formats are usually assigned with FORMAT statements that name a variable and the format to assign to that variable. Formats are made up of the format name and width. Numeric formats also have an optional decimal specification. A period is always required after the width. An example FORMAT statement is shown below.

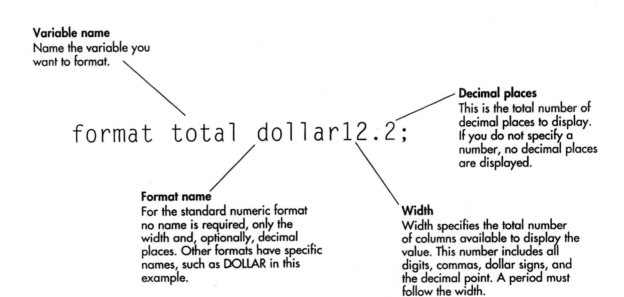

Variable name
Name the variable you want to format.

Decimal places
This is the total number of decimal places to display. If you do not specify a number, no decimal places are displayed.

```
format total dollar12.2;
```

Format name
For the standard numeric format no name is required, only the width and, optionally, decimal places. Other formats have specific names, such as DOLLAR in this example.

Width
Width specifies the total number of columns available to display the value. This number includes all digits, commas, dollar signs, and the decimal point. A period must follow the width.

Displaying dollar signs

Use a FORMAT statement with the DOLLAR format to display numeric values with dollar signs and commas.

```
00001   title "State Revenues";
00002
00003   proc gmap data=lib1.jobrev  map=maps.us all;
00004      format revenues dollar12.2;
00005      id state;
00006      choro revenues /
00007         levels = 5
00008         coutline = black
00009      ;
00010   run;
00011   quit;
```

FORMAT statement
The FORMAT statement assigns the DOLLAR12.2 format to the variable REVENUES.

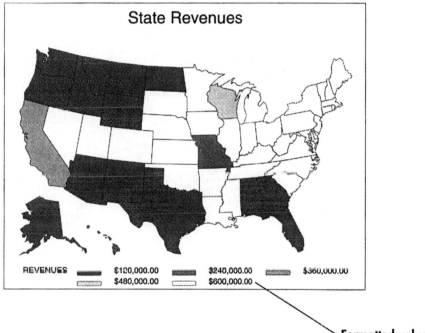

Formatted values
The values of the variable REVENUES are displayed with dollar signs and two decimal places, as specified in the FORMAT statement.

To eliminate decimal places, drop the decimal specification from the format. In the following example, the DOLLAR12. format is used instead of the DOLLAR12.2 format.

```
00001   title "State Revenues";
00002
00003   proc gmap data=lib1.jobrev  map=maps.us  all;
00004      format revenues dollar12.;
00005      id state;
00006      choro revenues /
00007         levels = 5
00008         coutline = black
00009      ;
00010   run;
00011   quit;
```

FORMAT statement
No decimal place specification follows the period in the DOLLAR12. format.

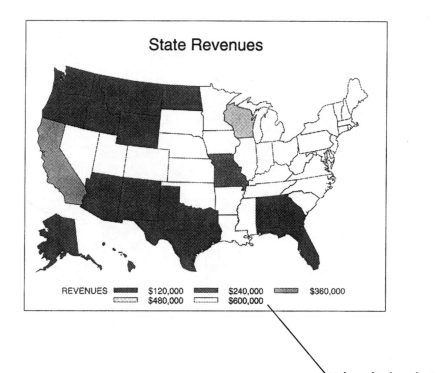

Values displayed without decimals
Compare this graph with the previous example.

More Information

SAS formats, description and list

"SAS Formats" in Chapter 3, "Components of the SAS Language", *SAS Language: Reference, Version 6, First Edition*, pp. 64-69

SAS formats, reference for individual formats

Chapter 14, "SAS Formats", *SAS Language: Reference*, pp. 673-713

COMMA format, reference

"COMMA$w.d$" in Chapter 14, "SAS Formats", *SAS Language: Reference*, p. 681

DOLLAR format, reference

"DOLLAR$w.d$" in Chapter 14, "SAS Formats", *SAS Language: Reference*, p. 684

PERCENT format, reference

"PERCENT$w.d$" in Chapter 14, "SAS Formats", *SAS Language: Reference*, p. 697

standard numeric format, reference

"$w.d$" in Chapter 14, "SAS Formats", *SAS Language: Reference*, p. 704

38 Displaying Dates with Plots and Charts

In This Chapter

- Placing dates on a plot axis
- Controlling the date format
- Formatted dates in charts

Placing dates on a plot axis

To control the display of dates on a plot axis, use the AXIS and FORMAT statements. In the following example, the AXIS1 statement defines a set of tick marks incremented by month ranging from January 1, 1995 to January 1, 1996. Dates are expressed with SAS date constants. The HAXIS= option applies this set of tick marks to the horizontal plot axis. The FORMAT statement assigns the DATE7. format to values of the variable DATE displayed with the tick marks. See Chapter 37 for more on using the FORMAT statement.

AXIS statement

FORMAT statement
The DATE7. format is assigned to the variable DATE.

```
00001   symbol1 interpol=join;
00002
00003   axis1 order=('01jan95'd to '01jan96'd by month);
00004
00005   title "Monthly Sales";
00006
00007   proc gplot data=lib1.monthly;
00008     format date date7.;
00009     plot sales*date /
00010       haxis=axis1
00011     ;
00012   run;
00013   quit;
```

ORDER= option
Tick marks are defined with a start and end date incremented by month.

HAXIS option
HAXIS=AXIS1 applies the AXIS1 settings.

You can use the AXIS statement with both PROC GCHART and PROC GPLOT. Axis definitions can be applied to either the horizontal axis, vertical axis, or both. Keep in mind that the ORDER= option defines an arbitrary set of tick marks. Make sure your data values match the tick marks. If they don't, you will get incomplete or confusing results.

Plot with date display

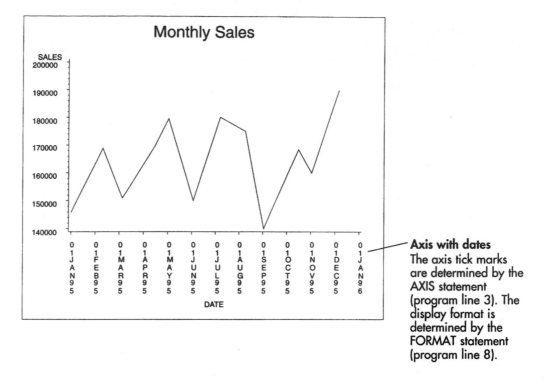

Axis with dates
The axis tick marks are determined by the AXIS statement (program line 3). The display format is determined by the FORMAT statement (program line 8).

Controlling the date format

The tick mark values defined in the ORDER= option are independent of how the tick marks are displayed. In the following example, the tick mark values are the same as in the previous example, but displayed with the WORDDATE3. format instead of the DATE7. format.

AXIS statement
The tick mark values are the same as in the previous example.

```
00001   symbol1 interpol=join;
00002
00003   axis1 order=('01jan95'd to '01jan96'd by month);
00004
00005   title "Monthly Sales";
00006
00007   proc gplot data=lib1.monthly;
00008      format date worddate3.;
00009      plot sales*date /
00010         haxis=axis1;
00011   run;
00012   quit;
```

FORMAT statement
The FORMAT statement displays the values of the variable DATE with the WORDDATE3. format.

Plot with changed date format
Compare this output with the previous example.

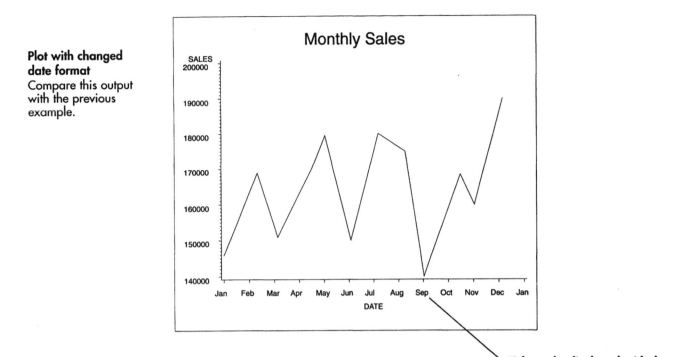

Tick marks displayed with the WORDDATE3. format

Formatted dates in charts

You can use the FORMAT statement with PROC GCHART to group date-based data. The LIB1.MONTHLY data, used in this example, are shown below.

LIB1.MONTHLY data set
The variable DATE is shown in the MMDDYY8. format.

```
           LIB1.MONTHLY

  OBS        DATE        SALES

   1       01/01/95     145830
   2       02/10/95     168930
   3       03/05/95     150922
   4       04/16/95     170082
   5       05/02/95     179500
   6       06/03/95     150040
   7       07/07/95     180090
   8       08/09/95     175035
   9       09/02/95     140010
  10       10/16/95     168500
  11       11/02/95     159950
  12       12/06/95     190010
```

In the data set LIB1.MONTHLY, sales figures are recorded for each month, but not necessarily on the same day of each month. These data can be charted quarterly with the SAS QTR1. format. The QTR format translates each date to a value from 1 to 4 representing the quarter of the year. When charted with the DISCRETE option, PROC GCHART uses the formatted values of the charting variable DATE, instead of the actual values. The formatted values are quarters: 1, 2, 3, or 4.

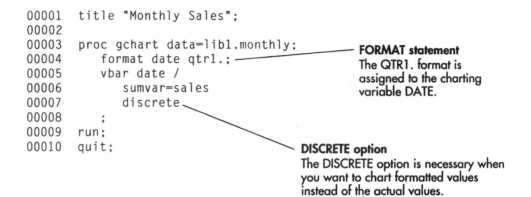

```
00001    title "Monthly Sales";
00002
00003    proc gchart data=lib1.monthly;
00004       format date qtr1.;
00005       vbar date /
00006          sumvar=sales
00007          discrete
00008       ;
00009    run;
00010    quit;
```

FORMAT statement
The QTR1. format is assigned to the charting variable DATE.

DISCRETE option
The DISCRETE option is necessary when you want to chart formatted values instead of the actual values.

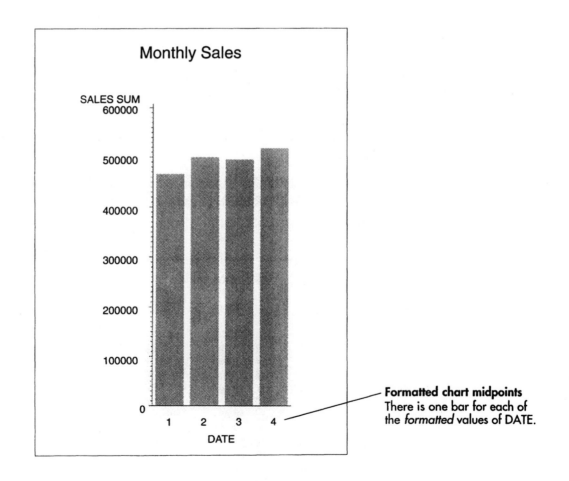

Formatted chart midpoints
There is one bar for each of the *formatted* values of DATE.

More Information

SAS date formats, description and list
"SAS Formats" in Chapter 3, "Components of the SAS Language", *SAS Language: Reference, Version 6, First Edition*, p. 68

SAS formats, reference for individual formats
Chapter 14, "SAS Formats", *SAS Language: Reference*, pp. 673-713

DATE format, reference
"DATE*w*." in Chapter 14, "SAS Formats", *SAS Language: Reference*, p. 682

date constants
"Date and Time Constants" in Chapter 4, "Rules of the SAS Language", *SAS Language: Reference*, pp. 115-116

QTR format, reference
"QTR*w*." in Chapter 14, "SAS Formats", *SAS Language: Reference*, p. 698

WORDDATE format, reference
"WORDDATE*w*." in Chapter 14, "SAS Formats", *SAS Language: Reference*, p. 706

AXIS statement, general reference
Chapter 9, "The AXIS Statement", *SAS/GRAPH Software: Reference, Volume 1, Version 6, First Edition*, pp. 215-258

ORDER= option, AXIS statement, reference and date examples
"AXIS statement options" in Chapter 9, "The AXIS Statement", *SAS/GRAPH Software: Reference, Volume 1*, pp. 224-226

MAXIS= option, VBAR statement, reference
"Options" in Chapter 23, "The GCHART Procedure", *SAS/GRAPH Software: Reference, Volume 2*, p. 849 (HBAR p. 789)

using formats with PROC GCHART, example with the STAR statement
"Formatting the dates as months" in Chapter 12, "Introduction to Star Charts", *SAS/GRAPH Software: Usage, Version 6, First Edition*, pp. 158-159

using dates on plot axes, example
"Modifying the Axes" in Chapter 23, "Producing High-Low Plots", *SAS/GRAPH Software: Usage*, pp. 326-328

Controlling Axes on Plots and Charts

In This Chapter

- Using the AXIS statement
- Defining axis label text
- How to define plot tick marks
- Controlling tick mark labels and minor tick marks
- Changing bar chart axis labels

Using the AXIS statement

The AXIS statement defines axis settings for plots and charts. AXIS statement settings control the axis color, the color and size of tick marks, the order and value of the major tick marks, and the text attributes of the axis label and major tick marks.

AXIS statement settings are global. This means they are in effect from the point they appear in your program and remain in effect until explicitly changed or your SAS session ends. AXIS statement settings are independent of the input data so you need to establish settings that make sense for the data you are charting or plotting.

In addition to AXIS statements, you can use PLOT statement options such as VMINOR=, XTICKNUM=, and NOAXES to control plot axes from within the GPLOT procedure.

Defining axis label text

Use the AXIS statement LABEL= option to control axis label text. With this option, you can specify the label text itself plus all text attributes. In the following example, the AXIS1 statement sets the size (height) and font attributes for the axis label. The AXIS2 statement sets size, color, and label text. Font is not set in the AXIS2 statement, so the default font is used. The axis settings are applied with the VAXIS= and HAXIS= options.

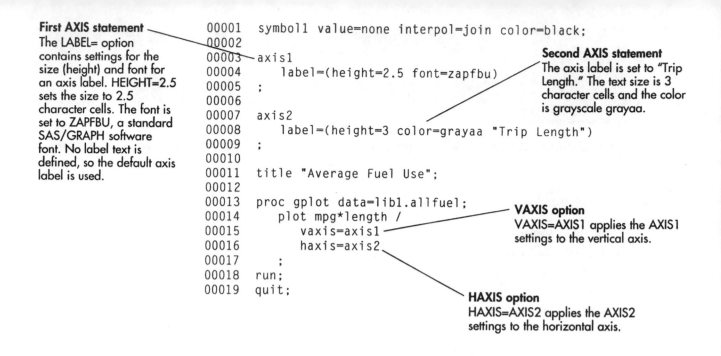

First AXIS statement
The LABEL= option contains settings for the size (height) and font for an axis label. HEIGHT=2.5 sets the size to 2.5 character cells. The font is set to ZAPFBU, a standard SAS/GRAPH software font. No label text is defined, so the default axis label is used.

Second AXIS statement
The axis label is set to "Trip Length." The text size is 3 character cells and the color is grayscale grayaa.

```
00001    symbol1 value=none interpol=join color=black;
00002
00003    axis1
00004        label=(height=2.5 font=zapfbu)
00005    ;
00006
00007    axis2
00008        label=(height=3 color=grayaa "Trip Length")
00009    ;
00010
00011    title "Average Fuel Use";
00012
00013    proc gplot data=lib1.allfuel;
00014        plot mpg*length /
00015            vaxis=axis1
00016            haxis=axis2
00017        ;
00018    run;
00019    quit;
```

VAXIS option
VAXIS=AXIS1 applies the AXIS1 settings to the vertical axis.

HAXIS option
HAXIS=AXIS2 applies the AXIS2 settings to the horizontal axis.

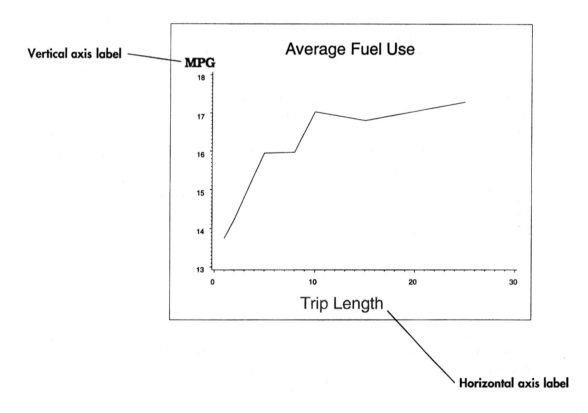

Vertical axis label

Horizontal axis label

How to define plot tick marks

Use the AXIS statement ORDER= option to control the order and value of major tick marks. There are several ways to define the tick marks. In the example below, the start-end-increment method is used. This method is preferred because it ensures that there will be equal increments between tick mark values. You can also list values individually.

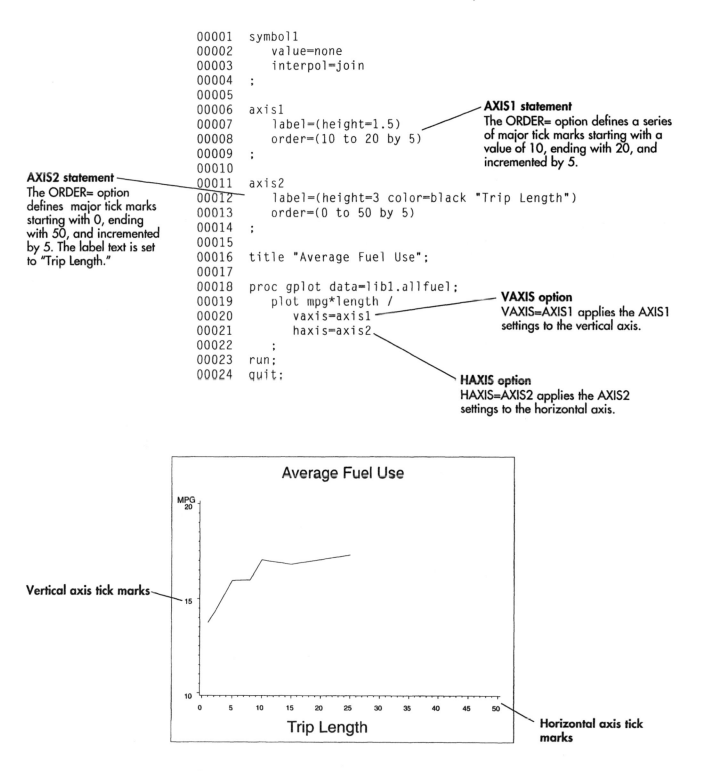

```
00001   symbol1
00002      value=none
00003      interpol=join
00004   ;
00005
00006   axis1
00007      label=(height=1.5)
00008      order=(10 to 20 by 5)
00009   ;
00010
00011   axis2
00012      label=(height=3 color=black "Trip Length")
00013      order=(0 to 50 by 5)
00014   ;
00015
00016   title "Average Fuel Use";
00017
00018   proc gplot data=lib1.allfuel;
00019      plot mpg*length /
00020         vaxis=axis1
00021         haxis=axis2
00022      ;
00023   run;
00024   quit:
```

AXIS1 statement
The ORDER= option defines a series of major tick marks starting with a value of 10, ending with 20, and incremented by 5.

AXIS2 statement
The ORDER= option defines major tick marks starting with 0, ending with 50, and incremented by 5. The label text is set to "Trip Length."

VAXIS option
VAXIS=AXIS1 applies the AXIS1 settings to the vertical axis.

HAXIS option
HAXIS=AXIS2 applies the AXIS2 settings to the horizontal axis.

Average Fuel Use

MPG

Vertical axis tick marks

Trip Length

Horizontal axis tick marks

Controlling tick mark labels and minor tick marks

The AXIS statement VALUE= option controls the attributes of major tick mark labels. You can change the color, font, and size of these labels. In the example, the AXIS1 VALUE= option sets the size of the tick mark labels. You can remove minor tick marks with the MINOR=NONE option as in the AXIS2 statement below.

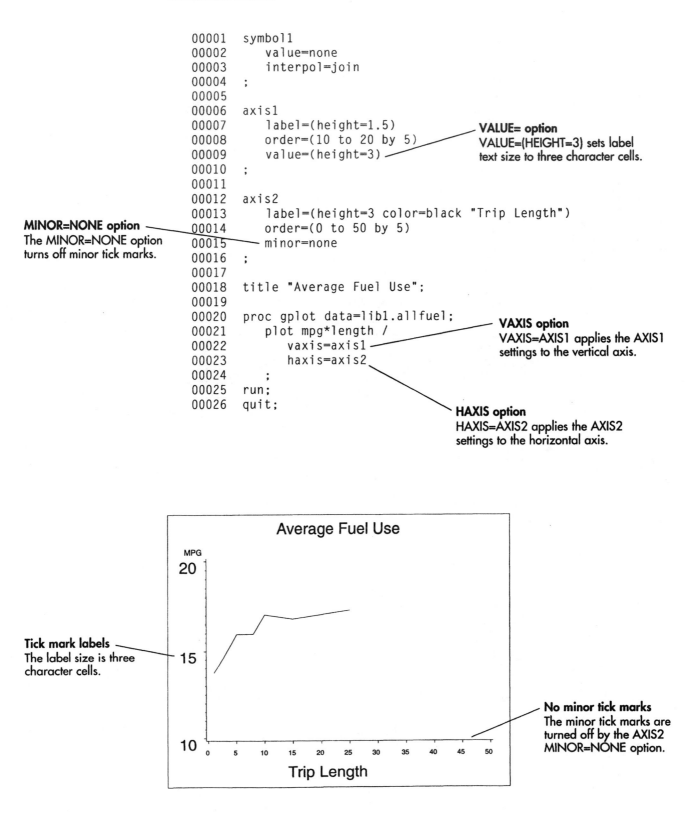

```
00001    symbol1
00002       value=none
00003       interpol=join
00004    ;
00005
00006    axis1
00007       label=(height=1.5)
00008       order=(10 to 20 by 5)
00009       value=(height=3)
00010    ;
00011
00012    axis2
00013       label=(height=3 color=black "Trip Length")
00014       order=(0 to 50 by 5)
00015       minor=none
00016    ;
00017
00018    title "Average Fuel Use";
00019
00020    proc gplot data=lib1.allfuel;
00021       plot mpg*length /
00022          vaxis=axis1
00023          haxis=axis2
00024       ;
00025    run;
00026    quit;
```

VALUE= option
VALUE=(HEIGHT=3) sets label text size to three character cells.

MINOR=NONE option
The MINOR=NONE option turns off minor tick marks.

VAXIS option
VAXIS=AXIS1 applies the AXIS1 settings to the vertical axis.

HAXIS option
HAXIS=AXIS2 applies the AXIS2 settings to the horizontal axis.

Tick mark labels
The label size is three character cells.

No minor tick marks
The minor tick marks are turned off by the AXIS2 MINOR=NONE option.

Changing bar chart axis labels

By default, PROC GCHART uses midpoint values to label bars. When the variable type is character, each unique value becomes a midpoint. For numeric variables, midpoints are calculated by the procedure unless you use the DISCRETE option. You can control the labeling of midpoints with the AXIS statement VALUE= option. The values listed in the VALUE= option label bars on a one-to-one, left-to-right basis. Keep in mind that AXIS statement settings are arbitrary. There is no cross-checking to make sure the bar labels make sense for the charting data. This means you must be familiar with the data before creating the bar labels.

AXIS1 statement
The LABEL= option assigns axis label text.

VALUE= option
The VALUE= option defines a series of three text strings to use as tick mark labels.

```
00001   axis1
00002       label=("Number of Meetings")
00003   ;
00004
00005   axis2
00006       label=(height=1.5 "Department")
00007       value=("Accounting" "Marketing" "Shipping")
00008   ;
00009
00010   title "Count of Meetings By Department";
00011
00012   proc gchart data=lib1.meetings;
00013       hbar dept /
00014           raxis=axis1
00015           maxis=axis2
00016       ;
00017   run;
00018   quit;
```

RAXIS option
RAXIS=HBAR applies the AXIS1 settings to the chart response axis. For horizontal bar charts, the response axis is the horizontal axis.

MAXIS option
MAXIS=HBAR applies the AXIS2 settings to the midpoint axis. For horizontal bar charts the midpoint axis is the vertical axis.

Midpoint tick mark labels
The label text from the AXIS2 statement is applied to the midpoint axis.

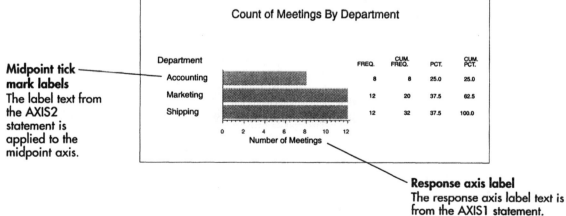

Response axis label
The response axis label text is from the AXIS1 statement.

⬚ More Information

AXIS statement, general reference

Chapter 9, "The AXIS Statement", *SAS/GRAPH Software: Reference, Volume 1, Version 6, First Edition*, pp. 215-258

axis components and terminology, visual reference and discussion

"AXIS Statement Description" in Chapter 9, "The AXIS Statement", *SAS/GRAPH Software: Reference, Volume 1*, pp. 218-220

LABEL= AXIS statement option, reference

"AXIS Statement Options" in Chapter 9, "The AXIS Statement", *SAS/GRAPH Software: Reference, Volume 1*, pp. 221-222

MAJOR= AXIS statement option, reference

"AXIS Statement Options" in Chapter 9, "The AXIS Statement", *SAS/GRAPH Software: Reference, Volume 1*, p. 223

MINOR= AXIS statement option, reference

"AXIS Statement Options" in Chapter 9, "The AXIS Statement", *SAS/GRAPH Software: Reference, Volume 1*, p. 223

ORDER= AXIS statement option, reference

"AXIS Statement Options" in Chapter 9, "The AXIS Statement", *SAS/GRAPH Software: Reference, Volume 1*, pp. 224-226

VALUE= AXIS statement option, reference

"AXIS Statement Options" in Chapter 9, "The AXIS Statement", *SAS/GRAPH Software: Reference, Volume 1*, pp. 227-228

axis text attributes, description and reference

"Text Description Parameters" in Chapter 9, "The AXIS Statement", *SAS/GRAPH Software: Reference, Volume 1*, pp. 228-231

tick mark attributes, description and reference

"Tick Mark Description Parameters" in Chapter 9, "The AXIS Statement", *SAS/GRAPH Software: Reference, Volume 1*, pp. 231-232

MAXIS= VBAR (or HBAR) statement option, reference

"Options" in Chapter 23, "The GCHART Procedure", *SAS/GRAPH Software: Reference, Volume 2*, p. 849, (p. 789 for HBAR)

RAXIS= VBAR (or HBAR) statement option, reference

"Options" in Chapter 23, "The GCHART Procedure", *SAS/GRAPH Software: Reference, Volume 2*, pp. 852-853, (pp. 792-793 for HBAR)

CAXIS= PLOT statement option, reference

"Options" in Chapter 31, "The GPLOT Procedure", *SAS/GRAPH Software: Reference, Volume 2*, p. 1104

HAXIS= PLOT statement option, reference

"Options" in Chapter 31, "The GPLOT Procedure", *SAS/GRAPH Software: Reference, Volume 2*, pp. 1105-1106

HMINOR= PLOT statement option, reference

"Options" in Chapter 31, "The GPLOT Procedure", *SAS/GRAPH Software: Reference, Volume 2*, p. 1106

NOAXES PLOT statement axis control option, reference

"Options" in Chapter 31, "The GPLOT Procedure", *SAS/GRAPH Software: Reference, Volume 2*, p. 1107

VAXIS= PLOT statement option, reference

"Options" in Chapter 31, "The GPLOT Procedure", *SAS/GRAPH Software: Reference, Volume 2*, p. 1107

controlling chart axes, example

"Modifying the Axes" in Chapter 5, "Producing Horizontal Bar Charts", *SAS/GRAPH Software: Usage, Version 6, First Edition*, pp. 56-59

"Modifying the Axes" in Chapter 6, "Producing Vertical Bar Charts", *SAS/GRAPH Software: Usage*, pp. 73-77

controlling plot axes, example

"Modifying the Axes" in Chapter 19, "Introduction to Plots", *SAS/GRAPH Software: Usage*, pp. 246-252

using the AXIS statement, examples

Chapter 51 "Modifying Axes", *SAS/GRAPH Software: Usage*, pp. 681 707

Controlling Legends

Using the LEGEND statement

LEGEND statements do not create legends. Rather, LEGEND statements define a group of legend settings that may be assigned to the legends created by GPLOT, GCHART, GMAP, and other SAS/GRAPH procedures. To use a LEGEND statement, you must first enter LEGEND statement settings; then, assign those settings with an option within a graphics procedure. With the LEGEND statement you can control the legend label, the label for each legend item, the color, the position, all text attributes, and the size of legend symbols.

LEGEND statements are global. This means they are in effect from the point they appear in your program until you explicitly change them or your SAS session ends. There are defaults for all legend settings. If defaults are satisfactory, then LEGEND statements are not necessary.

Several LEGEND statement options are shown in the following examples. Even though the options are used with different procedures, most options can be used in any combination with any procedure.

How to define legends for plots

Plots created with the third-variable plot request in the PLOT statement have a legend describing each line or set of points in the plot. You can apply LEGEND statement settings to this legend with the LEGEND= option in the PLOT statement.

```
00001    symbol1 interpol=join value=diamond
00002       height=1 line=1 color=black;
00003
00004    symbol2 interpol=join value=circle
00005       height=1 line=3 color=black;
00006
00007    symbol3 interpol=join value=dot
00008       height=1 line=5 color=black;
00009
00010    symbol4 interpol=join value=star
00011       height=1 line=8 color=black;
00012
00013    title "Fuel Use and Car Type";
00014
00015    legend1
00016       across=2
00017       value=(height=2 color=gray99)
00018    ;
00019
00020    proc gplot data=lib1.typefuel;
00021       plot mpg*length=type /
00022          legend=legend1
00023       ;
00024    run;
00025    quit;
```

LEGEND statement
The ACROSS=2 option displays a maximum of two columns of legend entries. Additional rows of entries are generated as needed to accommodate all legend symbols. The VALUE= option controls legend value labels. The value text size is set to two character cells and the grayscale color gray99.

LEGEND= option
LEGEND=LEGEND1 applies the LEGEND1 settings to the plot legend.

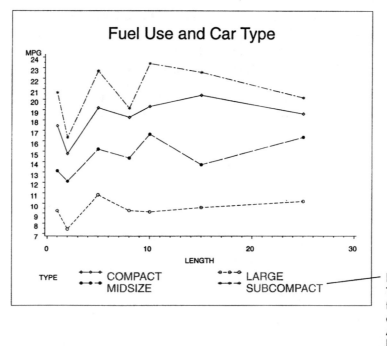

Resulting legend
The plot legend shows two columns of entries, as specified by the ACROSS=2 option. Labels are the size and color specified in the VALUE= option.

Setting legend labels

You can set the legend label with the LABEL= option. The label text itself plus all text attributes can be changed.

```
00001    symbol1 interpol=join value=diamond
00002       height=1 line=1 color=black;
00003
00004    symbol2 interpol=join value=circle
00005       height=1 line=3 color=black;
00006
00007    symbol3 interpol=join value=dot
00008       height=1 line=5 color=black;
00009
00010    symbol4 interpol=join value=star
00011       height=1 line=8 color=black;
00012
00013    title "Fuel Use and Car Type";
00014
00015    legend1
00016       label=(height=2 font=zapfbu "Car Type")
00017       across=2
00018       value=(height=1.5 color=gray99)
00019    ;
00020
00021    proc gplot data=lib1.typefuel;
00022       plot mpg*length=type /
00023          legend=legend1
00024       ;
00025    run;
00026    quit;
```

LEGEND= option
LEGEND=LEGEND1 applies the LEGEND1 statement settings to the plot legend.

LABEL= option
The LABEL= option controls legend label text. Here the label is set to "Car Type" in the ZAPFBU font with a size of two character cells.

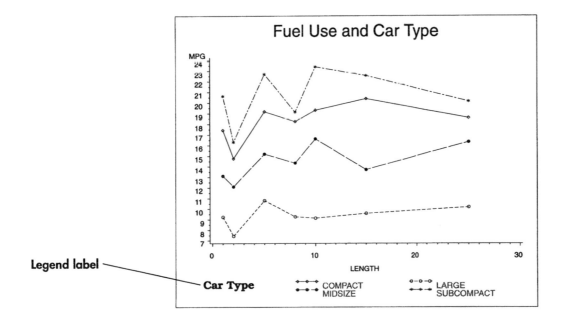

Legend label

Controlling the size of point markers

You can enlarge (or reduce) the size of the plot point markers displayed in the legend. This is often useful to help distinguish the markers, when several sets of points are displayed in a single set of axes. Use the SHAPE=SYMBOL option in the LEGEND statement to control the size of the symbols. The SHAPE=SYMBOL option controls the size of the entire symbol display, not just the size of each point marker. Remember that the SHAPE=SYMBOL option affects the legend only, not points in the plot.

The SYMBOL specification is made up of two values in parentheses. The first is the width of each legend item; the second is the height. Default units are character cells, but you can specify any other valid height unit.

```
00001    symbol1 interpol=join value=diamond
00002        height=1 line=1 color=black;
00003
00004    symbol2 interpol=join value=circle
00005        height=1 line=3 color=black;
00006
00007    legend1
00008        shape=symbol(10,4)
00009    ;
00010    title "Fuel Use and Car Type";
00011
00012    proc gplot data=lib1.typefuel;
00013        where (type="LARGE" or type="COMPACT");
00014
00015        plot mpg*length=type /
00016            legend=legend1
00017        ;
00018    run;
00019    quit;
```

SHAPE= option
The symbol size is set to 10 character cells wide by 4 character cells high.

LEGEND= option
LEGEND=LEGEND1 applies the LEGEND1 statement settings to the plot legend.

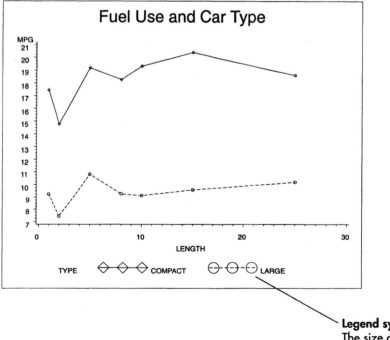

Legend symbol items
The size of each legend item is 10 x 4 character cells.

Defining bar chart legends

LEGEND statement settings can be applied to bar charts generated with the SUBGROUP= option. Subgroup chart legends distinguish each bar segment. Use the VBAR or HBAR LEGEND= option to apply LEGEND statement settings.

In the example below, the SHAPE=BAR option controls the size of each pattern swatch displayed in the legend. Default width and height units, in parentheses, are character cells but you can use other valid units as well. The LABEL= option controls the legend label text. The POSITION= option controls the position of the legend within the graphics display area. See "More Information" for details on using these options for other possible settings.

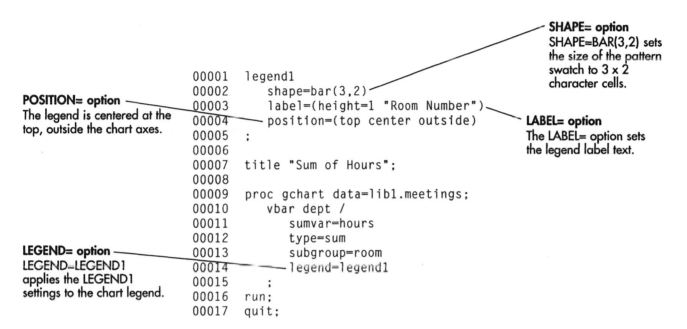

SHAPE= option
SHAPE=BAR(3,2) sets the size of the pattern swatch to 3 x 2 character cells.

POSITION= option
The legend is centered at the top, outside the chart axes.

LABEL= option
The LABEL= option sets the legend label text.

LEGEND= option
LEGEND=LEGEND1 applies the LEGEND1 settings to the chart legend.

```
00001    legend1
00002        shape=bar(3,2)
00003        label=(height=1 "Room Number")
00004        position=(top center outside)
00005    ;
00006
00007    title "Sum of Hours";
00008
00009    proc gchart data=lib1.meetings;
00010        vbar dept /
00011            sumvar=hours
00012            type=sum
00013            subgroup=room
00014            legend=legend1
00015        ;
00016    run;
00017    quit;
```

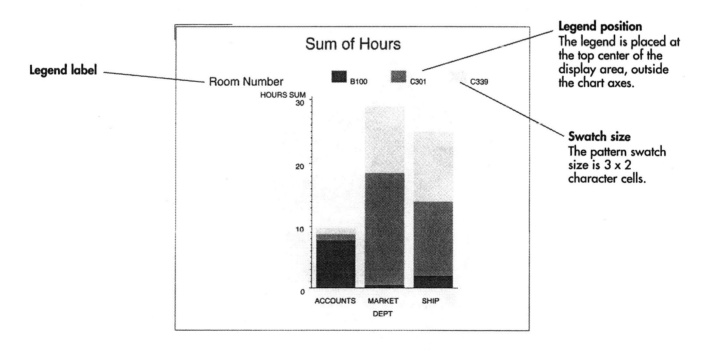

Legend label

Legend position
The legend is placed at the top center of the display area, outside the chart axes.

Swatch size
The pattern swatch size is 3 x 2 character cells.

Defining legends on maps

Map legends describe each fill pattern used in the map. LEGEND statement settings are applied to choropleth map legends with the CHORO statement LEGEND= option.

In the example below, the SHAPE=BAR option is used to set the size of the map pattern swatch displayed in the legend. The numbers in parentheses are the width and height of the swatch. Character cells are the default units, but you can use any other valid units. The FRAME option draws a box around the legend. The VALUE= option sets the labels for each legend item on a one-to-one, left-to-right basis.

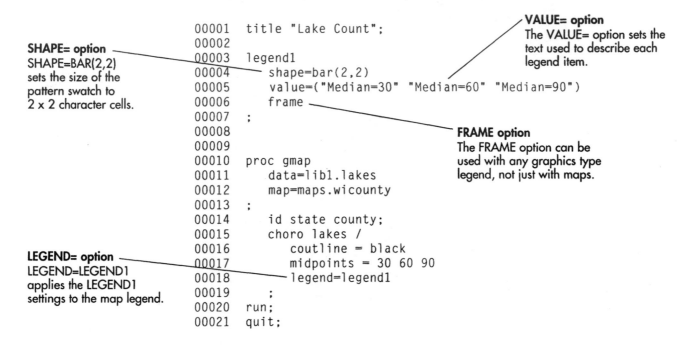

SHAPE= option
SHAPE=BAR(2,2) sets the size of the pattern swatch to 2 x 2 character cells.

VALUE= option
The VALUE= option sets the text used to describe each legend item.

FRAME option
The FRAME option can be used with any graphics type legend, not just with maps.

LEGEND= option
LEGEND=LEGEND1 applies the LEGEND1 settings to the map legend.

```
00001    title "Lake Count";
00002
00003    legend1
00004      shape=bar(2,2)
00005      value=("Median=30" "Median=60" "Median=90")
00006      frame
00007    ;
00008
00009
00010    proc gmap
00011       data=lib1.lakes
00012       map=maps.wicounty
00013    ;
00014       id state county;
00015       choro lakes /
00016          coutline = black
00017          midpoints = 30 60 90
00018          legend=legend1
00019       ;
00020    run;
00021    quit;
```

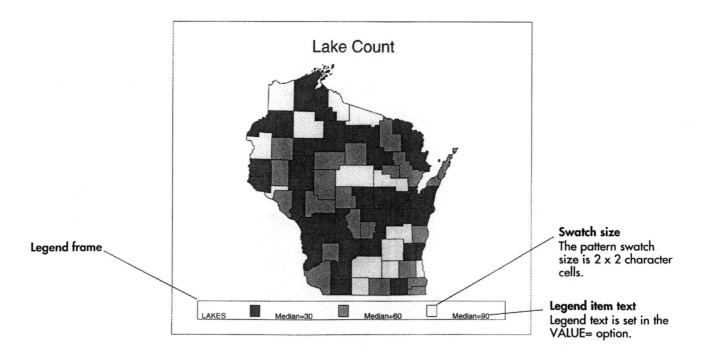

Legend frame

Swatch size
The pattern swatch size is 2 x 2 character cells.

Legend item text
Legend text is set in the VALUE= option.

More Information

LEGEND statement, general reference
>Chapter 13, "The LEGEND Statement", *SAS/GRAPH Software: Reference, Volume 1, Version 6, First Edition*, pp. 303-345

legend components, description and visual reference
>"LEGEND Statement Description" in Chapter 13, "The LEGEND Statement", *SAS/GRAPH Software: Reference, Volume 1*, pp. 306-308

ACROSS= LEGEND statement option, reference
>"LEGEND Statement Options" in Chapter 13, "The LEGEND Statement", *SAS/GRAPH Software: Reference, Volume 1*, p. 309

LABEL= LEGEND statement option, reference
>"LEGEND Statement Options" in Chapter 13, "The LEGEND Statement", *SAS/GRAPH Software: Reference, Volume 1*, p. 309

FRAME LEGEND statement option, reference
>"LEGEND Statement Options" in Chapter 13, "The LEGEND Statement", *SAS/GRAPH Software: Reference, Volume 1*, p. 309

POSITION= LEGEND statement option, reference
>"LEGEND Statement Options" in Chapter 13, "The LEGEND Statement", *SAS/GRAPH Software: Reference, Volume 1*, p. 312

SHAPE= LEGEND statement option, reference
>"LEGEND Statement Options" in Chapter 13, "The LEGEND Statement", *SAS/GRAPH Software: Reference, Volume 1*, pp. 312-313

SYMBOL LEGEND statement option, reference
>"LEGEND Statement Options" in Chapter 13, "The LEGEND Statement", *SAS/GRAPH Software: Reference, Volume 1*, p. 313

legend text control options, sizing unit options
>"Text Description Parameters" in Chapter 13, "The LEGEND Statement", *SAS/GRAPH Software: Reference, Volume 1*, pp. 314-318

LEGEND= option, PROC GCHART, HBAR statement
>"Options" in Chapter 23, "The GCHART Procedure", *SAS/GRAPH Software: Reference, Volume 2*, p. 789 (VBAR p. 849)

LEGEND= option, PROC GMAP, CHORO statement
>"Options" in Chapter 29, "The GMAP Procedure", *SAS/GRAPH Software: Reference, Volume 2*, p. 1033

LEGEND= option, PROC GPLOT, PLOT statement
>"Options" in Chapter 31, "The GPLOT Procedure", *SAS/GRAPH Software: Reference, Volume 2*, p. 1106

using the LEGEND statement with plots, example
>"Modifying a Legend" in Chapter 21, "Producing Plots with Legends", *SAS/GRAPH Software: Usage, Version 6, First Edition*, pp. 288-290

using the LEGEND statement with maps, example
>"Modifying the Legend" in Chapter 28, "Producing Choropleth Maps", *SAS/GRAPH Software: Usage*, pp. 392-393

using the LEGEND statement with SAS/GRAPH procedure, discussion and examples
>Chapter 52, "Modifying Legends", *SAS/GRAPH Software: Usage*, pp. 709-726

Creating Multiple Graphs from a Single Data Set

In This Chapter

- Using BY groups
- How to create multiple graphs with BY groups
- Suppressing the BY line

Using BY groups

SAS/GRAPH procedures allow you to use BY group processing to create multiple graphs from a single input data set. BY groups are groups of observations that share a common value for one or more variables called BY variables. In the examples that follow, REGION is the BY variable. Data sets used for BY group processing must be sorted in BY variable order. You do not have to sort the data set each time you use it. If it is already in the correct order, you can use it without sorting. BY group processing works with all SAS/GRAPH procedures that generate graphics output from a SAS data set.

BY group processing is particularly useful when you are handling large amounts of data. For example, you may want to generate a sales chart for each of the 50 states from a single SAS data set that contains sales data for the entire United States. You can run PROC GCHART with a BY statement to create 50 charts with one procedure step.

How to create multiple graphs with BY groups

In the following example, the data set LIB1.DEER is first sorted by REGION, to ensure that it is in proper order. Next, PROC GCHART with a BY statement creates a chart for each unique value of REGION. Each graph is displayed on a separate page.

PROC SORT step
The SORT procedure sorts the data set LIB1.DEER by the variable REGION. This ensures that the data in LIB1.DEER are in the proper order when REGION is used as the BY variable in the following step.

```
00001   proc sort data=lib1.deer out=plotit;
00002      by region;
00003   run;
00004
00005   title "Deer Type Count";
00006
00007   proc gchart data=plotit;
00008      by region;
00009      vbar type /
00010         sumvar=pop
00011      ;
00012   run;
00013   quit;
```

BY statement
The BY statement requests separate procedure output for each region. All procedure statements and options are in effect for each BY group.

Procedure output
Three charts are generated, one for each unique value of the BY variable REGION. Each chart is on a separate page.

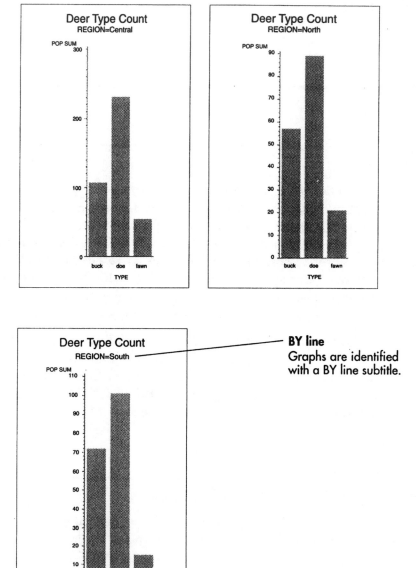

BY line
Graphs are identified with a BY line subtitle.

Suppressing the BY line

To suppress the BY line use the HBY=0 GOPTION to set the height of the BY line to 0. HBY= is one of three BY line attribute graphics options. The others are FBY=, which sets the BY line text font; and CBY=, which sets the BY line text color. HBY= is a global option, meaning it remains in effect until you change it or your SAS session ends.

```
00001   proc sort data=lib1.deer out=plotit;
00002      by region;
00003   run;
00004
00005   goptions hby=0;                          HBY=0 option
00006                                            HBY=0 sets the height of
00007   title "Deer Type Count";                 any BY line text to 0. This
00008                                            suppresses BY line display.
00009   proc gchart data=plotit;
00010      by region;
00011      vbar type /
00012         sumvar=pop
00013      ;
00014   run;
00015   quit;
```

No BY line
The HBY=0 option eliminates the BY line. Compare this chart with the previous example.

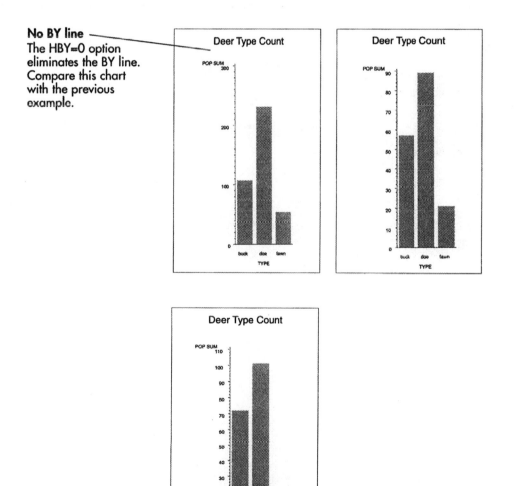

More Information

using the BY statement in SAS/GRAPH procedures, general reference and discussion

Chapter 10, "The BY Statement", *SAS/GRAPH Software: Reference, Volume 1, Version 6, First Edition*, p. 259-269

BY line graphics options, description

"Using Graphics Options" in Chapter 10, "The BY Statement", *SAS/GRAPH Software: Reference, Volume 1*, p. 263

using the BY statement with graphics procedures, examples and discussion

"Example" in Chapter 10, "The BY Statement", *SAS/GRAPH Software: Reference, Volume 1*, pp. 265-268

"Producing Separate Graphs for Groups of Data" in Chapter 47 "Special Techniques for Producing Graphics Output", *SAS/GRAPH Software: Usage, Version 6, First Edition*, pp. 640-648

GOPTIONS statement, general reference

Chapter 12, "The GOPTIONS Statement", *SAS/GRAPH Software: Reference, Volume 1*, pp. 291-302

CBY= option, reference

"CBY" in Chapter 5, "Graphics Options and Device Parameters Dictionary", *SAS/GRAPH Software: Reference, Volume 1*, p. 89

FBY= option, reference

"FBY" in Chapter 5, "Graphics Options and Device Parameters Dictionary", *SAS/GRAPH Software: Reference, Volume 1*, p. 104

HBY= option, reference

"HBY" in Chapter 5, "Graphics Options and Device Parameters Dictionary", *SAS/GRAPH Software: Reference, Volume 1*, p. 121

Saving and Reviewing Graphs

Why save graphs?

You can save graphics procedure output in a SAS catalog. These saved graphs can be displayed or "replayed" without re-creating the graph from the original data. This is useful when re-creating the graph would require costly computer resources or the original data are no longer available. Saved graphs can also be used to create presentations or publications.

How to save graphs in a SAS catalog

To save graphs, use the GOUT= option in any SAS/GRAPH procedure that generates graphics output. Output is saved in the SAS catalog named in the GOUT= option. In the following example, graphs are saved in the catalog named LIB1.MYGRAFS.

To store graphs in a permanent SAS catalog, you must first create or have write access to a permanent SAS library and establish a libref referring to that library. As with SAS data sets, permanent SAS catalogs have a two-level name made up of the libref (LIB1) and the member name (MYGRAFS.) Levels are separated by a period. SAS graphics catalogs can contain one or more entries. Each entry is a stored graph.

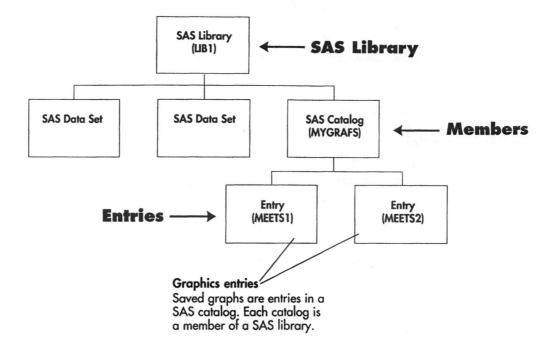

Graphics entries
Saved graphs are entries in a
SAS catalog. Each catalog is
a member of a SAS library.

In the following example, two pie charts are generated. The first chart is displayed on the screen *and* stored as an entry in the LIB1.MYGRAFS catalog. The entry name is MEETS1. The next chart is stored in LIB1.MYGRAFS under the entry name MEETS2. This second chart is not displayed because the NODISPLAY option is set, before the second PROC GCHART step is run. You can use the DEVICE= and DISPLAY/NODISPLAY options in any combination, depending on whether or not you want to preview the graphs stored in the GOUT= catalog.

 The GREPLAY procedure has many functions not covered in this chapter. PROC GREPLAY can create templates that allow you to display and position multiple graphs on a page. There are other features that help you manage graphics entries. See "More Information" PROC GREPLAY references.

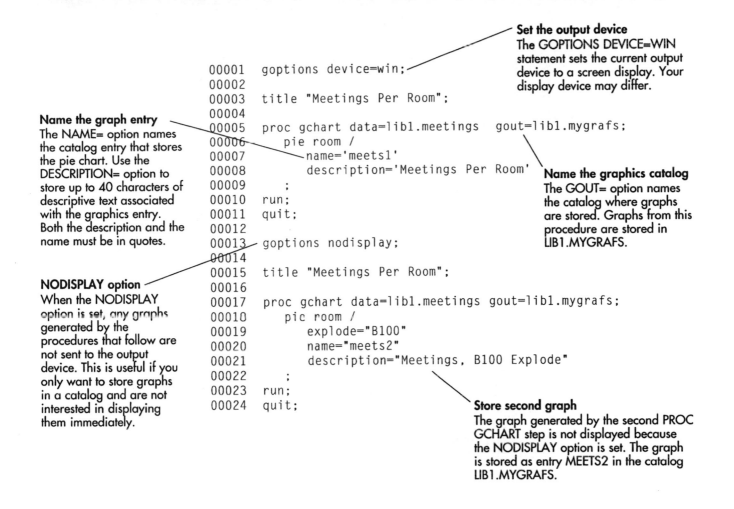

Set the output device
The GOPTIONS DEVICE=WIN statement sets the current output device to a screen display. Your display device may differ.

Name the graph entry
The NAME= option names the catalog entry that stores the pie chart. Use the DESCRIPTION= option to store up to 40 characters of descriptive text associated with the graphics entry. Both the description and the name must be in quotes.

NODISPLAY option
When the NODISPLAY option is set, any graphs generated by the procedures that follow are not sent to the output device. This is useful if you only want to store graphs in a catalog and are not interested in displaying them immediately.

Name the graphics catalog
The GOUT= option names the catalog where graphs are stored. Graphs from this procedure are stored in LIB1.MYGRAFS.

Store second graph
The graph generated by the second PROC GCHART step is not displayed because the NODISPLAY option is set. The graph is stored as entry MEETS2 in the catalog LIB1.MYGRAFS.

```
00001    goptions device=win;
00002
00003    title "Meetings Per Room";
00004
00005    proc gchart data=lib1.meetings  gout=lib1.mygrafs;
00006       pie room /
00007          name='meets1'
00008          description='Meetings Per Room'
00009       ;
00010    run;
00011    quit;
00012
00013    goptions nodisplay;
00014
00015    title "Meetings Per Room";
00016
00017    proc gchart data=lib1.meetings gout=lib1.mygrafs;
00018       pic room /
00019          explode="B100"
00020          name="meets2"
00021          description="Meetings, B100 Explode"
00022       ;
00023    run;
00024    quit;
```

Given the names used in this example, you can check the graphics catalog entries from the SAS Display Manager System as follows: Use the LIB command to display the current libraries in the LIBNAME window. To view a list of the entries, select the LIB1 library, then select the MYGRAFS catalog in the DIR window. See "Listing cataloged graphs" below, for an example of how to list graphics entries in batch mode.

LIBNAME window
Select the LIB1 library to see a directory of members.

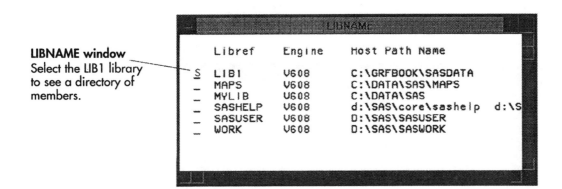

```
Libref: LIBI
Type: ALL

       SAS File   Memtype    Indexed

  _    ALLFUEL    DATA
  _    ALLFUEL1   DATA
  _    CARCOUNT   DATA
  _    DATA1      DATA
  _    DATA2      DATA
  _    DATA3      DATA
  _    DATA4      DATA
  _    DATA5      DATA
  _    DEER       DATA
  _    FUEL       DATA
  _    FUEL2      DATA
  _    JOBREV     DATA
  _    JOBSITES   DATA
  _    LAKES      DATA
  _    MEETING1   DATA
  _    MEETINGS   DATA
  _    MONTHLY    DATA
  S    MYGRAFS    CATALOG
  _    REVENUES   DATA
  _    SALESQ1    DATA
  _    SALESREP   DATA
  _    TYPEFUEL   DATA
  _    TYPEFUL1   DATA
  _    UTILITY    DATA
  _    UTILYEAR   DATA
  _    VEHICLES   DATA
```

Member list
Select the MYGRAFS
catalog to view a list
of entries.

CATALOG window
MEETS1 and MEETS2
are listed as GRSEG
entries. GRSEG entries
are saved graphs.

```
Libref: LIBI
Catalog: MYGRAFS

     Name      Type      Description

  L  MEETS1    GRSEG     Meetings Per Room
  _  MEETS2    GRSEG     Meetings, B100 Explode
```

Description text
The description text
is set with the
DESCRIPTION=
option. See program
lines 8 and 21.

Replaying cataloged graphs

Stored graphs can be replayed at any time. Replaying means sending the graph to an output device. The device can be your screen or any supported hard-copy device. You can select a different device for each replay.

To select graphs for replay, use PROC GREPLAY from the display manager:

Replaying graphs in interactive mode
When you run PROC GREPLAY in interactive mode, the GREPLAY window is displayed.

```
00001    proc greplay igout=libl.mygrafs;
00002    run;
00003    quit;
```

PROC GREPLAY with IGOUT= option
Name the catalog you want to work with in the IGOUT= option.

GREPLAY window
The GREPLAY window lists graphics entries. To replay an entry, enter "s" in the Sel field.

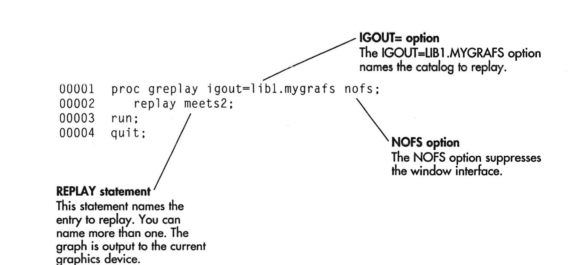

Current device
You can change the output device by typing over the name in the Device field. Here the output device is set to HPLJS3.

To replay a graph in batch mode, use PROC GREPLAY with a REPLAY statement. The NOFS option suppresses the PROC GREPLAY interactive windows.

Replaying graphs in batch mode
When you replay graphs in batch mode, they are sent directly to the current output device.

IGOUT= option
The IGOUT=LIB1.MYGRAFS option names the catalog to replay.

```
00001    proc greplay igout=libl.mygrafs nofs;
00002        replay meets2;
00003    run;
00004    quit;
```

NOFS option
The NOFS option suppresses the window interface.

REPLAY statement
This statement names the entry to replay. You can name more than one. The graph is output to the current graphics device.

Listing cataloged graphs

To generate a list of cataloged graphs in batch mode use PROC GREPLAY with the LIST IGOUT statement. The list is sent to the SAS log. The NOFS option suppresses the window interface.

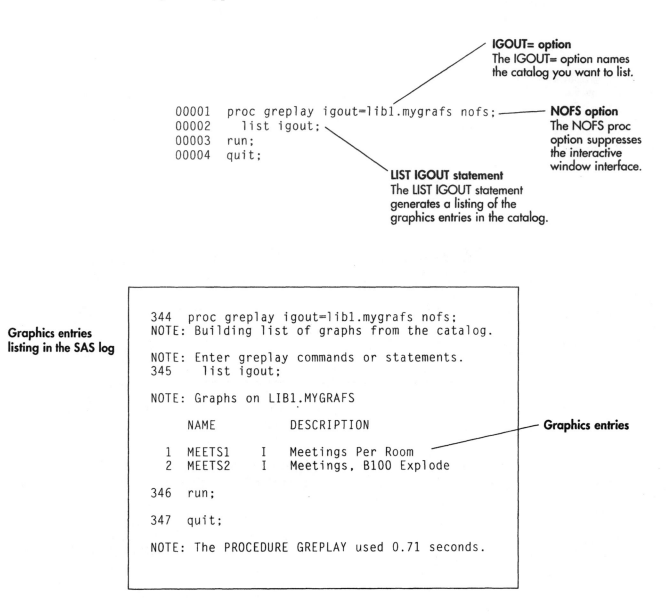

IGOUT= option
The IGOUT= option names the catalog you want to list.

NOFS option
The NOFS proc option suppresses the interactive window interface.

LIST IGOUT statement
The LIST IGOUT statement generates a listing of the graphics entries in the catalog.

```
00001   proc greplay igout=lib1.mygrafs nofs;
00002     list igout;
00003   run;
00004   quit;
```

Graphics entries listing in the SAS log

```
344   proc greplay igout=lib1.mygrafs nofs;
NOTE: Building list of graphs from the catalog.

NOTE: Enter greplay commands or statements.
345     list igout;

NOTE: Graphs on LIB1.MYGRAFS

        NAME            DESCRIPTION

    1   MEETS1      I   Meetings Per Room
    2   MEETS2      I   Meetings, B100 Explode

346  run;

347  quit;

NOTE: The PROCEDURE GREPLAY used 0.71 seconds.
```

Graphics entries

More Information

PROC GREPLAY, general reference

Chapter 36, "The GREPLAY Procedure", *SAS/GRAPH Software: Reference, Volume 2, Version 6, First Edition*, pp. 1191-1257

IGOUT= option, reference

"Options" in Chapter 36, "The GREPLAY Procedure", *SAS/GRAPH Software: Reference, Volume 2*, p. 1201

NOFS option, reference

"Options" in Chapter 36, "The GREPLAY Procedure", *SAS/GRAPH Software: Reference, Volume 2*, p. 1201

LIST statement, reference

"LIST" in Chapter 36, "The GREPLAY Procedure", *SAS/GRAPH Software: Reference, Volume 2*, pp. 1211-1212

REPLAY statement, reference

"REPLAY" in Chapter 36, "The GREPLAY Procedure", *SAS/GRAPH Software: Reference, Volume 2*, p. 1215

PROC GREPLAY window interface, discussion and command reference

"GREPLAY Procedure Windows" in Chapter 36, "The GREPLAY Procedure", *SAS/GRAPH Software: Reference, Volume 2*, pp. 1231-1245

PROC GREPLAY window interface, usage examples

"Using the GREPLAY Procedure Windows" in Chapter 36, "The GREPLAY Procedure", *SAS/GRAPH Software: Reference, Volume 2*, pp. 1245-1257

replaying saved graphs from the GREPLAY window, example

"Listing the Catalog Entries Containing Graphics Output" and "Replaying the Entries in the List" in Chapter 36, "The GREPLAY Procedure", *SAS/GRAPH Software: Reference, Volume 2*, pp. 1246-1247

NAME= PIE statement option (usage is the same in all graphics output procedures)

"Options" in Chapter 23, "The GCHART Procedure", *SAS/GRAPH Software: Reference, Volume 2*, p. 815

DESCRIPTION= PIE statement option (usage is the same in all graphics output procedures)

"Options" in Chapter 23, "The GCHART Procedure", *SAS/GRAPH Software: Reference, Volume 2*, p. 813

GOUT PROC GCHART proc statement option (usage is the same in all graphics output procedures)

"PROC GCHART Statement" in Chapter 23, "The GCHART Procedure", *SAS/GRAPH Software: Reference, Volume 2*, p. 767

sending graphics output to catalogs, discussion

"Catalog Output" in Chapter 3, "Graphics Output", *SAS/GRAPH Software: Reference, Volume 1*, pp. 61-65

DISPLAY graphics option, reference

"DISPLAY" in Chapter 5, "Graphics Options and Device Parameters Dictionary", *SAS/GRAPH Software: Reference, Volume 1*, p. 102

GOUTTYPE= graphics option, reference

"GOUTTYPE" in Chapter 5, "Graphics Options and Device Parameters Dictionary", *SAS/GRAPH Software: Reference, Volume 1*, p. 113

SAS catalogs, discussion

"SAS Catalogs" in Chapter 6, "SAS Files", *SAS Language: Reference, Version 6, First Edition*, p. 206-207

using graphics catalogs and PROC GREPLAY, window interface, discussion and examples

Chapter 45, "Reviewing Graphics and Managing Catalogs in a Windowing Environment", *SAS/GRAPH Software: Usage, Version 6, First Edition*, pp. 607-624

using graphics catalogs and PROC GREPLAY, batch interface, discussion and examples

Chapter 46, "Reviewing Graphics and Managing Catalogs in a Line-Mode Environment", *SAS/GRAPH Software: Usage, Version 6, First Edition*, pp. 625-636

Data Used in Examples

In This Chapter

- **LIB1.ALLFUEL**
- **LIB1.DEER**
- **LIB1.FUEL2**
- **LIB1.JOBREV**
- **LIB1.JOBSITES**
- **LIB1.LAKES**
- **LIB1.MEETINGS**
- **LIB1.MONTHLY**
- **LIB1.REVENUES**
- **LIB1.SALESQ1**
- **LIB1.SALESREP**
- **LIB1.TYPEFUEL**
- **LIB1.UTILITY**
- **LIB1.UTILYEAR**

LIB1.ALLFUEL

```
                    LIB1.ALLFUEL

        OBS     LENGTH     TOTAL      MPG

         1         1      0.08035    13.7487
         2         2      0.15603    14.2366
         3         5      0.34026    15.9502
         4         8      0.54998    15.9710
         5        10      0.64835    17.0327
         6        15      0.99652    16.8029
         7        25      1.59152    17.2900
```

LIB1.DEER

```
                    LIB1.DEER

     OBS    REGION      TYPE      POP

      1     North       buck       57
      2     North       doe        89
      3     North       fawn       21
      4     Central     buck      107
      5     Central     doe       231
      6     Central     fawn       54
      7     South       buck       72
      8     South       doe       101
      9     South       fawn       15
```

LIB1.FUEL2

```
                  LIB1.FUEL2

     OBS    SUBCOM      LARGE     LENGTH

      1    20.6352     9.2401        1
      2    16.3122     7.4282        2
      3    22.6963    10.8119        5
      4    19.1297     9.2644        8
      5    23.3921     9.1327       10
      6    22.5562     9.5771       15
      7    20.1433    10.1883       25
```

LIB1.JOBREV

```
                    LIB1.JOBREV

       OBS    STATE      REVENUES

        1      55      456403.66
        2      56       30605.71
        3      36      678889.72
        4       6      385398.77
        5      38       31030.22
        6      16       81181.69
        7      12      121911.87
        8      29      183142.11
        9      15       10643.04
       10       2       20874.58
       11       1      101325.51
       12      13      141819.66
       13      48       61358.05
       14       4       10198.75
       15      35       10900.19
       16      41       20981.68
       17      53       10731.77
       18      30       10176.05
```

LIB1.JOBSITES

```
                   LIB1.JOBSITES

          OBS    STATEZIP    SITES    STATE

           1       WI         45       55
           2       WY          3       56
           3       NY         67       36
           4       CA         38        6
           5       ND          3       38
           6       ID          8       16
           7       FL         12       12
           8       MO         18       29
           9       HI          1       15
          10       AK          2        2
          11       AL         10        1
          12       GA         14       13
          13       TX          6       48
          14       AZ          1        4
          15       NM          1       35
          16       OR          2       41
          17       WA          1       53
          18       MT          1       30
```

LIB1.LAKES

```
                   LIB1.LAKES

          OBS    STATE    COUNTY    LAKES

           1      55        1        51
           2      55        3        17
           3      55        5        68
           4      55        7         6
           5      55        9        15
           6      55       11        46
           7      55       13        33
           8      55       15        33
           9      55       17        28
          10      55       19        68
          11      55       21         1
          12      55       23         9
          13      55       25        80
          14      55       27        84
          15      55       29        71
          16      55       31        96
          17      55       33        48
          18      55       35         7
          19      55       37        30
          20      55       39        90
          21      55       41        72
          22      55       43        48
          23      55       45        91
          24      55       47        38
          25      55       49        42
          26      55       51        83
          27      55       53        72
          28      55       55        81
          29      55       57         8
          30      55       59        58
          31      55       61        37
```

(continued on next page)

```
32        55        63        17
33        55        65         2
34        55        67        38
35        55        69        52
36        55        71        34
37        55        73        76
38        55        75         7
39        55        77        74
40        55        78        63
41        55        79        77
42        55        81        14
43        55        83        58
44        55        85         2
45        55        87        27
46        55        89        21
47        55        91        94
48        55        93         0
49        55        95        77
50        55        97        40
51        55        99        30
52        55       101        60
53        55       103        48
54        55       105        61
55        55       107         4
56        55       109         3
57        55       111        10
58        55       113        85
59        55       115        86
60        55       117        52
61        55       119        65
62        55       121        44
63        55       123        42
64        55       125        80
65        55       127        12
66        55       129        25
67        55       131        11
68        55       133        57
69        55       135        26
70        55       137        20
71        55       139        27
72        55       141        56
```

LIB1.MEETINGS

LIB1.MEETINGS

OBS	DATE	DEPT	ROOM	HOURS
1	10JAN95	ACCOUNTS	C339	1.00
2	24JAN95	ACCOUNTS	B100	0.50
3	30JAN95	SHIP	C339	2.00
4	24FEB95	MARKET	C301	3.50
5	28FEB95	SHIP	C339	4.00
6	01MAR95	MARKET	C301	4.00
7	03MAR95	ACCOUNTS	B100	3.50
8	08MAR95	ACCOUNTS	B100	0.50
9	21MAR95	ACCOUNTS	B100	0.25
10	27MAR95	SHIP	C301	1.50
11	29MAR95	ACCOUNTS	C301	0.50
12	12APR95	SHIP	C339	0.50
13	25APR95	MARKET	C301	1.50
14	02MAY95	MARKET	B100	0.50
15	12MAY95	SHIP	C301	2.50
16	25MAY95	MARKET	C301	3.50

(continued on next page)

```
17   01JUN95   SHIP       C301   2.00
18   07JUN95   SHIP       C339   3.00
19   14JUN95   SHIP       C301   2.00
20   12JUL95   MARKET     C339   0.50
21   03AUG95   ACCOUNTS   B100   3.00
22   14AUG95   SHIP       C301   2.50
23   28AUG95   SHIP       C339   1.50
24   15SEP95   MARKET     C339   3.00
25   28SEP95   ACCOUNTS   C301   0.50
26   11OCT95   MARKET     C301   3.00
27   01NOV95   SHIP       C301   1.50
28   15NOV95   MARKET     C339   1.00
29   21NOV95   SHIP       B100   2.00
30   22NOV95   MARKET     C339   3.50
31   05DEC95   MARKET     C339   2.50
32   21DEC95   MARKET     C301   2.50
```

LIB1.MONTHLY

```
                    LIB1.MONTHLY

         OBS       DATE       SALES

          1     01/01/95     145830
          2     02/10/95     168930
          3     03/05/95     150922
          4     04/16/95     170082
          5     05/02/95     179500
          6     06/03/95     150040
          7     07/07/95     180090
          8     08/09/95     175035
          9     09/02/95     140010
         10     10/16/95     168500
         11     11/02/95     159950
         12     12/06/95     190010
```

LIB1.REVENUES

```
                  LIB1.REVENUES

       OBS      DATE     REGION    REVENUE

        1     01/01/95    West      10391
        2     01/01/95    East      19045
        3     02/01/95    West      12750
        4     02/01/95    East      25905
        5     03/01/95    West      15755
        6     03/01/95    East      27900
        7     04/01/95    West      16995
        8     04/01/95    East      21000
        9     05/01/95    West      12225
       10     05/01/95    East      23565
       11     06/01/95    West      17890
       12     06/01/95    East      30560
```

LIB1.SALESQ1

```
                LIB1.SALESQ1

        OBS    MONTH    AMOUNT

         1      JAN       823
         2      JAN      1093
         3      JAN       971
         4      JAN      1121
         5      FEB       623
         6      FEB      1200
         7      MAR       789
         8      MAR       450
         9      MAR      1301
        10      MAR       808
        11      MAR       950
```

LIB1.SALESREP

```
                LIB1.SALESREP

        OBS    NAME       STATE

         1     Collins       1
         2     Collins       5
         3     Collins      13
         4     Collins      28
         5     Collins      37
         6     Collins      45
         7     Collins      29
         8     Plotnik       2
         9     Plotnik      53
        10     Plotnik      41
        11     Plotnik      16
        12     Arno         56
        13     Arno          8
        14     Arno         30
        15     Arno         38
        16     Arno         46
```

LIB1.TYPEFUEL

```
                     LIB1.TYPEFUEL

    OBS    TYPE          LENGTH    TOTAL      MPG

     1     SUBCOMPACT       1     0.04846   20.6352
     2     SUBCOMPACT       2     0.12261   16.3122
     3     SUBCOMPACT       5     0.22030   22.6963
     4     SUBCOMPACT       8     0.41820   19.1297
     5     SUBCOMPACT      10     0.42750   23.3921
     6     SUBCOMPACT      15     0.66500   22.5562
     7     SUBCOMPACT      25     1.24111   20.1433
     8     COMPACT          1     0.05733   17.4432
     9     COMPACT          2     0.13546   14.7641
    10     COMPACT          5     0.26073   19.1771
    11     COMPACT          8     0.43838   18.2490
```

(continued on next page)

```
12   COMPACT      10    0.51789   19.3090
13   COMPACT      15    0.73605   20.3790
14   COMPACT      25    1.34418   18.5986
15   MIDSIZE       1    0.07625   13.1145
16   MIDSIZE       2    0.16520   12.1067
17   MIDSIZE       5    0.32908   15.1936
18   MIDSIZE       8    0.55777   14.3429
19   MIDSIZE      10    0.60147   16.6259
20   MIDSIZE      15    1.09434   13.7068
21   MIDSIZE      25    1.53006   16.3392
22   LARGE         1    0.10822    9.2401
23   LARGE         2    0.26925    7.4282
24   LARGE         5    0.46245   10.8119
25   LARGE         8    0.86352    9.2644
26   LARGE        10    1.09496    9.1327
27   LARGE        15    1.56623    9.5771
28   LARGE        25    2.45379   10.1883
```

LIB1.UTILITY

```
                        LIB1.UTILITY

OBS    QUARTER    EBGAS    EBELEC    WBGAS    WBELEC

 1      QTR1      1433      780      2052      1148
 2      QTR2      1555      821      2239      1246
 3      QTR3      1051      682      1789      1017
 4      QTR4       850      652      1154       908
```

LIB1.UTILYEAR

```
                      LIB1.UTILYEAR

OBS    YEAR     GAS     ELEC    TELE

 1     1990     5600    1250    2450
 2     1991     6250     950    3000
 3     1992     6100    1025    3400
 4     1993     6450    1175    3800
 5     1994     6575    1350    4200
 6     1995     6500    1425    4350
 7     1996     6450    1425    4775
 8     1997     6525    1500    5500
 9     1998     6600    1700    6550
10     1999     6750    1725    7500
```

Index

A

ACROSS= option
  controlling page layout for pie charts
      199–200
  displaying legends, example 248
  displaying multiple pie charts 199–200
ADMGDF graphics option 41
ALL option, GMAP procedure
  displaying empty map areas, examples 167,
      168
  forcing empty map areas to display 174
ANGLE= option
  changing location of first pie slice 208
  changing text orientation 222–223
  setting description and examples, table 220
area fill plots 139–142
  filling under multiple lines 140–141
  filling under single line 139–140
area plot, cumulative 143–147
  creating 144–146
  sample data set 144
AREAS= option, PLOT statement
  cumulative area plot, example 145
  filling area under multiple lines 140–141
  filling area under single line 139–140
ARROW value, pie slice labels
  arrow leaders and INSIDE location value
      196
  problems when using with OUTSIDE
      location 196
  specifying in SLICE=, VALUE=, and
      PERCENT= options 193
ASCENDING option, HBAR/VBAR statements
  displaying bars in order of length 77
  GAXIS= option not used with 78
ASPECT= graphics option 42
asterisk (*)
  representing comments in program code 18
  separating y and x variables in PLOT
      statement 110
AUTOCOPY graphics option 42
AUTOFEED graphics option 42
AUTOHREF option 149–150
AUTOVREF option 149–150
averages 57–58
  charting with TYPE=MEAN and SUMVAR=
      options 57
  showing means within groups 58
axes
  See also AXIS statement
  adding second axis 127–129
  controlling axes on plots and charts
      239–245
  drawing reference lines for plots, example
      150
  horizontal axis variable, illustration 110
  left and right plot axes, illustration 128
  placing date on plot axis 233–234
  setting origin to zero 151–152
  vertical axis variable, illustration 110
axis
  See axes
axis labels
  changing bar chart axis labels 243
  cumulative area plot, example 146
  defining axis label text 239–240
  grouped bar chart, example 51
  multiple plots on single set of axes,
      example 37
  response axis label, illustration 243
AXIS statement
  applying definitions to axes 233–234
  common text options, table 220
  controlling font, color, and size 219
  defining axis label text 239–240
  global nature 239
  purpose and use 239

B

bar charts
  See also bar fill patterns
  See also bar order
  averages, charting 57–59
  axes, controlling 239–245
  axis labels, changing 243
  bar fill patterns, controlling 99–106
  bar spacing, changing 83–84
  bar width, changing 81–82
  counts, charting 47–52
  data structure 28–30
  data structure, example 28
  default bar width 81, 82
  defining legends 251
  displaying statistics 67–72
  formatted dates 235–236
  numeric variables, charting 87–93
  order of bars, changing 73–79
  percentages, charting 61–66
  space between bar groups, controlling 84–85
  statistics displayed by default 47, 67
  sums, charting 53–56
  value ranges in charts 95–98
  variables for bar charts, table 30
bar fill patterns 99–106
  controlling pattern assignments 101–102
  controlling with PATTERN statement 99
  default patterns 100
  overriding default patterns 101
bar order 73–79
  changing 73–79
  controlling for character variables 74
  controlling for numeric variables 75

bar order *(continued)*
  default order 73
  displaying bars by length 77
  MIDPOINTS= option 74–76
  order of bar groups 78
  ORDER= option 76
BAUD= graphics option 42
block maps 163
BORDER graphics option 42
BOX= option, FOOTNOTE statement 221
boxes
  drawing around footnotes 221
  drawing around legends 252
BY groups
  assigning patterns to BY groups 104
  creating multiple graphs 255–256
  purpose and use 255
BY line, suppressing 257
BY statement, example 256
BY variables 255

C

CATALOG= option 24
CATALOG window 262
catalogs
  controlling with graphics options 41
  displaying cataloged graphs 262–263
  listing cataloged graphs 264
  replaying cataloged graphs 263
  saving graphs in catalogs 259–262
  saving modified driver in alternate catalog 24–25
  two-level names 259
CAXIS= option, table 152
CBACK= graphics option 41
CBY= graphics option 41, 257
CELL graphics option 42
CFRAME= option 150–151
CFREQ option, table 69
character cells
  units for SPACE= option 83
  units for WIDTH= option 82
  variation in size depending on value of options 84
character variables
  controlling bar order 74
  creating value ranges 97
  mapping 167
CHARACTERS graphics option 41, 42
chart legends
  See legends
chart variables
  bar chart, example 28
  determining default bar order 73
  location in data set, example 29
  pie chart, example 29
  using in bar charts, table 30
  using in pie charts, table 30
charts
  See bar charts
  See pie charts
CHARTYPE= graphics option 41, 42

CHORO statement
  DISCRETE option 166, 171
  specifying choropleth map, example 164, 167
  specifying map variable, example 168
  specifying response variable, example 32
choropleth maps 163
CHREF= option, table 152
CIRCLEARC graphics option 42
classification variable
  See also z variable
  location in code, example 34
  representation in plots, illustration 33
  using in plots, table 34
CO= option, SYMBOL statement 125
COLOR= option
  assigning color to axis labels, example 240
  controlling color in titles and footnotes 219
  description and examples, table 220
COLOR= option, PATTERN statement
  combining pie slice color and fill, example 214
  preventing unexpected results 177
  specifying map color 177–180
  specifying pie slice color 211–215
COLOR= option, SYMBOL statement
  changing plot symbol color 112
  effect on second axis 127–128, 130
  omitting from symbol definitions 112
colors
  assigning color to axis labels, example 240
  changing plot symbol color 112
  confidence limit line color 125
  controlling in pattern sequences 179, 214
  controlling with graphics options 41
  filling plot frames 150–151
  forcing use of single color in patterns 100
  map colors, changing 179
  map fill patterns, controlling 177–178
  omitting specification in patterns 102
  outline color for maps 164
  outlining pie slices 204
  pie chart fill colors, controlling 213–214
  plot appearance options, table 152
  specifying pie slice color, example 211, 213
  title and footnote colors, controlling 219
COLORS= graphics option 41, 42
  controlling colors in pattern sequences 179, 214
COMMA format 227
confidence limits, adding to regression plots 125
CONTENTS procedure 31
COPY statement, example 24, 25
counts 47–52
  charting 47–52
  comparing data groups side-by-side 51
  default for bar charts 47
  default for pie charts 185
  numeric variables 48
  showing percentage in bar chart 61
  showing subgroup contributions to total count 50
  weighting observations 49

COUTLINE= option
   outlining maps, example   164
   outlining pie slices   204
CPATTERN= graphics option   41
   controlling colors in pattern sequences   179, 214
   default behavior   100
   forcing use of single color   100
CPERCENT option, table   69
CSYMBOL= graphics option   41
CTEXT= graphics option   41
   controlling statistic text appearance   71
CTEXT= option, table   152
CTITLE= graphics option   41
cumulative area plot, creating   143–147
CVREF= option, table   152

D

DASH graphics option   42
DATA= option
   specifying data set for map, example   164
   specifying data set for plot, example   110
data set examples
   See SAS data set examples
DATA step
   creating data set for cumulative area plot   145–146
   restructuring data for graphs   35–36
   with FREQ= variable   62
data structure   27–37
   bar and pie charts   28–30
   examples   27
   maps   31–32, 157–158
   plots   33–34
   restructuring for cumulative area plot   145–146
   restructuring for graphs   35–36
dates   233–237
   controlling date format   234–235
   displaying with plots and charts   233–237
   formatted dates in charts   235–236
   placing on plot axis   233–234
   SAS date constants   233
DATE7. format   233
decimal places
   controlling   227–228
   dropping from format   230
   specifying with formats, example   228
dependent variable
   See y variable
DESCENDING option, HBAR/VBAR statements
   displaying bars by length   77
   GAXIS= option not used with   78
DESCRIPTION= option, catalog entries   261, 262
DEVADDR= graphics option   41
device drivers
   See display device drivers
   See output device drivers
DEVICE= graphics option   42
   combining with DISPLAY or NODISPLAY options   260

naming output device   14
previewing hardcopy output   17–18
saving graphs in catalogs   261
specifying default driver for previewing hardcopy   18–19
specifying graphics output device driver   23
DEVMAP= graphics option   42
DIAMOND symbol   116
DIR window   262
DISCRETE option, CHORO statement
   mapping formatted values, example   171
   overriding midpoints   166
DISCRETE option, HBAR/VBAR statements
   charting all values of numeric variables   89–90
   charting formatted values of dates, example   236
   charting formatted values of numeric variables   95–96
DISCRETE option, PIE statement   189
display device drivers
   checking with GTESTIT procedure   10
   using default driver for previewing hardcopy   18–19
DISPLAY graphics option   41
   combining with DEVICE= option   260
display manager
   See SAS Display Manager System
DOLLAR format   71, 229
DOT symbol   111
DOWN= option
   controlling page layout for pie charts   200–201
   displaying multiple pie charts on one page   199

E

EXPLODE= option, PIE statement   203

F

FBY= graphics option   41, 257
Federal Information Processing Standards (FIPS) codes
   See FIPS codes
fill color for pie charts
   combining with fill patterns   214
   varying   213
FILL graphics option   42
fill patterns, controlling
   bars   99–106
   maps   177–178
   pie charts   211–214
FILLINC= graphics option   42
filling area under lines
   See area fill plots
FIPS codes
   identifying states in map data sets   31
   using for ID variable   157
   using for ID variable, illustration   167

FONT= option
  compared with FTITLE= graphics option
    40
  controlling fonts in titles and footnotes 219
  description and examples, table 220
  overriding FTEXT= graphics option,
    example 71
fonts
  See also text
  controlling in titles and footnotes 219
  controlling with graphics options 41
FOOTNOTE statement
  adding footnotes 221
  common text options, table 220
  controlling font, color, and size 219
footnotes
  adding 221–222
  changing orientation 222–224
  changing text within a line 224–225
  controlling font, color, and size 219–220
  drawing box around, example 221
format labels
  creating for numeric variables 95–96
  maps 171
  maximum length 96
FORMAT procedure
  creating character value ranges in charts 97
  creating numeric value ranges in charts
    95–96
  creating value ranges for maps 171
FORMAT statement
  applying date format 233
  applying DOLLAR format in bar chart 71
  charting formatted values of character
    variables 97
  charting formatted values of numeric
    variables 95–96
  controlling date format 234–235
  mapping formatted values 171–172
  specifying formats, example 227
formats
  COMMA format 227
  components, example 228
  controlling date format 234–235
  DATE7. 233
  DOLLAR format 71, 229–230
  formatted dates in charts 235–236
  PERCENT format 227
  purpose and use 228
  QTR1. date format 236
  WORDDATE3. format 234
frame for plots, filling with color 150–151
FRAME option
  definition, table 152
  drawing box around legend 252
FREQ= option, HBAR/VBAR statements
  combining with TYPE=PERCENT option 62
  compared with WEIGHT statement 63
  confusion between TYPE=FREQ and
    FREQ= options 50
  showing percentage of sum 62
  weighting observations for bar charts 49
FREQ statistic option, table 69
FREQ= variable, use in DATA step 62

frequency
  See counts
FTEXT= graphics option 41
  controlling statistic text appearance 71
  overriding with FONT= option 71
  overriding with TITLE statement options 71
FTITLE= graphics option 41
  compared with FONT= option 40

G

GACCESS= graphics option 41, 42
GAXIS= option
  applying tick mark definitions to group axis
    78
  not allowed with DESCENDING,
    ASCENDING, and NOZERO options 78
GCHART procedure
  creating pie charts 185
  truncation of format labels 96
GCLASS= graphics option 41
GCOPIES= graphics option 42
GDDMCOPY= graphics option 41
GDDMNICKNAME= graphics option 41
GDDMTOKEN= graphics option 41
GDEST= graphics option 41
GDEVICE procedure 22
GDEVICE window 22–23
GDEVICE0 library 25
GEND= graphics option 42
GEPILOG= graphics option 42
GFORMS= graphics option 41
GFSPROMPT graphics option 42
global graphics options 40
GMAP procedure 31, 157
GOPTIONS statement
  changing default settings of graphics
    options 41
  commenting and uncommenting when
    previewing graphics 18
  listing of graphics options 41
  naming graphics output device driver 23
  overriding graphics output device driver
    settings 24
GOUT= option 259, 261
GOUTMODE= graphics option 41
GPLOT procedure
  creating plots, example 34
  PLOT statement 110–111
  use of symbol definitions 112
GPROJECT procedure 159–160
GPROLOG= graphics option 42
GPROTOCOL= graphics option 41
GRAPH windows 11
graphics catalogs
  See catalogs
graphics device drivers
  See display device drivers
  See output device drivers
graphics display 9–12
  See also hardcopy devices
  See also hardcopy, previewing
  checking display device driver 10
  controlling with graphics options 41, 42

using GRAPH windows 11
using with SAS/GRAPH software 9
graphics hardcopy devices
See hardcopy devices
graphics options 39–43
See also statement options
compared with SAS system options 39
effect on device drivers 14
global status 39
how to use 40
list of options grouped by category 41–42
listing current settings 40
resetting to default values 40
when to use global vs. statement options 40
graphics stream files, controlling with graphics
options 42
GRAPHRC graphics option 41
graphs
See also bar charts
See also pie charts
See also plots
creating multiple graphs with BY group
processing 255–258
listing cataloged graphs 264
replaying 263
saving 259–262
GREPLAY procedure
displaying multiple graphs 200
features 260
listing cataloged graphs 264
replaying cataloged graphs 263
GREPLAY window 263
GRID option, table 152
GROUP= option, HBAR/VBAR statements
avoiding cluttered chart 61
bar chart, example 28
comparing data groups side-by-side 51
controlling order of bar groups 78
controlling space between bar groups 84–85
grouped percentage bars, showing 63
means within groups, showing 58
percentage within data groups, showing 64
sums with groups charted side-by-side,
showing 55
GROUP= option, PIE statement
creating multiple pie charts 199–200
pie chart, example 29
group variables
bar chart, example 28
location in data set, example 29
pie chart, example 29
using in bar charts, table 30
using in pie charts, table 30
GSFLEN= graphics option 42
GSFMODE= graphics option 42
GSFNAME= graphics option 42
GSPACE= graphics option 84–85
GSTART= graphics option 42
GTESTIT procedure
checking display device drivers 10
testing hardcopy devices 14
GUNIT= graphics option 42
GWAIT= graphics option 41
GWINDOW option 11
GWRITER= graphics option 41

G100 option, HBAR/VBAR statements 64

H

HANDSHAKE= graphics option 42
hardcopy, previewing 17–19
commenting and uncommenting GOPTIONS
statement 18
reasons for previewing 17
sending final output to output device 18
specifying default display device 18–19
target-device emulation imperfections 17
TARGETDEVICE= option for previewing
17–18
hardcopy devices 13–15
See also graphics display
See also output device drivers
checklist for choosing 15
controlling with graphics options 42
how graphics device drivers work 13
testing with GTESTIT procedure 14
HAXIS= option
applying axis settings 239–240
applying tick marks to horizontal axis 233
controlling tick mark labels and minor tick
marks, example 242
defining tick marks, example 241
HBAR statement
See also bar charts
See also VBAR statement
charting averages, example 57
horizontal bar chart, example 67
slash (/) separating statement options 53
specifying chart variable, example 47
HBY= graphics option 41
suppressing BY line 257
HEIGHT= option
controlling text size in titles and footnotes
219
overriding HTEXT= graphics option,
example 71
specifying size of plot symbol 111
unit, setting description, and examples,
table 220
units of height 219, 221
units of height, table 220
HELP DEVICES command 14
HMINOR= option, table 152
HORIGIN= graphics option 42
horizontal axis variable, illustration 110
horizontal bar charts
See also bar charts
statistics displayed by default 47, 67
turning off all statistics 69
HPOS= graphics option 42
effect on character cells 84
HREF= option, table 152
HSIZE= graphics option 42
incorporating in modified device driver 25
overriding output device driver settings 24
HTEXT= graphics option 41
controlling statistic text appearance 71
overriding with HEIGHT= option 71
overriding with TITLE statement options 71

HTITLE= graphics option   41
HZERO option   151

I

ID statement, example   32, 164
ID variables
    controlling shape of maps   157
    location in data set, example   32
    matching in response and map data sets
        157, 158–159
    required by GMAP procedure   31
    specifying in ID statement, example   32
    U.S. map, example   .31
    using with GMAP procedure, table   32
IGOUT= option   263
independent variable
    See x variable
INSIDE value, pie slice labels   193, 196
INTERPOL= graphics option   42
    adding confidence limits to regression plots
        125
    using with LINE= option   119
interpolations, statistical   123
INTERPOL=JOIN option
    area fill plots, example   139
    connecting data points   115–116
    cumulative area plot, example   145
INTERPOL=R option   124
INTERPOL=RCCLM90 option   125
INTERPOL=SPLINE option   123–124
INVISIBLE= option, PIE statement   205

K

KEEP statement, example   145
KEYMAP= graphics option   41

L

LABEL= option, AXIS statement
    cumulative area plot, example   145
    defining axis label text   239–240
    defining axis label text, example   243
LABEL= option, LEGEND statement
    controlling legend label text   251
    setting legend labels   249
labels
    See also axis labels
    See also pie slice labels
    midpoint label   89, 186
    setting legend labels   249
LEGEND= option
    CHORO statement   252
    HBAR statement   251
    VBAR statement   251
LEGEND= option, PLOT statement
    applying customized legends   128, 136
    area fill plots, example   141
    controlling size of point markers   250
    cumulative area plot, example   145
    defining legends for plots   248

LEGEND option, PLOT statement
    generating legend for plot with two axes
        128–129
    identifying multiple overlay plots   136–137
LEGEND statement
    area fill plots, example   141
    common text options, table   220
    controlling font, color, and size   219
    creating customized legends   128
    cumulative area plot, example   145
    global nature   247
    purpose and use   247
legends   247–253
    chart legends generated by SUBGROUP=
        option   50
    chart legends generated by SUBGROUP=
        option, example   54
    controlling   247–253
    creating for plot with two axes   128–129
    cumulative area plot, example   146
    default legend for area fill plots, example
        140
    defining for bar charts   251
    defining for maps   252
    defining for plots   248
    generated with third-variable plot request,
        illustration   135
    identifying multiple overlay plots   136–137
    maps, example   164–167
    setting legend labels   249
    size of point markers, controlling   250
    suppressing for empty map, example   168
LEVELS= option
    HBAR statement   90–91
    PIE statement   187
    VBAR statement   90–91
LEVELS= option, CHORO statement
    specifying fill patterns for maps, example
        168, 178, 180
    specifying number of midpoints for maps
        166
LFACTOR= graphics option   42
LHREF= option   149
LIBNAME window   261
librefs
    MAPS libref for standard map library   160
    specifying for alternate graphics catalog   24
LINE= option, SYMBOL statements   119
line plots, creating   115–121
    adding data points   116
    changing line thickness   120
    changing line type   119
    connecting data points   115
    fixing zigzag line problem   117–118
    smoothing plot lines   123–126
    sorting data before plotting   117–118
    suppressing plot points   115
line types available for plots, illustration   119
LIST IGOUT statement   264
LIST statement, GDEVICE procedure   22
LVREF= option   149

M

mainframe computer graphics options 41
map data sets 157–161
　MAPS libref for standard map library 160
　matching variables in response data
　　158–159
　projecting data sets 159–160
　specifying, example 32
　structure 157–158
MAP= option, example 164
maps 157–181
　assigning empty pattern 179
　changing colors 179
　controlling fill patterns 177–178
　creating 163–170
　creating empty maps 168
　data structure 31–32
　default handling of empty areas 173–175
　default pattern selection 180
　defining legends 252
　formatting value ranges 171–172
　mapping character variables 167
　mapping numeric data 163–164
　specifying midpoints 165
　specifying number of midpoints 166
　types of maps 163
　user-defined pattern selection 180
　variables for maps, table 32
MATCHCOLOR option, PIE statement 206
MAXIS= option, HBAR/VBAR statements 76
MAXIS=HBAR option, AXIS statement 243
MEAN option
　definition, table 69
　requesting statistic for vertical bar chart,
　　example 70
mean statistic
　bar chart, example 57
　displaying as summary statistic 68
means
　charting with TYPE=MEAN and SUMVAR=
　　options 57
　showing with groups 58
midpoint label
　default numeric midpoints, illustration 89
　pie charts, illustration 186
midpoints
　confusing tick mark specifications with
　　midpoint specifications 76
　controlling labeling with VALUE= option
　　243
　default handling of numeric variables 87–89
　default value on pie charts, illustration 186
　overriding in CHORO statement 166
　representing count in bar charts 48
midpoints, specifying
　exploded pie slices 203
　maps 165, 166
　number of midpoint levels for bars 90–91
　pie charts 188
　values for midpoints 91–92
MIDPOINTS= option, CHORO statement 165
MIDPOINTS= option, HBAR/VBAR
　　statements
　confusing with ORDER= option 76

　controlling bar order for character
　　variables 74
　controlling bar order for numeric variables
　　75
　listing character variables in desired order,
　　example 74
　specifying values for midpoints 91–92
　specifying values for numeric variables,
　　example 75
MIDPOINTS= option, PIE statement
　controlling slice order 209
　specifying midpoints for pie charts 188
MINOR=NONE option, AXIS statement 242
MODIFY statement
　modifying graphics output device driver 24
MOVE= option, NOTE statement 224
multiple graphs, creating with BY group
　　processing 255–258
multiple pie charts per page
　controlling page layout 200–201
　creating 199–200
multiple sets of points, plotting 133–138
　area fill plot considerations 140
　controlling number of plots 135
　third variable for generating multiple plots
　　133–134
　using multiple plot requests and overlays
　　136–137

N

NAME= option, naming catalog entries 261
NEXTSCR command 22
NOAXES option 152
　AXIS statement 239
NODISPLAY option 260, 261
NOFS option 263, 264
NOGWINDOW option 11
NOHEADING option, PIE statement 207
NOLEGEND option 168
NOLOG option 41
NONE value, pie slice labels 193, 195
NOSTATS option 69
NOTE statement
　common text options, table 220
　controlling appearance of text 224
　controlling font, color, and size 219
notes
　See footnotes
NOZERO option 78
null TITLE statement 168
numeric variables 87–93
　bar charts 87–93
　charting all values 89–90
　charting counts by midpoint 48
　controlling bar order 74
　controlling number of pie slices 187
　creating value ranges 95–96
　default handling in bar charts 87–89
　mapping 163–164
　pie charts 186
　showing actual value in pie slices 189

numeric variables *(continued)*
    specifying midpoint values 91–92
    specifying number of midpoint levels 90–91

O

observations, restructuring for graphs 35
OFFSHADOW= graphics option 42
options
    See graphics options
    See SAS system options
    See statement options
OPTIONS statement 11
order of bars
    See bar order
ORDER= option, AXIS statement
    assigning dates to tick marks, example 233
    confusing with MIDPOINTS= option 76
output device drivers 21–26
    controlling with graphics options 42
    effect of graphics options 14
    getting more information 22–23
    how device drivers work 13, 21
    listing available device drivers 22
    modifying and saving in alternate catalog
        24–25
    naming in SAS programs 23
    overriding driver settings 24–25
OUTSIDE value, pie slice labels
    controlling placement 193
    problems when using with ARROW value
        196
OVERLAY option, PLOT statement
    generating legend for plot with two axes
        128–129
    placing plots on same set of axes 136–137

P

PAPERFEED= graphics option 42
PAPERLIMIT= graphics option 42
PATTERN statement
    area fill plots, example 139, 141
    changing order of pattern application 102
    color for maps, changing 179
    controlling bar patterns 99
    controlling pattern assignments 101–102
    creating empty map, example 168
    cumulative area plot, example 145
    default pattern selection for maps 180
    default patterns 100
    defining pattern sequences 179, 214
    empty pattern for maps, assigning 179
    global nature 99, 177
    limit for pattern settings 99
    map fill patterns, controlling 177–178
    maps, example 164–167
    omitting color specification 102
    overriding default bar patterns 101
    overriding pie chart default colors and fills
        211
    syntax, example 99, 177, 211
    user-defined pattern selection for maps 180

PATTERNID=BY option 104
PATTERNID=GROUP option 105
PATTERNID=MIDPOINT option 103
patterns
    See also PATTERN statement
    assigning empty pattern to maps 179
    assigning to bar groups 105
    assigning to BY groups 104
    controlling bar fill patterns 99–106
    controlling map fill patterns 177–178
    default pattern selection for maps 180
    resetting 100
    user-defined pattern selection for maps 180
PCLIP graphics option 41
PENMOUNTS= graphics option 42
PENSORT graphics option 42
PERCENT format 227
PERCENT= option, PIE statement 190,
    193–194
PERCENT option, table 69
percentage display, pie charts
    displaying only percentage values 195
    illustration 194
    specifying with PERCENT= option 190,
        193–194
percentages, charting 61–66
    grouped bars for showing percentages 63
    percentage of count 61
    percentage of sum 62
    percentage within each data group 64
    subgroup percentage with segmented bars
        65
PERCENT=ARROW option, PIE statement
    196
pie charts
    See also pie slices
    combining colors and fills 214
    controlling appearance 203–210
    controlling fill patterns 211
    creating 185–191
    data structure 28–30
    data structure, example 29
    multiple charts per page, creating 200–201
    numeric variables, charting 186
    selecting colors and fills 211–215
    specifying specific midpoints 188
    turning off chart type heading 207
    variables for pie charts, table 30
    varying fill color 213
    varying fill patterns 212
pie slice labels 193–197
    arrow leaders and INSIDE location value
        196
    creating 193–197
    default display, illustration 194
    illustration 185, 187
    matching text and slice color 206
    percentage display, illustration 194
    percentage values 195
    placement values for labels 193–194
    specifying value to display 193–194
    text obscured with inside display location
        196
pie slices
    adding exploded slices 203–204

changing location of first slice 208
controlling order of slices 209
controlling with numeric variables 187
default value, illustration 185
invisible slices 205
matching text and slice color 206
outlining slices 204
representing sums 190
showing all slices with numeric variable
  189
value, illustration 187–190
PIE statement
creating pie charts, example 185
specifying chart variable, example 29
PIEFILL graphics option 42
plot lines, smoothing 123–126
plot points, suppressing 115
PLOT statement, GPLOT procedure
creating legends for plots with two axes
  128 129
creating scatter plots 110–111
filling area under plot line 139–141
naming plotting variables 110
plot symbols
applying to two axes 128–129
available symbols, illustration 116
changing colors 112
changing symbol for plot lines 119
controlling size of point markers 250
controlling with SYMBOL statements 111
default symbol, illustration 110
DIAMOND 116
DOT 111
specifying in quotes 116
using any printable character for symbols
  111
plots
appearance options 149–153
appearance options, table 152
controlling axes on plots and charts
  239–245
cumulative area plot 143–147
data structure 33–34
defining legends 248
defining tick marks 241
drawing reference lines 149–150
filling area under lines 139–142
filling plot frame with color 150–151
line plots 115–121
multiple sets of points, plotting 133–138
regression lines, plotting 124
scatter plots 109–113
setting axes origin to zero 151–152
smoothing plot lines 123–126
PLOT2 statement 127–129
points, plotting multiple sets
See multiple sets of points, plotting
POLYGONCLIP graphics option 42
POLYGONFILL graphics option 42
POSITION= option, LEGEND statement 251
previewing hardcopy
See hardcopy, previewing
PRINT command 11
prism maps 163
projected map, illustration 160

PROMPT graphics option 42
PROMPTCHARS= graphics option 42

Q

QTR1. date format 236
quotation marks (") 116

R

ranges of values
See value ranges
RAXIS=HBAR option, AXIS statement 243
reference lines on plots, drawing 149–150
regression plots
adding confidence limits 125
plotting regression lines 124
REPLAY statement 263
replaying saved graphs
See GREPLAY procedure
RESET=ALL option 41
RESET=PATTERN option 100
response data set
matching ID variable in map data set 157
required by GMAP procedure 31, 157
specifying, example 32
structure, example 32
response variable 31
location in data set, example 32
specifying in CHORO statement, example 32
U.S. map, example 31
using with GMAP procedure, table 32
ROTATE= graphics option 42
changing text orientation 222–224
setting description and examples, table 220

S

SAS catalogs
See catalogs
SAS data set examples
LIB1.ALLFUEL 109, 267
LIB1.ALLFUEL1 117
LIB1.DEER 256, 268
LIB1.FUEL2 136, 268
LIB1.JOBREV 268
LIB1.JOBSITES 269
LIB1.LAKES 163, 269–270
LIB1.MEETINGS 88, 270–271
LIB1.MONTHLY 235, 271
LIB1.REVENUES 271
LIB1.SALESQ1 272
LIB1.SALESREP 167, 272
LIB1.TYPEFUEL 133, 272–273
LIB1.UTILITY 273
LIB1.UTILYEAR 144, 273
MAPS.COUNTIES 158
MAPS.US 158
PLOTIT 146
SAS data sets
See also data structure

SAS data sets *(continued)*
   creating multiple graphs from single data set 255–258
   map data sets 157–161
   sorting data before plotting 117–118
SAS date constants 233
SAS Display Manager System
   displaying saved graphs in catalogs 261–262
   getting information on device drivers 22–23
   GRAPH windows 11
SAS/GRAPH software
   checklist for requirements 7
   components 2
   graphics display requirements 9
   relation to SAS System 5
   requirements for running 6
SAS system options
   compared with graphics options 39
SASHELP.DEVICES catalog
   access protection 25
   storing modified device driver 25
scatter plots, creating 109–113
   changing color of plot symbol 112
   changing plot symbol 111
   default settings 109–110
second axis
   adding with PLOT2 statement 127–128
   identifying each plot with legends 128–129
   right axis, illustration 128
   SYMBOL2 statement ignored if COLOR= option omitted 130
shape of graphs, controlling with graphics options 42
SHAPE= option, LEGEND statement 141
SHAPE=BAR option, LEGEND statement
   bar chart legends 251
   map legends 252
SHAPE=SYMBOL option, LEGEND statement 250
SIMFONT= graphics option 41, 42
size of graphs, controlling with graphics options 42
slash (/)
   HBAR statement 53, 57
   PIE statement 187, 194
   PLOT statement 137
   VBAR statement 53, 57
SLICE= option, PIE statement 193
SLICE=INSIDE option, PIE statement 196
smoothing plot lines
   See plot lines, smoothing
SORT procedure, example 118
space between bar groups, controlling 84–85
SPACE= option, HBAR/VBAR statements 83–84
spacing of bars, changing 81–86
SPEED= graphics option 42
statement options
   See also graphics options
   slash (/) separating statement options 53, 57, 137, 187, 194
   when to use global vs. statement options 40
statistical interpolations 123
statistics 67–72
   controlling appearance of text 71

   default in horizontal bar charts 67
   default in horizontal bar charts, illustration 47
   default statistics, illustration 67
   displaying in bar charts 67–72
   displaying on vertical bar charts 70
   displaying summary statistic 68
   height of bar not related to statistic value 70
   requesting specific statistics 68–69
   statistic request options 69
   turning off all horizontal bar chart statistics 69
structure of data
   See data structure
SUBGROUP= option, HBAR/VBAR statements
   assigning patterns to each subgroup segment 101
   bar chart, example 28
   showing subgroup bar segments, example 54
   showing subgroup contribution to total count 50
   showing subgroup percentages with segmented bars, example 65
   using with TYPE=MEAN option 58
subgroup variables
   bar chart, example 28
   location in data set, example 29
   using in bar charts, table 30
   using in pie charts, table 30
subgroups
   See also SUBGROUP= option, HBAR/VBAR statements
   contribution to total count in bar charts 50
   showing bar segments for sums 54
   showing subgroup percentages with segmented bars 65
SUM option, table 69
summary statistic, displaying in bar charts 68
summary variables
   bar chart, example 28
   location in data set, example 29
   pie chart, example 28
   using in bar charts, table 30
   using in pie charts, table 30
sums 53–56
   See also SUMVAR= option, HBAR/VBAR statements
   charting 53–56
   contribution of subgroup bar segments to sum 54
   representing in pie slices 190
   showing in bar groups 55
   showing percentage in bar chart 62
   using TYPE=SUM and SUMVAR= options 53–54
SUMVAR= option, HBAR/VBAR statements
   bar chart, example 28
   charting averages 57
   charting sums, example 53
   displaying summary statistic 68
   pie chart, example 29
   showing means within groups, example 58

showing subgroup bar segments, example 54

showing sums with groups charted side-by-side 55

when to use with statistic request options, table 69

SUMVAR= option, PIE statement

representing sums in pie slices 190

using with TYPE=MEAN option 190

surface maps 163

SWAP graphics option 41, 42

SYMBOL graphics option 42

SYMBOL statement

See also INTERPOL= graphics option

applying plot symbols to two axes 128-129

area fill plots, example 139, 141

changing line type 119

changing plot line thickness 120

changing plot symbols 111

COLOR= option in plots with two axes 127-128, 130

controlling display of data points 115

controlling size of point markers 250

cumulative area plot, example 145

effect of omitting COLOR= option 112, 130

multiple plots in single set of axes, example 134, 135, 137

omitting plot points 115

use of symbol definitions by GPLOT procedure 112

symbols

See also plot symbols

See also SYMBOL statement

available symbols, illustration 116

defining with VALUE= and COLOR= options 112

DIAMOND 116

DOT 111

specifying in quotes 116

using any printable character for 111

T

TARGETDEVICE= graphics option 41, 42

global status 18

previewing hardcopy output 17-18

resetting to null 18

text

See also fonts

changing orientation 222-224

changing text within a line 224-225

controlling font, color, and size in titles and footnotes 219-220

controlling statistic text appearance 71

defining axis label text 239-240

matching pie slice text and color 206

third-variable plot requests

See also z variable

area fill plot considerations 140

controlling number of plots generated 135

cumulative area plot, example 145

generating multiple plots in single set of axes, example 134

multiple plot requests and OVERLAY option 136-137

tick marks

assigning dates to tick marks, example 233

confusing tick mark and midpoint specifications 76

controlling tick mark labels and minor tick marks 242

defining for plots 241

drawing reference lines at major tick marks 149-150

TITLE statement

adding titles 221

common text options, table 220

controlling font, color, and size 219

null TITLE statement 168

number of title lines allowed 221

overriding FTEXT= and HTEXT= option settings, example 71

titles

adding 221-222

changing orientation 222-224

changing text within a line 224-225

controlling font, color, and size 219-220

TRANTAB= graphics option 41

TYPE= option

HBAR statement 70

PIE statement 190

VBAR statement 70

TYPE=FREQ option, HBAR/VBAR statements

confusion with FREQ= option 50

specifying frequency chart, example 49

TYPE=MEAN option, HBAR/VBAR statements

charting averages 57

displaying summary statistic 68

showing means within groups, example 58

using with SUBGROUP= option 58

TYPE=MEAN option, PIE statement

using with SUMVAR= option 90

TYPE=PERCENT option, HBAR/VBAR statements

combining with FREQ= option 62

showing percentage of count 61

showing percentage of sum 62

showing percentages with grouped bars 63

showing percentages within data groups, example 64

showing subgroup percentages with segmented bars, example 65

TYPE=SUM option, HBAR/VBAR statements

charting sums, example 53

default when TYPE= option used with SUMVAR option 53

showing subgroup bar segments, example 54

showing sums with groups charted side-by-side 55

U

unprojected map, illustration 159

V

VALUE= option, AXIS statement
  controlling tick mark labels and minor tick
    marks 242
  labeling of midpoints 243
VALUE= option, LEGEND statement
  controlling legend value labels, example 248
  cumulative area plot, example 145
  specifying text for legend items, example
    252
VALUE= option, PATTERN statement
  setting map fill pattern, example 177
  setting pie slice fill pattern, example 211,
    212
VALUE= option, PIE statement 193
VALUE= option, SYMBOL statement
  always using for symbol definitions 112
  specifying plot symbols 111, 116
value ranges 95–98
  character charting variables 97
  creating with FORMAT procedure 95
  maps 171–172
  numeric charting variables 95–96
VALUE=EMPTY option, PATTERN statement
  179
VALUE=NONE option, SYMBOL statement
  115
VALUE=SOLID option, PATTERN statement
  179
VAXIS= option
  applying axis settings 239–240
  controlling tick mark labels and minor tick
    marks, example 242
  cumulative area plot, example 145
  defining tick marks, example 241
  multiple plots on single set of axes,
    example 137
VBAR statement
  See also bar charts
  See also HBAR statement
  naming chart variable, example 28
  requesting statistics, example 70
  showing percentage of count, example 61
  slash (/) separating statement options 53
  specifying numeric variable 48
  SUMVAR= option, example 53
  TYPE=SUM option, example 53
vertical axis variable, illustration 110
vertical bar charts
  See also bar charts
  displaying statistics 70
VMINOR= option 152
  AXIS statement 239
VORIGIN= graphics option 42
VPOS= graphics option 42
  effect on character cells 84
VREF= option, table 152
VREVERSE option, table 152
VSIZE= graphics option 42
VZERO option 151–152

V5COMP graphics option 42

W

WEIGHT statement, compared with FREQ=
  option 63
weighted frequency, example 49
WHERE statement
  controlling number of plots generated using
    third variable 135
  selecting observations for area fill plots 139
  subsetting map data set, example 160
width
  bar width, changing 81–82
  plot line width, changing 120
  specifying in formats, example 228
WIDTH= option, HBAR/VBAR statements
  changing bar width 81–82
  character cells used as units 82
WIDTH= option, SYMBOL statement 120
WORDDATE3. format 234

X

x variable
  location in code, example 34
  represented on horizontal axis, illustration
    33
  using in PLOT statement 110
  using in plots, table 34
XTICKNUM= option, AXIS statement 239

Y

y variable
  location in code, example 34
  represented on vertical axis, illustration 33
  using in PLOT statement 110
  using in plots, table 34

Z

z variable
  area fill plot considerations 140
  controlling number of plots generated 135
  generating multiple plots in single set of axes
    133–134
zero, setting axes origin to 151–152

Special Characters

" (quotation marks) 116
/ (slash)
  See slash (/)
* (asterisk)
  See asterisk (*)

Books Available from SAS Press

Advanced Log-Linear Models Using SAS®
by **Daniel Zelterman**

Analysis of Clinical Trials Using SAS®: A Practical Guide
by **Alex Dmitrienko, Geert Molenberghs, Walter Offen,** and **Christy Chuang-Stein**

Annotate: Simply the Basics
by **Art Carpenter**

Applied Multivariate Statistics with SAS® Software, Second Edition
by **Ravindra Khattree**
and **Dayanand N. Naik**

Applied Statistics and the SAS® Programming Language, Fourth Edition
by **Ronald P. Cody**
and **Jeffrey K. Smith**

An Array of Challenges — Test Your SAS® Skills
by **Robert Virgile**

Carpenter's Complete Guide to the SAS® Macro Language, Second Edition
by **Art Carpenter**

The Cartoon Guide to Statistics
by **Larry Gonick**
and **Woollcott Smith**

Categorical Data Analysis Using the SAS® System, Second Edition
by **Maura E. Stokes, Charles S. Davis,**
and **Gary G. Koch**

Cody's Data Cleaning Techniques Using SAS® Software
by **Ron Cody**

Common Statistical Methods for Clinical Research with SAS® Examples, Second Edition
by **Glenn A. Walker**

Debugging SAS® Programs: A Handbook of Tools and Techniques
by **Michele M. Burlew**

Efficiency: Improving the Performance of Your SAS® Applications
by **Robert Virgile**

The Essential PROC SQL Handbook for SAS® Users
by **Katherine Prairie**

Fixed Effects Regression Methods for Longitudinal Data Using SAS®
by **Paul D. Allison**

Genetic Analysis of Complex Traits Using SAS®
Edited by **Arnold M. Saxton**

A Handbook of Statistical Analyses Using SAS®, Second Edition
by **B.S. Everitt**
and **G. Der**

Health Care Data and SAS®
by **Marge Scerbo, Craig Dickstein,**
and **Alan Wilson**

The How-To Book for SAS/GRAPH® Software
by **Thomas Miron**

In the Know ... SAS® Tips and Techniques From Around the Globe
by **Phil Mason**

Instant ODS: Style Templates for the Output Delivery System
by **Bernadette Johnson**

Integrating Results through Meta-Analytic Review Using SAS® Software
by **Morgan C. Wang**
and **Brad J. Bushman**

Learning SAS® in the Computer Lab, Second Edition
by **Rebecca J. Elliott**

The Little SAS® Book: A Primer
by **Lora D. Delwiche**
and **Susan J. Slaughter**

The Little SAS® Book: A Primer, Second Edition
by **Lora D. Delwiche**
and **Susan J. Slaughter**
(updated to include Version 7 features)

The Little SAS® Book: A Primer, Third Edition
by **Lora D. Delwiche**
and **Susan J. Slaughter**
(updated to include SAS 9.1 features)

Logistic Regression Using the SAS® System: Theory and Application
by **Paul D. Allison**

Longitudinal Data and SAS®: A Programmer's Guide
by **Ron Cody**

Maps Made Easy Using SAS®
by **Mike Zdeb**

Models for Discrete Data
by **Daniel Zelterman**

Multiple Comparisons and Multiple Tests Using SAS®
Text and Workbook Set
(books in this set also sold separately)
by **Peter H. Westfall, Randall D. Tobias,
Dror Rom, Russell D. Wolfinger,**
and **Yosef Hochberg**

Multiple-Plot Displays: Simplified with Macros
by **Perry Watts**

Multivariate Data Reduction and Discrimination with
SAS® Software
by **Ravindra Khattree**
and **Dayanand N. Naik**

Output Delivery System: The Basics
by **Lauren E. Haworth**

Painless Windows: A Handbook for SAS® Users, Third Edition
by **Jodie Gilmore**
(updated to include Version 8 and SAS 9.1 features)

The Power of PROC FORMAT
by **Jonas V. Bilenas**

PROC TABULATE by Example
by **Lauren E. Haworth**

Professional SAS® Programming Shortcuts
by **Rick Aster**

Quick Results with SAS/GRAPH® Software
by **Arthur L. Carpenter**
and **Charles E. Shipp**

Quick Results with the Output Delivery System
by **Sunil K. Gupta**

Quick Start to Data Analysis with SAS®
by **Frank C. Dilorio**
and **Kenneth A. Hardy**

Reading External Data Files Using SAS®: Examples Handbook
by **Michele M. Burlew**

Regression and ANOVA: An Integrated Approach Using
SAS® Software
by **Keith E. Muller**
and **Bethel A. Fetterman**

SAS®Applications Programming: A Gentle Introduction
by **Frank C. Dilorio**

SAS® for Forecasting Time Series, Second Edition
by **John C. Brocklebank**
and **David A. Dickey**

SAS® for Linear Models, Fourth Edition
by **Ramon C. Littell, Walter W. Stroup,**
and **Rudolf J. Freund**

SAS® for Monte Carlo Studies: A Guide for Quantitative
Researchers
by **Xitao Fan, Ákos Felsővályi, Stephen A. Sivo,**
and **Sean C. Keenan**

SAS® Functions by Example
by **Ron Cody**

SAS® Guide to Report Writing, Second Edition
by **Michele M. Burlew**

SAS® Macro Programming Made Easy
by **Michele M. Burlew**

SAS® Programming by Example
by **Ron Cody**
and **Ray Pass**

SAS® Programming for Researchers and Social Scientists,
Second Edition
by **Paul E. Spector**

SAS® Survival Analysis Techniques for Medical Research,
Second Edition
by **Alan B. Cantor**

SAS® System for Elementary Statistical Analysis,
Second Edition
by **Sandra D. Schlotzhauer**
and **Ramon C. Littell**

SAS® System for Mixed Models
by **Ramon C. Littell, George A. Milliken, Walter W. Stroup,**
and **Russell D. Wolfinger**

SAS® System for Regression, Third Edition
by **Rudolf J. Freund**
and **Ramon C. Littell**

SAS® System for Statistical Graphics, First Edition
by **Michael Friendly**

The SAS® Workbook and Solutions Set
(books in this set also sold separately)
by **Ron Cody**

Selecting Statistical Techniques for Social Science Data:
A Guide for SAS® Users
by **Frank M. Andrews, Laura Klem, Patrick M. O'Malley,
Willard L. Rodgers, Kathleen B. Welch,**
and **Terrence N. Davidson**

Statistical Quality Control Using the SAS® System
by **Dennis W. King**

A Step-by-Step Approach to Using the SAS® System
for Factor Analysis and Structural Equation Modeling
by **Larry Hatcher**

A Step-by-Step Approach to Using SAS® for Univariate and
Multivariate Statistics, Second Edition
by **Norm O'Rourke, Larry Hatcher,**
and **Edward J. Stepanski**

Step-by-Step Basic Statistics Using SAS®: Student Guide
and Exercises
(books in this set also sold separately)
by **Larry Hatcher**

Survival Analysis Using the SAS® System:
A Practical Guide
by **Paul D. Allison**

support.sas.com/pubs

Tuning SAS® Applications in the OS/390 and z/OS Environments, Second Edition
by **Michael A. Raithel**

Univariate and Multivariate General Linear Models: Theory and Applications Using SAS® Software
by **Neil H. Timm**
and **Tammy A. Mieczkowski**

Using SAS® in Financial Research
by **Ekkehart Boehmer, John Paul Broussard,**
and **Juha-Pekka Kallunki**

Using the SAS® Windowing Environment: A Quick Tutorial
by **Larry Hatcher**

Visualizing Categorical Data
by **Michael Friendly**

Web Development with SAS® by Example
by **Frederick Pratter**

Your Guide to Survey Research Using the SAS® System
by **Archer Gravely**

JMP® Books

JMP® for Basic Univariate and Multivariate Statistics: A Step-by-Step Guide
by **Ann Lehman, Norm O'Rourke, Larry Hatcher,**
and **Edward J. Stepanski**

JMP® Start Statistics, Third Edition
by **John Sall, Ann Lehman,**
and **Lee Creighton**

Regression Using JMP®
by **Rudolf J. Freund, Ramon C. Littell,**
and **Lee Creighton**

Printed in the United States
44088LVS00002B/11-12